A MISFIT IN MOSCOW

HOW BRITISH DIPLOMACY
IN RUSSIA FAILED
2014-2019

IAN PROUD

ISBN Paperback: 978-1-7395431-0-5
ISBN Ebook: 978-1-7395431-1-2

CONTENTS

PREFACE

Since the Cold War, Russia has held an unshakeable and outsized power to strike fear and trembling into the hearts of western citizens. Staring at a map, we marvel at the enormity of a country which stretches from Norway to Japan. We ponder its seemingly bottomless reserves of every natural resource on the planet, then dwell on its oligarchs, with their football clubs, Belgravia mansions and supermodel mistresses.

Anxiety rising in our throats, our attention shifts to the sturdy intimidating walls of the Kremlin in Moscow. Inside, like a Seventies Thunderbirds villain, an embittered man with a dodgy accent and a red star on his hat plots the downfall of the detested collective West. He signs off every despicable act of his massive intelligence and security empire. His grub-like finger hovers over a giant button that in an instant might launch six thousand nuclear missiles in our direction.

Western media and social media reinforce these and other urban myths about Putin on a daily basis: he'll likely die at any moment from a terrible illness and is having his final psychotic hurrah; his support in Russia is evaporating fast but he'll terrorise his citizens until he's got the job done; once he's finished in Ukraine, we'll see Russian tanks in Estonia; although, hang on a minute, his army will run out of precious ammunition stocks by Tuesday teatime.

Everything we witness today, through the lens of a heartless war in Ukraine, therefore makes sense to us, even if we've never met a Russian person or visited their country. We believe that Putin was always going to do this; we've heard he has a bigger and more-dastardly plan. So, every like-minded country must spend more on defence to stop the Bearzilla. We need more NATO, not less. And, whatever we do, never talk to the odious Slavic 'other' that is Putin, because that will make him stronger, and he'll just hate us more. If we keep doing what we've been doing for the past ten years, then eventually Putin will be gone, and we can usher in a new era of peace.

But having studied Putin and Russia for the past decade, I take a different view. I watched Putin shaking hands with David Cameron on the lawn at Lough Erne at the G8 Summit in 2013, at a time when UK-Russia relations were going through a periodic thaw. I served at the British Embassy in Moscow from 2014 through to early 2019. I endured the low point of the Salisbury nerve agent attack and the loss of almost eighty colleagues from the Embassy in the subsequent diplomatic fall-out. I kept the understaffed Embassy afloat through the FIFA World Cup of 2018 and until reinforcements trickled in at the end of that year. Since my return to London, among other things, I authorised a significant proportion of all the sanctions placed on Russian citizens, including since the outbreak of war in February 2022.

So, I've done my bit to maintain a UK foreign policy towards Russia that has been practically unchanged for a decade. I've had my run ins with Russian intelligence agents on the streets of Moscow and other Russian cities. I don't present myself as a corduroy-wearing pacifist who thinks, perhaps, that Putin wasn't cuddled enough as a child and that we maybe need to be kinder to him. I condemn the invasion of Ukraine and the conflict since 2014 that has killed thousands of innocent civilians, including and especially children. It's an outrage that this has happened, and I call for all those responsible for war crimes and other crimes against humanity - on both sides of the conflict - to face justice.

However, I am also a realist. I believe the core purpose of diplomacy – and indeed statesmanship - is to manage relationships between states, to prevent conflict. It seems the utmost folly to believe that we could resolve our disputes with Russia through isolation and cancellation. That does not mean we should necessarily like Putin or the leaders of other states where our relations are most troubled. But our primary goal is not to fix Russia's internal problems or make Putin a better man.

So, I ask myself how we have ended up with a full-scale war in Europe for the first time in almost thirty years? Over the past decade, I've watched as UK Ministers were so consumed by Cold War zeitgeist that they could not take a step back and look at the bigger picture.

Russia is undoubtedly still a powerful country, but it is in secular decline. Its economy is about the size of South Korea's, its workforce is shrinking, and life expectancy is around ten years lower than the OECD average. NATO is at least ten-times greater, economically: it has three times more active military personnel, five times more combat aircraft and four times the number of ships. And NATO has access to more modern and sophisticated weaponry across most systems.

Putin isn't bent on world domination nor the recreation of the Soviet Union. Of the fourteen other former-Soviet countries, Russia can only count on Belarus to act as a compliant buffer, although retains significant influence in Moldova and Armenia. To its underpopulated east, Russia is vastly overmatched by China, also ten-times larger economically, and is progressively being overtaken by India.

As I left King Charles Street for the final time, at the end of a twenty-four-year career in HM Diplomatic Service, I paused to look at a digital display of the Foreign Office's priorities. Bearded and grimacing, James Cleverly – Britain's then seventh (of eight) Foreign Secretary since 2014 – stared out at me as if to emphasise the importance of our mission. And I saw that the UK's top foreign policy priority is to 'Deter Russia and support Ukraine.' Makes sense, you might think. We should support Ukraine.

But then I asked myself, 'deter Russia from what?' We didn't 'deter' Russia in 2022 or, indeed, in 2014. One-fifth of Ukraine is occupied by a Russian Army that appears content to wage an attritional war that depletes Ukrainian supplies at a time western military aid is dwindling.

Despite tidal waves of upbeat commentary in the press and from politicians, Ukraine does not have the economic or military clout to inflict a decisive defeat on Russia without direct NATO military involvement. And we know that, despite doomsday predictions of a Russian economic implosion, it has the resources to keep fighting at least through 2025.

So, what, then, of our deterrence? Even if you didn't think Ukrainian membership of NATO was a core strategic threat to Russia before, you might be wondering now. The UK, together with the US, has refused to acknowledge or try substantively to address Russia's concerns over the past decade. Because of this, I have watched as inescapable sanctions and megaphone diplomacy made Putin more hostile and more emboldened to take a stand, with the tragic consequences we see today. It is pure fantasy to believe that the UK has deterred Russia in the past or can in the future.

And despite all the advantages being stacked against Putin, global isolation, flight bans, ICC indictments, and even exclusion from Eurovision, he has one trump card; his sovereign ability to decide Russia's unilateral response. In the grand game of chess between Russia and the much more powerful NATO, Putin sits across from a team of thirty-one players and their unelected Captain, arguing loudly for weeks before each move, with a disenfranchised Ukrainian criticising them if they don't move the pieces he wants.

And it all comes down to this. Despite our collective strength in the West, our innate multilateralism means we will never be quick enough to outsmart Putin. We clearly don't want to send our troops to fight Russia in Ukraine, despite the absolute certainty from the progress of the war to date, that Russia would be no match for NATO in a conventional face off. Unable to outsmart Putin and unwilling to fight we should, for the first time in a decade, push for a ceasefire and support Ukraine in negotiating a just peace.

Not talking to Putin and hoping he'll eventually die from a mysterious and unspeakable illness, is not a strategy. And the longer the 'guns not butter' Tories encourage the war to continue, pumping billions of pounds' worth of weapons into Ukraine with few conditions attached, the less safe Britain becomes.

Working at the British Embassy in Russia must be the toughest overseas gig for a member of HM Diplomatic Service. You are followed constantly and very occasionally harassed by Russian intelligence. Deal with an oppressive security culture inside the Embassy with the Security Officer watching the Brits just as much as they watch the Russian staff. Colleagues are kicked out the Embassy at a moment's notice for all manner of transgressions and compromising situations.

Throughout, a constantly changing cast of Prime Ministers and Ministers flip-flop on policy, while studiously refusing the talk to their Russian counterparts. At an executive level, the Foreign Office has been paralysed since the 2020 merger, and drifts without a rudder or a compass. There remain some truly brilliant and decent diplomats and development experts in the FCDO, although they are a dying breed. A two-decade disinvestment in skills at the foreign office means that, often, we send inexperienced officers to work overseas singularly unprepared to be diplomats.

But would I recommend a career in diplomacy? Hell yeah! You can travel the world, meet people of all nationalities, cultures and religions and work on issues that really matter. Plus, work with some of the most talented, passionate, committed and just plain nice British and Country-Based colleagues you could ever hope to meet. And it doesn't matter if you didn't go to Eton or have rich parents: I was constantly amazed by the number of people who immediately assumed that I met both criteria. You must be that person who is relentlessly curious to understand better the rich diversity of our global community, in the interests of advancing greater mutual understanding and, you got it, world peace.

This is not an academic book or a forensic picking apart of the UK's activity in Russia; the limitations of the Official Secrets Act and the Radcliffe Rules would prevent that. I wrote this account entirely from memory, and from open-source research when I needed to check specific details or data. While this is principally a book about British diplomacy in Russia, I have woven in a small number of flashbacks to personal experiences that may help readers understand why I think the way that I do.

While I was careful to draft a book that would not unstitch the straitjacket of British government censorship, I cleared my manuscript through the Cabinet Office, in the usual way, and agreed to cut four thousand words from the text. There are some passages where I consider the scalpel of censorship cut too deeply, and I have indicated these.

However, my intention was foremost to express an opinion, and not to share secrets that would compromise British interests. I also wanted to write a memoir that anyone could pick up and read, to understand what it's really like to be a British Diplomat in Russia. And suggest, with the greatest of respect, that UK foreign policy there has failed. For this is my story: a bullied working-class boy from Southampton who became *The Misfit in Moscow*.

Ian T Proud

Overton, Hampshire| August 2023

PROLOGUE

In the rear-view mirror I watched the Volkswagen Touareg pull away from the kerb. Two men in woolly hats glared at me from the front seats. They looked like hoods from a dodgy heist movie. But the knot in my stomach told me they were agents of Russia's domestic intelligence service, the Federalnaya Sluzhba Byezopasnosti. Part-successor to the Soviet KGB, the FSB has a similar role to MI5 in the UK but with added responsibilities for border control. They are also alleged to have their grubby mitts in all manner of illicit activity such as arms smuggling, pimping and money laundering. Surveillance is a dull and unprofitable part of their day job. But today was anything but dull.

My alert level clicked to amber as I pulled onto the "garden ring," a sixteen-lane, ten-mile loop of concrete and tarmac around the heart of Moscow. There was no point in trying to get away from them. It wasn't just that at nine-thirty on a Saturday morning the enormous highway was almost empty. Where would I go? They knew where I lived and, anyway, I had my wife and our kids in the car. One diplomat who'd tried to shake off an FSB tail car got home to his apartment a few days later to find a turd in the middle of his bed. It was a calling card that gave off the stinking message, "Don't fuck us around again."

I sat in the middle lane and stuck to the speed limit. With the adrenaline pumping, my world slowed, and I was alive to everything in my direct and peripheral vision. The Volkswagen was never more than two cars behind. As a senior British diplomat, I was used to the unwanted advances of Russian intelligence agencies after almost four years in Moscow. But this day was different. It was Saturday 17 March 2018. The Russian Ministry of Foreign Affairs (MFA) was about to announce the expulsion of an unknown number of diplomats from the British Embassy. Laurie Bristow, Her Majesty's Ambassador to Russia, had been summoned at noon to be given the list of those people barred from Russia for at least five years. Our kids hummed along to Russian pop songs in the back seat, blissfully unaware.

Thirteen days earlier, a former Russian intelligence officer had collapsed in Salisbury city centre with his daughter, who was visiting him from Russia. Sergei and Yulia Skripal were clinging to life in hospital. Tests by the UK chemical warfare laboratory in Porton Down had confirmed that they were poisoned by a military-grade nerve agent called Novichok, produced in Russia during the Soviet period. Whoever had delivered the nerve agent had intended it to kill the Skripals and it seemed likely that they would succeed. No one else in the centre of Salisbury had suffered the same catastrophic symptoms,[1] although a Wiltshire police detective would later fall seriously ill after he visited Sergei Skripal's home.

In the British Embassy and in the corridors of Whitehall, there were huge questions about who'd done this. I didn't assume the Russian state had tried to assassinate the Skripals, but the investigation would have to explore that avenue. History is littered with spectacular "statement" killings signed off or supported by the Russians. Trotsky succumbed to a botched bludgeoning by ice-axe in Mexico in 1940, on the orders of Stalin. Bulgarian dissident Georgi Markov was killed in 1978 in London after a ricin pellet was fired into his leg from an umbrella supplied by the KGB. The UK was still arguing with the Russian state about how a former FSB officer, Alexander Litvinenko, had been given nuclear tea in a London

---

1 Dawn Sturgess, a woman from Amesbury, died in July 2018 after a friend gave her the discarded bottle containing the Novichok nerve agent, believing it to be perfume.

hotel in 2006, leading to his slow and painful death. There is a casebook of unsolved investigations into the mysterious and often grisly deaths of Russian residents of the UK. And there's a chilling pattern in the choice of new and more horrendous techniques for killing so-called traitors. Death to traitors sits at the farthest end of the Russian punishment spectrum from a shit on the bed for a minor offence.

In 2010, Putin famously said on TV that traitors would kick the bucket and choke on the pieces of silver paid them by foreign intelligence agencies. But would a senior figure in the Kremlin have authorised the use of a military nerve agent on an ex-Russian spy in sleepy Salisbury during daylight hours? Russian intelligence agencies don't appear as constrained by ministerial and parliamentary oversight as their UK rivals, so it might have been a rogue state actor. Another possibility was a non-state actor, possibly from a mafia group or an agent of a different country altogether, who had gained access to the nerve agent through illicit means. Corruption is so widespread in Russia that the sale of deadly nerve agents from the Soviet era is not inconceivable. It would have been obvious to the attackers that any hint of Russian involvement would provoke a British backlash.

Looking back on the reaction of the Kremlin and Russia's military intelligence apparatus, which suffered a huge fall from grace after Salisbury, I think a unit from Russian military intelligence was freelancing without proper authorisation. They would have done this either because they were liberally interpreting the mood of an essentially hostile Kremlin policy towards the UK or because they were looking to derail an improvement in UK–Russia relations that had started in mid-2017. The conspiracy theories bounced all over the place in those first few hours and days. But whichever theory you believed, it would be months before the Metropolitan Police had identified the attackers.

Laurie Bristow went into Russia's Foreign Ministry to seek an official response from Russia on the question of how a Soviet-era nerve agent had come to be used on UK soil and while he was doing so the Russian Ambassador to London was called into the Foreign Office to be presented with the same question. The essence was that the Salisbury attack could only have happened in one of two ways: either an agent of the Russian state had done this, or Russia had allowed a lethal nerve agent to get into the hands of an illicit actor who had done the deed. What was Russia's assessment? While there was a certain logic in the question, it was a bit like asking a man, "Have you stopped beating your wife?" The Russians were never going to engage with a question to which any answer implied they were to blame, either directly or indirectly. So, rather than answer, the Kremlin propaganda machine leapt into action to scream indignation through every available media outlet at this so-called provocation by foggy Albion. All windows into a sensible discussion with Russia on what had happened were slammed shut and what little remained of Laurie's influence in Moscow disappeared. In fairness, a different Ambassador may not have fared any better. The Russian state setting, with boring predictability, had been switched to deny and deflect.

With the request for information being stonewalled, the British government mulled over what it should do next. It had been stung by criticism that its response to the murder of Alexander Litvinenko in 2006 was too slow and too soft; the press and the hawks in Cabinet wanted a tough response and they wanted it now. Instead, the government settled on the lowest common denominator option in a diplomatic dispute. On 14 March 2018, Prime Minister Theresa May stood at the despatch box in Parliament and announced that the UK would expel twenty-three undeclared intelligence officers from the Russian Embassy in London. They had seven days to pack their bags and leave the UK.

As I trundled up Leningrad Prospekt at a steady eighty kph, my mind turned over why this had happened. Why would the Kremlin sign off on an assassination attempt in the UK just a month before Russia's presidential election? It was entirely possible that some

deranged strategist in the presidential administration on Staraya
Square had conjured up the scenario of a domestic electoral boost
from slotting a traitor abroad. But internationally, the Kremlin was
going hell for leather to deliver a football World Cup that showed a
more open and welcoming side of Russian people to the hundreds
of thousands of fans who'd be visiting the country for the first time.
Nerve agent attacks weren't great for tourist promotion.

And while UK–Russia relations had been frostier than a Yakutsk
winter since Russia's annexation of Crimea, there had been modest
signs of improvement at the end of 2017. The press was reporting
that, since his appointment as Foreign Secretary in the summer
of 2016, an unstoppable Boris Johnson had been blocked from
reaching out to Moscow by an immovable Prime Minister Theresa
May. Tory party in-fighting and Theresa May's hard-line stance was
leaving the UK increasingly isolated within the EU on Russia policy.
With the Prime Minister's authority dented by an ill-timed general
election that left the Conservatives governing without an overall
majority, I pressed on the need for higher levels of engagement.

Slowly, Whitehall was beginning to move and in November 2017,
junior FCO minister Sir Alan Duncan travelled to Moscow for the
first ministerial visit to Russia in two years. He visited Moscow's
Luzhniki Stadium to see preparations for the 2018 football World
Cup. He also sealed a new diplomatic visa deal between the UK
and Russia after a twelve-month blockage which had left the
Embassy in Moscow chronically short-staffed. Shortly afterwards,
the Archbishop of Canterbury, Justin Welby, arrived in Moscow for
a visit described as "pastoral, ecumenical and political." And then
in December and at the third attempt, Boris Johnson paid the first
Cabinet-level visit to Russia for five years for talks with his counterpart, Sergey Lavrov. Planning was launched for Prince William
to attend the World Cup in his role as President of the FA, most
likely to watch the England v Belgium group match in Kaliningrad.
After an almost four-year perma-chill in the relationship, this was
a positive tidal wave of diplomatic engagement. So, against the

backdrop of a slight thawing of relations, the "Kremlin did it" thesis didn't completely add up to me, although I didn't discount Russian state involvement in some way.

In the four days since Theresa May's announcement, I had swung on a regular basis between a conviction that I would be kicked out and a belief that I would not be declared persona non grata. On the one hand, as the Economic Counsellor[2] at the Embassy, I was responsible for advising London about sanctions against Russia, specifically how they were working and where to focus next. On the other hand, I was the most dovish diplomat at the British Embassy, constantly travelling around Russia's regions, building contacts wherever I could. I believed then and believe now – especially against the backdrop today of full-blown war in Ukraine – that the UK must engage with Russia. That position is the antithesis of a Tory foreign policy that still insists – even today – that direct engagement with Russia shows weakness. It also put me at odds with political colleagues who rarely left the Embassy building, let alone Moscow, and accepted the hard-line UK policy without question. However, it was far from clear that my dovishness would sway the cold calculations of the counter-intelligence analysts at the FSB who'd draw up the shitlist. Whatever happened, I just wanted the uncertainty to end. Stay or go, I knew the next card in the biggest tit-for-tat expulsion of Russian and British diplomats for thirty-three years was about to be played.

Ben MacIntyre's *The Spy and the Traitor* recalls how in 1985, KGB Colonel Oleg Gordievsky had been smuggled across the Finnish border from the Soviet Union in the boot of an MI6 officer's car. He'd been spying for Britain for over ten years and was forced to defect after his cover was blown, ironically through the actions of

---

2 Diplomatic ranks are confusing to some people. In a large embassy a Counsellor is a senior diplomat who counsels the Ambassador on a specialist area of work. Other ranks include Attaché, Third Secretary, Second Secretary and First Secretary. We shorten titles: for example, Second Sec or Two Sec for a Second Secretary.

Aldrich Ames at the CIA, who was a Soviet spy.[3] The Soviet Union responded by expelling twenty-five British diplomats, including the MI6 officers who had smuggled Gordievsky out, and the UK reciprocated in kind. On this occasion, the UK had fired the first salvo of diplomatic expulsions. But the process was the same. You kick out ours, we'll kick out yours.

It was a sunny March morning and the snow had started its slow retreat from the streets of Moscow. I glanced across and watched the tail car carry on up the road as I pulled into the kids' school in the north of the city. We enjoyed our weekend routine of taking the kids for swimming lessons at the school. Sod it, I thought; life had to continue as normal, so we'd just go. If I had to receive bad news, I'd sooner do something nice beforehand rather than stew at home. I'd rush back to the Embassy after swimming class.

Travelling back from the school there was no tail car. I dropped the family at home, then took the short drive to the Embassy. All the British diplomats and many spouses were milling around. It was like the end of an episode of *The Great British Bake Off*, with contestants waiting to hear whether they'd be kicked out of the tent.

"Oh, I hope it isn't you," one would say to another.

"You don't deserve to go, you've been so amazing, babes," another would say, secretly praying that they themselves wouldn't have to miss Biscuit Week.

Laurie Bristow was still at the sandstone monstrosity that serves as the Russian Foreign Ministry building, the least beautiful but possibly most imposing of the Seven Sisters, statement buildings constructed in the early 1950s to please the ailing Stalin. People were asking nervously when the Ambassador would be back.

I could see a heavy cloud of fear descending, so I went up to my office for a more productive distraction. As I locked my phone, Bluetooth headphones and car keys outside the Chancery, my mind

---

3 Ames was eventually arrested by the FBI in 1994, having spied for the Soviet Union for nine years.

mulled over the various "What next?" scenarios. I never thought the Russians would close the British Embassy and break off diplomatic relations with the UK just because we had kicked out twenty-three of their spooks. But just in case they did, and even before Theresa May had stood up to make her announcement to Parliament, a mass shredding of classified documents had started. We had a lot of documents in Chancery and if the Embassy had to shut up shop at a moment's notice, we wanted to go with our heads held high and avoid the unedifying prospect of a document bonfire on the Embassy terrace.

So, I gathered up a stack of papers from my desk and walked them along the corridor to the industrial shredder, which vibrated as each document disappeared into its mechanical mouth. As the shredder ate my papers, I wondered how I'd feel to be expelled. I'd enjoyed four years in Russia, and it would have been disappointing to miss the World Cup. But my posting was due to finish in July 2018 anyway. And in truth it was our family life in Russia that I'd enjoyed, more than my life inside the Chancery; being a lone dove in a top-secret nest of hawks was hard work and made me stick out as the misfit in Moscow.

There had been heated debate about how people would be told their fate. I thought it would be a bad idea to call in officers one at a time. With around fifty British diplomats in Moscow, imagine being the first person called in? And worse, the last. I joked it might end up like *The X Factor*, with the Ambassador playing the role of Simon Cowell.

"Well, the Russians have come to their decision. If I could keep everyone here at the Embassy, I would. Look, there's no easy way to do this, but I have some bad news. You're STAYING with me in Moscow!"

Laurie agreed to my suggestion that we call in teams to hear the news.

Now, I heard the outer door click open, anxious voices and the movement of people. Laurie was back and he looked pale as a sheet. Everyone wanted to get it over with, so the Chancery team, by far the largest group at the Embassy, were the first to file into the meeting room. As was custom, I sat directly opposite Laurie at the large table next to my political opposite number, with the collective Chancery team arrayed on either side. The heavy door clunked shut. Laurie made brief remarks, in which he regretted we were in this situation; he confirmed that twenty-three British diplomats were to be kicked out of Russia then read out the list of names.

PART ONE

1. KOMPUTER SAYS "*NYET*"

On 16 December 1998, at the height of impeachment proceedings, President Bill Clinton launched four days of air strikes against Iraq – degrading their chemical capabilities to cover degrading revelations of a biological strike on Monica Lewinsky's dress. Holed up in a dingy hotel in Shepherd's Bush, I stayed up most of the night glued to TV news coverage, taking notes. I was competing in the Civil Service Selection Board ("sizbee") to join the Foreign Office fast stream.

I was elated when I drove home at the end of two hard days with Steps blaring out of the car radio. While I thought I'd failed selection, I didn't care; I couldn't have tried harder and had gone toe to toe with candidates from better backgrounds than mine.

For me, joining "the Office" wasn't preordained by a childhood of privilege, good connections and an easy sail through public school and Oxbridge. I defy the *Daily Mail* stereotype of a Foreign Office toff.

My parents grew up in working-class families, Dad in a colliery village in the north-east and Mum in a village close to Southampton docks, where her father was a carpenter until he died of asthma aged just thirty-two. Mum's stepdad, the "Gramp" I adored as a child, was a big-hearted stevedore who couldn't read. Neither of my parents had the opportunity to study beyond secondary school.[4] But my dad is gifted in maths and languages; he used to do MENSA tests for fun. My mum had a photographic memory and a love of reading. I seem to have inherited these gifts from parents who ensured that my two brothers and I wanted for nothing. I feel blessed with the deck of cards I was handed in life.

My first memory is of being with my parents in the car, in Germany. A few months after I was born, our family moved to Monchengladbach, near to the Dutch border where Dad was to be stationed with the British Army on the Rhine. Growing up on an army base was an endless adventure, with "army stuff" happening all around and school fairs livened up by a tank or military helicopter. Our family didn't have a lot of money, but we had a nice life, with a bit to spare for camping holidays in Bavaria and Italy, plus trips back to visit grandparents in the UK.

It was the height of the Cold War and in the back of my mind loomed the repressive, nuclear-tipped shadow of the Soviet Union, a term that I interchanged freely with Russia without knowing why. The nuance didn't seem important; it was sufficient to know that the Russians were the enemy, and we were the good guys. My dad told me that if nuclear war hadn't happened by 1984, it never would. This was before Francis Fukuyama's prophecy that Western liberal democracy would establish itself as a final form of human government and effectively consign war to the dustbin of history. The rise of China has proved Fukuyama wrong. And while I trust my dad completely, my confidence in his earlier prediction about the risk of nuclear war isn't as solid as it was when I was nine.

After we returned to the UK, the asthma that I'd inherited from Mum made life a struggle. I was physically small until my mid-teens and painfully introverted. So, I was bullied a lot, including by my PE teacher at secondary school. Mr Wade used to make me stand

---

4 I remain the only member of my immediate family to have completed a university education. My older brothers have followed careers as tradesmen, the eldest specialising in metals, and my middle brother as an accomplished car mechanic.

on the centre circle of the hockey pitch all afternoon if I couldn't do PE because I was chesty. Having grown up with a respect for authority, I was terrified to ask when I could go home, and by the time I summoned up the courage, it invariably turned out that wanker Wade already had. I didn't just stand out on the hockey pitch. I supported Borussia Mönchengladbach football team, could speak some German, liked politics and news coverage of Prime Minister's Questions. People who stick out in life are an easy target, so with studied care I learned to blend in and not be noticed. But I also inherited my mum's stubbornness and being bullied made me determined never to follow the crowd. So, I was destined to be a misfit from an early age.

But the bullying took its toll and having been in all the top sets at school when we moved back to the UK, I finished school with only two O levels and a CSE grade 1 in drama. In the sixth form I managed to add two AS levels before dropping out of my A level courses. I didn't have the option of going to university and was disillusioned with education anyway, so when I reached eighteen, I had to get a job. I tried selling expensive German hoovers but sold none. I'd stacked vegetables at Asda part-time while at Sixth Form but didn't see myself doing that as a career. So, I got a place on Hampshire County Council's clerical trainee scheme. Manually writing out rail season tickets for schoolkids was a huge reality check. I didn't want to do this for the rest of my life. For two years I worked hard to achieve a day-release qualification that gave me the equivalent of A levels. My teacher on that programme was a former Member of Parliament and he organised a trip to Parliament, where he gave me and my classmates a personal tour. I also got a ticket for Prime Minister's Questions and watched with eyes like saucers as Margaret Thatcher and Neil Kinnock went head-to-head over the despatch box. Life in the big city seemed so exciting.

With a new qualification under my belt, I was invited to interview for an office manager job with the Hampshire Constabulary, in a unit that oversaw internal investigations into complaints against police officers. I was completely unqualified for the job and only twenty years old. But at interview, I talked in detail about the provisions for handling complaints against police officers, as set out in the *1984 Police and Criminal Evidence Act*. I'd spent ages conducting research at the library to prepare me for the interview; it seemed like no one else had, so I was offered the job. I was in awe of the Chief Superintendent, Eddie Day, a larger-than-life character who liked me and trusted me to do my job. I thrived in this environment and my career went from strength to strength. The police sponsored me to study towards a degree in public policy in Southampton on day release, and after a five-year slog I passed with first-class honours.

I enjoyed eleven happy years as a civilian with the Old Bill working in various police stations across Hampshire. By the age of thirty, I was overseeing one hundred civilian support staff within Southampton Division. I was enjoying life, had a terrific boss in Chief Superintendent Graham Wyeth, and top mates, like Ted Sethi, the Property Centre Manager. But my career had gone as far as it could go as a "civvy." Several senior officers suggested I join the police. But as I was mulling my options, I wandered into Southampton Library and saw a pamphlet about the Civil Service fast stream. It was a eureka moment.

The Foreign and Commonwealth Office jumped out of the page at me as the best option. I'd always loved politics, and since I'd grown up overseas, the idea of getting paid to live and work abroad really appealed. A gruelling nine-month period followed in which I was put through a succession of tests, assessment centres and interviews. For the two-day Civil Service Selection Board in December 1998, I had researched weapons inspections in Iraq as my thematic topic for one of various interviews. Luckily, I nailed my interview better than the US President nailed his intern.

Just a couple of days later, a letter arrived informing me that I'd made it to the final selection board, ironically called the FSB. There were in fact a few more hurdles to jump over, including a language aptitude test, which judged my ability to make sense of random sentence structures in Kazakh. But one sunny afternoon in June 1999, a message appeared on my desk at work to call a number in London. It was a lady at the Foreign Office with a desperately sophisticated voice, offering me a job. I was over the moon and my parents were both so proud, in more than just name. Two months later, I moved into a bedsit near Woolwich and started work at the FCO office in Palace Street, which, as the name hints, is next to Buckingham Palace. I opened a new bank account at the branch on Buckingham Palace Road. I'd come a long way from being a bullied kid who left school with two O levels. How ironic to think that Monica Lewinsky gave me a happy ending too.

Having travelled on police business to places like Wakefield and Lincoln, I was suddenly jetting off on an induction visit to Mexico, Atlanta and Washington DC. A few months after I joined, my boss asked if I could cover for her at a conference the following week. She apologised for the desperately short notice.

"Where is it?" I asked.

"Melbourne."

Trying to keep a straight face and sucking my teeth about the inconvenience, I checked my calendar before agreeing. "Yes!"

Three days later, as I sipped on champagne before take-off, I thought I'd made it in life.

Fast-forward six years: I was three years into a posting to the British Embassy in Bangkok and was preparing for my first visit to Moscow, a prospect I'd never imagined while growing up in Germany during the Cold War. The occasion was a G8 working-level meeting of the Counter-Terrorism Action Group (CTAG). As Head of the Political Section, I'd coordinated joint activity on counter-terrorism in Thailand with other G8 embassies during the UK presidency of the G8 in 2005. Thailand was a priority country for the CTAG, with a focus on countering identity document fraud: that is, clamping down on fake passports and other fake personal identity documents that terrorists use to ghost around the globe.

South-east Asia had been the focus of terror attacks since the rise of the militant group Jemaah Islamiyah, who wanted to create a pan-Islamic caliphate in the region. Hambali, the mastermind behind the 2002 Bali bombing, had been arrested in the ancient capital of Ayutthaya, fifty miles north of Bangkok, just months after I had arrived in Thailand. He had been plotting to bomb the 2003 Asia Pacific Economic Cooperation (APEC) summit in Bangkok, which would be attended by the leaders of twenty-one countries, including the US President.

As Russia was a G8 member, I'd been working closely with diplomats at the Russian Embassy in Bangkok. They were serious and eager to collaborate. Of course, they would have been FSB, which has responsibility in Russia for border control. But back then the UK–Russia relationship was in a better state. I was therefore pleased when they invited me to Moscow in February 2006 for a working-group meeting under Russia's G8 presidency. I was intrigued by the prospect of visiting Russia for the first time. Cold country, cold people. Still stuck in the Soviet era. Everything is backward and not as good as in the UK. Korruption, krime and killings: this neatly summarises the stereotypes and prejudices that shaped my view of Russia and Russian people in February 2006.

I love travelling on planes, including the whole process of going to the airport. The large grey Aeroflot jet parked up at Don Mueang Airport looked modern yet unfamiliar. I would be travelling on an Ilyushin – how exciting – another new experience! But the Russian airliner had none of the frills and comforts of a modern Boeing or Airbus jet. As far as I was concerned, it was the aviation equivalent of a Lada. The interior was dark and there was little separating the passenger compartment from the roof of the fuselage. While the old-fashioned business-class seats were generous in width, they had the same legroom as economy class. So, if the passenger in front reclined their seat, you would be forced to do the same, and end up stacked, chevron-fashion, like swaddled newborns in a Soviet nursery. In a miracle of Soviet-style engineering, it would end up somehow less comfortable than in economy class. Luckily, I was able to switch seats so there was no passenger in front of me.

Upon arrival, Sheremetyevo 2 Airport was as dark and dingy as I'd imagined it would be. The immigration officer wore a sneer and a Soviet-style uniform. It all felt intimidating and alien. It was minus twenty degrees when I stepped out of the terminal building, and I'd never felt so cold. With no warm clothing in my Bangkok wardrobe, I'd put on extra T-shirts under my thin sweater, but it wasn't enough. The craggy-faced driver grunted and ushered me to follow him across the freezing snow-covered car park to his beaten-up Lada. I stared out of partially iced-up windows as we drove into the centre of Moscow along Leningrad Prospekt. The architecture further out towards the airport was grim and Soviet. Closer to the centre, I was surprised to see grander pre-revolutionary buildings with the odd café and restaurant lit up and filled with people enjoying their Sunday night.

A stereotypically beautiful yet cold-faced receptionist stared blankly at me when I staggered into the hotel lobby. She had no record of my booking. When I offered three different variants of how my booking may have been recorded, the komputer said *nyet!* We reached a stand-off, and she stood in sullen silence across the desk from me. I could almost read her thoughts: *Man dressed in thin sweatshirt and no fur hat, clearly does not have money enough to stay at prestige hotel like Kyempinski.* I stared back at the receptionist with a determined jaw. "Do you have any spare rooms?"

"Yes, we have."

I learned my first important lesson about Russian people. Russians don't do shades of grey. Things are either correct or they are not. If you ask a closed question, you will get a closed, yes-or-no response. A yes answer in any language is easy to package. People like the answer yes. Following more than seventy years of Soviet rule, Russian people became used to the word no, and they don't try to sugarcoat it.

I learned this same lesson from the FSB agent who had been sent to follow me wherever I went. For a bit of fun, I walked up to him outside the hotel and asked him to take a photo of me with the Kremlin in the background across the frozen river. "*Nyet.*"

I was on the ground in Moscow for less than twenty-four hours, most of which I spent sleeping or at G8 meetings. The only Brit I met was an official from the Home Office. She was clueless about the work we were doing on counterterrorism in Thailand but breathlessly told me about a strategy document I'd never read. I passed up the offer of vodka shots that the waiting staff carried round on trays loaded with wine glasses and orange juice during the business buffet lunch. It felt about as Russian an experience as I imagined it would be.

Just as I was about to leave Moscow, I got a glimpse of something more positive. I realised my passport was missing as I was about to board the flight home. The last thing I wanted was to get stranded in this Godforsaken miserable freezing country for a minute longer. So, I instinctively went back to the shop where I'd bought souvenirs. The babushka at the counter spotted me, beamed and waved my passport in the air. I thanked her profusely as she babbled happily in Russian. As the plane left the frozen landscape of Moscow behind in its jet stream, my interest in Russia ran cold for the next six years.

2. VLADIMIR PUTIN VISITS NORTHERN IRELAND

Enniskillen, Northern Ireland, 18 June 2013

"Git yer hands out yer pockets!" a Secret Service agent shouted at me.

Barack Obama strolled easily down the driveway of the hotel in shirtsleeves, his two guards giving him plenty of width. We were in the safest place on the planet at that time.

I reached out my right hand for the US President to shake. A touch taller than me, Obama smiled and said, "You've done a great job."

Staff poured out of the hotel entrance to get their Obama moment. While all this was happening, I spotted a short, tubby man walking by with his entourage, waving at the assembled scrum. No one else noticed President Hollande of France.

In July 2012, I'd been appointed to lead delivery of the G8 summit working out of the Cabinet Office and reporting to 10 Downing Street. After a roller-coaster thirteen years in the Diplomatic Service, this was a dream job for me. I could never have imagined that I'd one day organise a summit of world leaders. It was also the second time that my work had touched on Russia.

In one of my first appointments, I popped across to No. 10 for a coffee with David Cameron's special adviser Liz Sugg. She was Cameron's general fixer and was made a baroness in his "medals for mates" resignation honours list.[5] Direct and occasionally abrasive, Liz started from the view that the FCO would strive to deliver a solution that offered every benefit except satisfaction. But once I'd convinced her that, despite my FCO background, my only priority was delivering an outcome that the Prime Minister wanted, she was a pleasure to work with.

She made it clear that my top priority was to find a venue. The FCO had spent two years combing through a hundred venues without success. Cameron had been impressed by the 2012 Camp David G8 summit in which he got to stay in his own cabin. She suggested I look at Northern Ireland.

So, the day after the London 2012 Olympics finished, I flew to Belfast. I met up with officials from No. 10 and from the FCO Protocol Directorate, which organises most major international events for the British government. We looked at several hotels across Northern Ireland, but in the end the Lough Erne Resort in County Fermanagh was the stand-out choice. It had turret-like cabins next to the main hotel building. It was by Lough Erne, which made it work from a security point of view. Enniskillen, the nearby town, was held by a republican Sinn Féin Member of Parliament, making it "interesting," politically. It was by the border with Ireland, making the optics of inviting the Irish Taoiseach work. A snag was that the hotel was in administration. But we thought we could carve a good story out of the UK government supporting a struggling business in Northern Ireland. Everything clicked. Liz loved it and she was the person who would make the final recommendation to Cameron. What could go wrong?

The announcement would be made on Tuesday 20 November 2012. Cameron was visiting Northern Ireland for talks with the First and deputy First Ministers of the Northern Ireland Executive,

Peter Robinson and the late Martin McGuinness. He would pop into Lough Erne first thing in the morning to check that he was happy with the venue and then announce it at a factory before his talks with McGuinness and Robinson. Simple.

As I got in a taxi at seven o'clock in the morning on 19 November, my phone rang. It was Trevor Andrews from FCO Protocol, calling from Lough Erne. Without ceremony he announced that the hotel was on fire. Holy shit!

I told him to get the team to a safe place and wait for instructions. I phoned Liz and she asked me not to fly to Northern Ireland. No. 10 was alive with the damp clammy sound of hands being wrung. This was as I pulled into Heathrow Terminal 1.

I said something along the lines of, "Look, Liz, we have staff out there and I need to make sure they are safe. Plus, Northern Ireland is the prize, not Lough Erne. So, I'll visit the back-up venue [Hillsborough Castle] and start to talk about Plan B." She was content for me to fly but decided to wait in London for further news. I called the Assistant Commissioner of Police, Alistair Finlay, in charge of policing for the summit. He reported that there was nothing suspicious, just an electrical fire at the hotel. I texted Liz. "Electrical fire. No suggestion of terrorism."

By the time I landed in Belfast, the storm in Whitehall had passed. David Cameron's visit was back on, and Liz flew out in the afternoon with one of the Prime Minister's police protection officers. I visited the Northern Ireland Office at Stormont before collecting Liz and the cop at Belfast City Airport in the late afternoon. It was getting dark, and I hammered down the M1 in the rain at high speed in my rented Peugeot, overtaking on the inside lane. Blue police lights flashed in my rear-view mirror.

I pulled over and wound down the window. The officer bellowed that my "driving was atrocious." I apologised profusely. The officer in the rear seat of my car held up his Metropolitan Police warrant card and said, "Just making you aware."

The Northern Irish police officer looked at his London counterpart.

He looked at Liz, who had her face down tapping furiously into her BlackBerry, wishing a hole would appear in the floor of the car and swallow her up. Then he looked at me.

"So where are you headed then?" he asked.

"To Enniskillen."

"On security business, is it?"

"Yep."

He must have known something important was afoot in Enniskillen; he flapped his notebook shut and sent us on our way.

We made it to Lough Erne. Ferghal Purcell, the general manager of the hotel, was rushing here and there, getting a meal service up for the small number of remaining guests – mostly my staff – in the golf clubhouse. His face red and his voice hoarse, he looked wound up and stressed out. When Liz told him that David Cameron would be popping in to visit in the morning, he almost burst a vein.

The weather was glorious when I stepped out of the hotel the following day. I'd received a heads-up that Cameron's helicopter had landed nearby. A police helicopter hovered overhead, much to my annoyance. I had asked the police to ensure the Prime Minister's brief visit was low-key. I suppose they didn't want to take any chances of an IRA terrorist getting intelligence of the visit and planning a spontaneous attack.

Despite the scorch marks and soot, the hotel looked lovely in the autumn sun. David Cameron turned up and with me, Ferghal, Liz, Trevor and some police officers, and had a tour. He loved the hotel and chatted happily with the staff, who appeared bemused. Later that morning, on 20 November 2012, he announced the hosting of the G8 summit at Lough Erne.

The summit opened on 17 June 2013 with the sun shining on Northern Ireland, after a week of foul weather. It had been a hectic nine months, but once the leaders were all on the ground, I could relax a bit and let the FCO protocol team do what it does best. I'd gone for a snooze at lunchtime, having worked most of the night before getting everything ready. A mechanical clicking roused me from my slumber. I slipped out of bed dressed only in my underpants, hair in a mess, knelt by the open window and peered out. Stephen Harper, then Prime Minister of Canada, was shaking David Cameron's hand directly below my window; the press pack was clamouring to capture the perfect photograph. It was the classic arrivals handshake shot that you see at every major summit, except with Ugly Naked Guy staring out of the window. One by one, nine world leaders walked out and met the Prime Minister halfway across the lawn. One of the guests was Vladimir Putin of Russia. He shook Cameron's hand, said a few words and pointed at the lake beside the garden with a smile.

Cameron had taken an early morning swim before the summit started. I can imagine Putin was saying something like, "Did you catch fish with teeth before wrestling bear?" An Irish journalist joked that Putin, known for his macho photoshoots, would arrive at the summit in Speedos, surfing across Lough Erne on the backs of dolphins. He arrived by helicopter like everyone else. But there and then, fully clothed and looking a manly couple, the Prime Minister of the United Kingdom and the President of the Russian Federation seemed at ease in each other's company.

Cameron had invested political capital in building a relationship with Putin. UK–Russia relations had been frosty since 2006 when two former FSB agents had assassinated Alexander Litvinenko in London, using tea laced with radioactive polonium-210. Cameron had visited Moscow in September 2011, the first visit by a UK Prime Minister to Moscow for six years. He got nowhere on Litvinenko, but he'd opened a channel of communication with Putin, who was then Prime Minister while the diminutive Dmitry Medvedev pretended to be President. At that time, it was a requirement of Russia's constitution that Presidents could serve only two consecutive terms, much as in the US.[6] After Putin's four-year sabbatical as Prime Minister, Medvedev had nominated Putin to stand for election again in 2012 and, surprise, he won by a landslide. So, in the summer of 2012, Putin visited Cameron and they watched a judo match together at the London 2012 Olympics, following talks in Downing Street. Cameron again visited Russia in May 2013 for talks with Putin in Sochi, largely focused on Syria. Putin had taken him on a helicopter tour of the Winter Olympic Park and given him a bottle of Ararat brandy, proudly announcing that it was Winston Churchill's favourite.

After the G8 at Lough Erne, Cameron would go on to St Petersburg in September 2013 for the Russian-hosted G20 summit. In the space of two years, the two leaders met five times in each other's countries. There was cautious optimism in Whitehall about the scope to strengthen bilateral relations. The UK and Russia are two of the five Permanent Members of the UN Security Council, the P5. Russia has the largest stockpile of nuclear weapons in the world, which are pointed at Europe and the US. It's vitally important that two of the largest global military powers maintain a healthy dialogue, at the very least to minimise the risk of escalation.

The mutual suspicion that exists between Russia and the West is as fuelled by a tendency in the West to view Russia as desperately foreign and hostile as it is by Russian paranoia about so-called NATO encirclement and suspicion of the UK as a historical competitor. But however difficult the relationship, you need grown-up leaders who can cut through the white noise and work through the toughest issues, to avoid a state of permanent mutual hostility. You need statesmanship. In the eighties, Margaret Thatcher and Mikhail Gorbachev could not have been more different ideologically. But they built a personal relationship that helped them to navigate

---

6 Russia's constitution has recently been amended to allow Putin to remain in power for a further two terms, making a total of four terms, should he put himself up for re-election.

UK–Soviet relations through a particularly tense period of the Cold War. Thatcher and Gorbachev could argue heatedly for hours, but through that they had forged some areas of common understanding and grudging admiration. The total collapse in the UK relationship with Russia – and related to that, the gradual and dangerous escalation of the Ukraine crisis - has in part been caused by a statesmanship vacuum in the UK; successive members of the current government have actively chosen not to talk to Russia when tensions were at their highest.

Building any sort of diplomatic relationship with Russia is tough, given the fundamental lack of trust on both sides. Russia will never engage with us solely on our terms. Tony Blair had briefly built a rapport with Putin, but this had fallen apart after the UK gave refuge to oligarch Boris Berezovsky, for whom Alexander Litvinenko had been working when he was invited for his terminal cup of tea. Cameron had recognised the need to have a go with Putin. Before the annexation of Crimea, UK–Russia relations were in better shape than they'd been for some time and that was partly down to the tone set by both leaders.

In June 2013, I'd just applied to work at the British Embassy in Moscow as the Economic Counsellor. I'd be the senior diplomat at the Embassy charged with – as the job description set out – "thickening" UK–Russia economic relations. Prior to the Ukraine war, the UK had the largest foreign investment in Russia, through BP's 19.75% investment in state oil giant Rosneft. British high-end goods, together with consultancy, law and engineering firms, are extremely popular in Russia. But there was scope to do more.

Various strands of economic and cultural cooperation were marshalled under an Intergovernmental Steering Committee (ISC), jointly chaired by Russia's Deputy Prime Minister, Igor Shuvalov, and, at that time, Sir Vince Cable, Business Secretary during the Tory–Lib Dem coalition. As always, the Russian side focused on the format and the need for dialogue as an end, while the Foreign Office spent its time evaluating outcomes to justify whether the dialogue was worthwhile. On the practicalities, the ISC worked through issues, such as: increasing two-way commercial flights between the UK and Russia and Siberian overflight slots for UK airlines on the lucrative routes into Asia; establishing a mechanism for cooperation on financial services regulation between the City of London and Moscow's financial centre; and working through specific blockages and barriers on the two-way export of goods, including British pig semen.

Animal genetics aside, it was exciting. Until that point, my FCO career had been focused on Asia. Then Foreign Secretary William Hague had placed a premium on senior diplomats getting relevant trade and economic experience. When the Moscow job came up, it offered me the chance to work on economic issues for a while and attend the 2014 G8 summit, which was scheduled to take place in Sochi, Russia. Two G8 summits for the price of one, or so I thought. Plus, I could learn about a new country and language, which is one of the benefits of an FCO career. Russia seemed like the perfect next step.

With the summer sun shining on Lough Erne, the final G8 summit ran like clockwork. I notched it up as an unforgettable career experience. After my Obama moment, I chatted with Cameron in the garden and he joked that my next task was to sell the hotel, which remained in administration.

The following day, I hammered down the M1 at speed. I was headed for police headquarters in Belfast for tea with the Assistant Commissioner Alistair Finlay, whom I wanted to thank for everything the Police Service of Northern Ireland had done to make the summit a success.

As I approached Belfast, blue lights flashed in my rear-view mirror. The police officer came to my window and told me that my driving had been "atrocious." He asked me where I was going.

"I'm going to police headquarters."

"Who are you going to see there, then?"

"Er, Mr Finlay."

He paused. "Do you think Mr Finlay would be happy with you driving like that?"

"I don't think that he would, Officer," I replied, with genuine contrition. I explained that I was exhausted after the summit and just wanted to pop in to say thanks to the police for an amazing job before flying home. He sent me on my way. My second close shave with the law in Northern Ireland.

I enjoyed a pleasant tea with Alistair Finlay, during which I kept quiet about my atrocious driving. As I drove back to Belfast City Airport for the last time, my mind was already on my next assignment. Within three months, I'd be studying Russian full-time at the Foreign Office language school. The next exciting stage of my diplomatic career – a four-year posting to Moscow – was on the horizon. What could go wrong?

3. FUCK THE EU!

Hillsborough Castle, Northern Ireland, October 2013

From across the crowded reception room, through florid-faced revellers in black tie and ballgown, two men clocked me and walked across. We'd never met. Or at least not in person. They introduced themselves as Messrs Lebedev and Ledenev from the Russian Embassy in London. I'd recently submitted my diplomatic visa application for Russia. How sweet of them to notice.

One was the director of the Russian trade delegation and the other a First Secretary from the Economic Department. As we sized each other up over small talk about the delights of Jamie Oliver's latest cooking show, I wondered whether Tweedledum or Tweedledee worked for Russia's foreign intelligence service, the SVR.[7]

The event, a gala dinner ahead of an investment promotion conference the following day at Belfast's Titanic Centre, was hosted by Peter Robinson and Martin McGuinness. Despite their polar-opposite politics, there was barely a fag-paper-thin difference between their speeches; I was impressed that the Unionist and Republican warhorses were able to put on a united front to promote a more positive future for Northern Ireland. While the G8 summit in June had filled all the hotels for three days and attracted global media coverage, the direct economic benefits were limited. So,

---

7 Sluzhba Vneshney Razvedki (Service of Foreign Intelligence).

I had succeeded in getting 10 Downing Street's agreement for David Cameron to return to Belfast in the autumn to bang the drum for foreign investors. It's ironic that the Prime Minister who took the UK into a fateful Brexit referendum put so much effort into promoting a prosperous Northern Ireland and positive relations with the Republic.

London

One month earlier, I'd started Russian-language training at the Old Admiralty Building by the entrance to the Mall. Veronika, a well-to-do lady from Kyiv was to be one of two teachers, working with me for four hours on alternate days. The following day I met Nadia, my second teacher, the no-nonsense Cambridge-educated linguist from the eastern Ukrainian city of Donetsk. Over the following nine months I grew fond of them both, though they couldn't have been more different. Those differences would become magnified by events.

Within weeks, we moved to the Foreign Office's gleaming new language school in the basement of King Charles Street. New Labour had closed the Diplomatic Service Language School on Millbank in the noughties. This sent an unhelpful signal that monoglot Britain didn't see foreign language use as a vital component of diplomacy. William Hague arrived as Foreign Secretary in 2010, determined to rebuild the reputation of HM Diplomatic Service as the best in the world.[8] A new language school was therefore established, and I was one of its first students.

As I sat at home in Surrey in late 2013, poring over Russian grammar exercises, I was gripped by the media frenzy that accompanied the run-up to the Eastern Partnership[9] summit in Vilnius. A

---

8 The Foreign Office has improved its performance in language learning since 2010. But even today, over a third of British diplomats paid full-time to learn Russian for fourteen months either fail their final exams or, worse still, don't get around to sitting them.

9 In 2009, the EU established the Eastern Partnership with six former Soviet states including Ukraine but excluding Russia. The other countries are Moldova, Belarus, Armenia, Azerbaijan and Georgia.

verbal punch-up was kicking off between Russia and the EU about whether the coiffured President of Ukraine, Viktor Yanukovych, should sign an EU association agreement. This would usher in a "deep and comprehensive" free-trade deal between Ukraine and the EU and visa-free travel in both directions and allow for a gradual political convergence. It reopened an old and fraught debate across Ukraine which had been suppressed during the Soviet period: did the country's future lie with Europe or with Russia?

As a language student, I wasn't copied into much reporting on Ukraine or Russia and what I did see was below confidential.[10] So, these are armchair perspectives leavened by four and a half years of having my nosed pressed up against the detailed policy discussions from Moscow.

Self-evidently, Ukraine will benefit from a strengthened economic relationship with Europe, and I hope when the fog of war subsides, it joins the EU eventually. Neighbouring Poland's economy is now significantly larger, having been a similar size when the Warsaw Pact collapsed. That isn't just down to the undoubted talents and endeavour of the Polish people. Ukraine has a similarly well-educated and industrious workforce but was struggling to cast off the rusted shackles of Soviet-era economic mismanagement.

The Western press depicted Vilnius as a zero-sum tussle between the EU and Russia over Ukraine. A UK newspaper before the summit bore a photo of Putin with the headline "Don't let him win," or something to that effect.

Viktor Yanukovych faced a zero-to-hero moment. His European counterparts courted the corrupt Ukrainian to sign and bring his country closer to Europe's orbit. Had he signed, he'd have been feted and welcomed in all the major European capitals. In the end, he went from hero to zero. Russia opened her generous purse, offering a new deal on subsidised gas and a loan of $15 billion

---

10 The confidential classification has been retired by the FCO and the term secret is now used in its place.

with no strings attached. Viktor decided Vladimir was his best bet. As the Eurocrats in Brussels cried into their moules frites, Russia paid the first tranche of $3 billion to Ukraine.

Enraged that the President had not signed the agreement, pro-European activists set up camp on Maidan Square in central Kyiv. The protest grew in scale and volume, capturing the attention of the world's media. Anti-Maidan protestors were made up of pro-government activists and Russian nationalists. Clashes between both sides grew in frequency.

This tension played itself out for me daily in the classroom. Veronika started to bring in anti-Russian cartoons and poke fun at Putin, although it was clear she didn't consider Russia's behaviour funny. Nadia complained that the news coverage in the UK was lopsided and that surely Putin wasn't that bad. They stopped talking directly and instead communicated through me. I was living in a microcosm of the Maidan Square arguments, without the violence.

The other Russian teachers were often in huddles in the library area, split into distinct pro-EU and pro-Russia groups. They reflected the clear divide in Ukraine: in Kyiv and in the west of the country, the Ukrainian language is widely spoken, and people more naturally incline to Europe than to Russia; in the east and south, including Crimea, Russian is the lingua franca and large swathes of industry were tied into Russian supply chains. And unlike some of the loony fringe elements in both camps in the Maidan, our teachers were well-educated, sophisticated Ukrainians who'd lived in the UK for many years.

Time and again I would hear colleagues either at the British Embassy in Kyiv or at the FCO in London talking emotionally about Ukraine's European "choice." But it was clear that not everyone in Ukraine saw Europe as their first or best option. The western media often depicts Ukraine as culturally and politically homogenous, with a citizenry unified in its desire to sever all connections with Russia, but this is grossly inaccurate. British and European diplomacy should have focused on building the same sort of economic relationship with Russia that it was working towards with Ukraine, so no one had to choose sides.

Meanwhile, Americans were working behind the scenes to steer any resolution of the conflict on terms acceptable to them. A transcript of a bugged call between US Assistant Secretary of State Victoria Nuland[11] and US Ambassador to Ukraine Geoffrey Pyatt was released in early February 2014. They were plotting which Maidan leader should be elevated to the role of Ukrainian Prime Minister after Yanukovych's removal. Nuland wanted Arseniy "Yarts" Yatsenyuk and was keen to get her plan signed off by then Vice President, Joe Biden. "Fuck the EU," she says, an indication of how the US saw their role in finding a solution to the crisis. European leaders, including Angela Merkel, condemned these remarks.

When people were shot and killed by unidentified snipers in Maidan Square, it was clear that Yanukovych was losing his grip on the presidency. Following intervention by the governments of Germany and Poland, Yanukovych signed an agreement on 21 February with opposition leaders. He agreed to reinstate the 2004 constitution, pass more powers back to Parliament and hold presidential elections by no later than December. Yanukovych had effectively set a date for his leaving office. It was a terrific example of European leadership by two key member states.

However, that same night Yanukovych's convoy was attacked as he left Kyiv bound for another city in Ukraine and his mansions were occupied by the oppositionists. The following day, he fled the country. He was voted out of office by the Ukrainian Parliament the day after with a vote tally that fell slightly short of that required under the impeachment provisions in Ukraine's constitution.

I remember thinking at the time, *The Russians aren't going to like this.* Had Yanukovych signed the association agreement and been ousted by pro-Russian extremists, it would have been

---

11 Having been side-lined by Trump, Nuland returned to steer US policy towards Russia after Biden's election as President.

condemned from the rooftops of the Berlaymont and the Capitol. Instead, Western diplomats shrugged their shoulders when the 21 February agreement was binned. Arseniy Yatsenyuk was ushered into power as Prime Minister, with presidential elections set for May.

At best, this process had taken place in a constitutionally questionable way. Putin convinced himself that he had proof of his long-held suspicion: Western countries were happy to see the removal of Russian-leaning leaders of other countries by undemocratic means. To this day, Russia refers to the removal of Yanukovych as an "illegal coup d'etat." While the origins of the Ukraine conflict go back much further, this was the flashpoint that lit the slow-burning fuse to eventual war.

One can't help but wonder how differently the Ukraine crisis would have run had matters been allowed to follow the course charted by the German and Polish Foreign Ministers on 21 February. It's significant that Putin's representative at the negotiations that fateful night did not sign the agreement. Russia may have tried to slow down implementation of the agreement later. But it's hard to see how Yanukovych could have clung to power without a more violent resurgence of the Maidan movement. The point is academic now.

Buoyed by anti-Russian sentiment, Ukraine's Parliament cancelled a law giving regions of Ukraine the right to have a second official language. This meant that in places like Crimea and eastern Ukraine, Russian could not be recognised as an official second language even though it was the language that most people used. It was a move of monumental stupidity; it alienated a significant proportion of Ukraine's population[12] and played into Putin's narrative of a hostile west bent on destroying Russia and Russian speakers. Western powers should have called it out at the time.

Yanukovych's ouster and the abolition of the language law destroyed an equilibrium that had been in place since Ukraine

---

12 Estimates vary on the total number of Russian speakers in Ukraine, but Ukraine's only census of 2001 listed ethnic Russians as 17.8% of the population.

gained independence in 1991. Major protests erupted throughout the Russian-speaking parts of Ukraine. The Russian military massed along the border and the global press wondered where they might strike. Crimea was a popular holiday destination for Russians and Ukrainians alike. Ethnic Russians constitute the largest group of people in Crimea. The Russian Black Sea Fleet had a longstanding basing agreement at Sevastopol. Hindsight's a wonderful thing.

On 27 February 2014, shortly after the curtains had closed on the Winter Olympics in nearby Sochi, Russian troops without insignia on their green uniforms took over key sites in Crimea. Russia had annexed the sovereign territory of her neighbour, gambling correctly that NATO wouldn't fight for it.

The EU imposed its first sanctions on Russia and Russia's membership of the G8 was suspended. A hastily rigged referendum in Crimea voted in favour of integration with Russia. On 21 March 2014, Crimea was formally absorbed when Russia's Federation Council rubber-stamped a treaty of accession.

In the Foreign Office language centre, tensions increased. Veronika and the pro-European teachers were furious that Russia had stolen Ukrainian territory. I steered clear of the subject to avoid an angry tirade about Russian repression. Nadia would shrug her shoulders and say, "What did they expect, after what happened to Yanukovych?" My job was to learn Russian, and I wasn't going to take sides.

The move on Crimea proved popular with ordinary Russians who considered the peninsula part of Russia going back to the days of Catherine the Great. It gave a huge boost to President Putin's popularity rating, which had been in slow and steady decline since 2009. By Western standards, an approval rating of 61% in 2013 was high. After Crimea, it bounced up to 87%.

A live-fire conflict then erupted in eastern Ukraine, in an area collectively known as the Donbass.[13] Full-blown war was being waged in Europe for the first time since the Balkans conflict ended twenty years earlier. A bloody line of contact was frozen into the earth that barely shifted until Russia's full-scale invasion in February 2022. For Veronika, the eastern separatists were terrorists, while Nadia was sad that she was no longer able easily to visit her relatives in Donetsk, which is now a war zone.

Russia has been cast firmly in the role of the revanchist aggressor by the West. Putin undoubtedly responded to the facts as they were presented to him by hawkish intelligence and military chiefs and saw an opportunity to give the West a bloody nose. But Europe's failure to push back against the Americans and hold Ukrainian protest leaders to the 21 February agreement was a tactical blunder with huge strategic consequences. And the tendency among western leaders since 2014 to put the blame completely in Russia's lap is one of the many reasons why Ukraine is a war zone today.

Towards the end of May 2014, a new President of Ukraine was elected: confectionery billionaire Petro Poroshenko. His arrival heralded a brief period of optimism. European leaders thought engagement between Poroshenko and Putin might start to cool the temperature of the war in the Donbass. President Hollande of France came up with a plan: both Putin and Poroshenko had confirmed their attendance at commemorations in France to mark the 70th anniversary of the D-Day Normandy landings. A new format of dialogue, to be named the Normandy Contact Group, would be established with the French and German leaders plus Putin and Poroshenko.

Around this time, David Cameron was preoccupied by his bid to stop Jean-Claude Juncker from becoming European Commission President. Cameron had single-handedly faced down EU member

---

13 After widespread protests, separatist groups in Luhansk and Donetsk provinces declared their independence from Ukraine and initially made significant territorial gains. When the Ukrainian Army regrouped and regained territory, Russia upped its involvement in the conflict.

states at the end of 2011, vetoing an attempted amendment to the Lisbon Treaty. The Germans, Swedes and Dutch had sympathy with the UK position on Juncker. But it was clear in Whitehall, which was being whipped into a diplomatic frenzy on the anti-Juncker campaign, that Cameron was never going to win this fight. Rather, he'd placed himself once more on the European naughty step and, whether knowingly or not, taken the UK one step closer to Brexit.

Spotting an ideal opportunity to blank the upstart *rosbif* on Ukraine policy, Hollande convened the first Normandy-format meeting with Merkel, Putin and Poroshenko on 6 June 2014, while Cameron enjoyed the military bands.

The UK, which had been the leading voice in imposing sanctions on Russia following Crimea, was caught flat-footed. Staffers at the Foreign Office would tell you, "Oh well, the Americans aren't in the Normandy format either, so why does it matter?" But the Americans were paddling their own canoe on Ukraine policy and didn't need to align with the EU to have talks with Poroshenko and Putin; the UK, on the other hand, was stuck in a policy no-man's land, a position that the Russians, French and Germans were happy for us to occupy. In King Charles Street, the Foreign Office Director covering Russia and Ukraine left suddenly and unexpectedly.

The British Ambassador in Moscow was thenceforth frozen out of senior-level dialogue with Russia on Ukraine, reliant on crumbs of insight from his German and French counterparts. Even before I'd arrived in Moscow, the UK had lost any influence it may have had. In the eight years between the start of the Ukraine crisis and Russia's eventual invasion in February 2022, Britain remained almost completely shut out of efforts towards a peaceful resolution of the conflict.

On 15 July 2014, Jean-Claude Juncker was elected as European Commission President. That same night, William Hague resigned from David Cameron's government, his departure packaged as part of a big reshuffle, branded by some as a new "night of the long knives." Cameron has said that Hague wanted to leave Parliament to pursue other interests. But it wasn't clear why a grandee of the Conservative Party would step down from his office of state ten months before the next general election. Rumour swirled that he'd fallen on his sword for Cameron's twin failures on Juncker and Ukraine policy.

Hague was the best Foreign Secretary during my career. He arrived at the Foreign Office after thirteen years of New Labour disinvestment in diplomacy, and breathed life and purpose back into the organisation. A political titan, he was replaced by "spreadsheet Phil" Hammond, who I hoped would be a short-lived stopgap. He wouldn't be the first square peg, after Margaret Beckett's meaningless caravan tour of King Charles Street in 2006/07.

I wasn't initially put off by the UK's self-imposed exclusion from the Normandy format, nor the loss of a great Foreign Secretary. With the foolish enthusiasm of a diplomat waiting to start a new overseas posting, I felt the need for diplomatic engagement with Russia was greater than ever.

4. WELCOME TO MOSCOW

Moscow, Russia, July 2014

"**D**id David Cameron send you?" Ivan Ivanovich boomed, as he opened the heavy wooden door to our apartment block. The building supervisor was a neat-as-a-pin sixty-year-old ex-Red Army soldier with close-cropped sandy hair. When he saw the kids, he descended into high-pitched grandpa Russian and gave them sweets, before walloping me on the shoulder with his massive hands and giving me a big smile.

"Do you like David Cameron then?" I countered in Russian.

He stood bolt upright, towering above me from the top step, index finger aloft and eyes wide. "No, I don't like David Cameron!" He fired off a salvo of reasons why he didn't and why Russia was a great country.

I shook his hand and said, "Don't worry about it. I'm pleased to be in Russia." First tip of diplomacy: always try to say nice things about the country you are living in.

Ivan heaved our collection of suitcases and pushchairs up the stairs. At the door to our apartment, he grinned and pinched the kids' cheeks before retreating. It was the first time I noticed Russians are great with kids. In a country where millions died during the Second World War, children are cherished and worshipped. I hadn't expected that.

With its high ceilings and unadorned walls, the apartment – built before the Russian Revolution – did not feel homely. It would be another month before our possessions arrived from the UK. We had a cup of tea, then wandered along the Old Arbat, where Ivan Bezdomny had chased the mysterious Woland and his entourage in Bulgakov's *The Master and Margarita*. Our life in Russia had begun.

Everyone who's applied to work at the British Embassy in Moscow knows there is a 5–10% chance the Russian state will refuse them a visa. If the British government blocks a Russian diplomatic visa application – normally because they think the applicant is an undeclared intelligence officer – the Russians will refuse one of our diplomats on a tit-for-tat basis. It's a lottery with the Damocles finger of "It Could Be You" hanging ominously over your head.

In July 2014, I'd been sweating for ten months, wondering if I was going to Russia or not. Then one day, halfway through a Russian lesson, a fellow student tapped my shoulder. He'd heard a rumour that my diplomatic visa had been issued. I almost sprinted down Whitehall to the Foreign Office travel centre at the Old Admiralty Building. Sure enough, my family's passports had arrived from the Russian Embassy, stamped with three-year visas.

Within days, my elation had evaporated. On 17 July 2014, Malaysian Airlines flight 17 from Amsterdam to Kuala Lumpur was shot down over eastern Ukraine by a Russian-made BUK missile. This reckless act led to the death of all 298 passengers and crew, including eighty children. As someone who enjoys air travel with my kids, that tragedy still makes me shudder. The separatists and Ukrainian government accused each other. Putin made a late-night TV appearance looking visibly shaken by the sudden outpouring of international condemnation.

Just days later, I paid a short visit to Moscow to find a place to live. Sheremetyevo Airport had been tarted up since my visit in 2006. I checked into a modern hotel near the Embassy where the receptionist complimented me on my Russian. On TV, state-run news channels were awash with reports from the Donbass of the CIA and MI6 supporting the conflict: an indignant reporter displayed fragments of an American-made munition or British medical pack, ostensibly found at the scene.[14] Russia's propaganda machine was in full swing.

Some colleagues took me for a meal at a Georgian restaurant on the Ukraine Boulevard. It was alive with the hubbub of young and trendy customers eating al fresco during the long summer night. During the grinding misery of the latter stages of the Soviet Union, Georgian restaurants were the most popular in Moscow. The meal was simple, hearty and delicious, and I returned to this restaurant many times with family.

The following day, I found a nice apartment fifteen minutes from the Embassy in the aptly named Denezhniy Pereulok, or Money Lane. I never wanted to live in one of the thirty purpose-built flats in the Embassy. British colleagues can cling to "compound life" and avoid immersion in the country to which they've been posted. If there's an Embassy pub, a shop with Walkers crisps and duty-free booze, life's good. But that's never appealed.

Under a warm summer sun, I walked to Red Square, past goose-stepping guards, and took the first of many selfies in front of the onion-domed St Basil's Cathedral. I enjoyed my first experience of the Moscow Metro then flew home. My second whirlwind 24-hour visit in eight years.

On 31 July 2014, the day the EU imposed its toughest sanctions yet on Russia, the British Economic Counsellor and family boarded a British Airways flight to Moscow. On their first ever flight, my son watched CBeebies, and my seven-month-old daughter crawled happily along the aisle. They've always been great travellers.

It was a glorious day when we landed in Moscow, without a cloud in the cornflower sky and temperatures in the high twenties. After a few days of settling in, I got into the low-level psychological

---

14 No military assistance was provided to Ukraine during the early period of the Donbass conflict. The UK approved a package of non-lethal military assistance including training to the Ukrainian military in February 2015 and the Trump administration agreed to the sale of Javelin anti-tank weapons in March 2018.

warfare of the daily tussle with the Russian diplomatic police at the front gate of the Embassy. They'd randomly stand in my way and insist on seeing my Embassy pass, even though they knew who I was and had no legal right to detain me. I'd drop a shoulder and shimmy past as the heavy metal gate whirred open to let me in. I'd smile and say, "Thanks for your help today" on my way home. The next day, they'd be waiting with a bigger smile, and a salute for good measure, before asking to see my staff pass. Despite this, the Embassy security guards had an amazing ability to let in suspicious-looking people without passes, with the diplomatic police nodding them through.

For over seventy years, the British Embassy operated out of the Ambassador's Residence on Sofiyskaya Embankment, with some offices dotted around the city. In 2000, a modern Embassy, composed of four metal and glass blocks, was opened on Smolenskaya Embankment. It's a stone's throw from the White House,[15] where President Yeltsin famously climbed on a tank in 1991 as an act of defiance against the attempted military coup. The materials and labour for the new building were trucked into Russia via Finland. Every dollop of cement was scrutinised, to prevent the introduction of listening devices and other sneaky tech. Steam billowed from the site during the winter, as heaters dried the foundations.

The largest of the four towers of the British Embassy – the office block – is split down the middle by a thick concrete and metal septum. It separates the East Wing from the West Wing. All Russian staff work in the East. The Ambassador, Chancery diplomats,[16] military and security types work in the West Wing.[17] It's a parody

---

15 The Russian White House is the seat of government in Russia, while the Kremlin is the Presidential Palace.

16 The term Chancery refers to the diplomatic service officers at an embassy who work principally on traditional diplomacy, diplomatic reporting and foreign policy development.

17 Yes, we really call it that.

of the Berlin Wall without the machine-gun towers.

It was the end of August and Moscow was waking up as ministers and government officials drifted back from their dachas. Tim Barrow, Her Majesty's Ambassador to Russia, had returned from his summer break. West Wing colleagues were on edge.

For up to ninety minutes, three days per week, the meeting room became the Roman Colosseum, with Emperor Tim watching imperiously over his gladiators. He'd start with a thirty-minute monologue, ranging over and connecting the various insights he'd gathered since the previous Chancery meeting. A tour-de-table followed, and everyone was expected to raise two or three issues.

With at least fifteen ambitious people at the table, there were never enough interesting stories to go around. Tim would lob in a difficult question to poleaxe officers who hadn't prepared. Martin Harris, Tim's deputy, and current British Ambassador to Ukraine, would probe gaps in logic or facts, to see if officers would stand their ground.

It was clear the larger political team saw themselves as top dogs. In my first month, my political oppo took pleasure in correcting me – the new guy – on points of detail about Russia or Russian policy. I decided to focus on the detail of my areas, so no one could out-manoeuvre me. Sanctions, Russia's energy sector and Ukraine's free-trade deal with Europe were sexy, high-profile issues; for want of a juicy story of their own, political colleagues often strayed into economics. I was soon correcting my political oppo. If political colleagues missed an interesting story in their area, a member of my team would throw it in. Tim grinned from ear to ear with each slap-down.

While the rules of engagement were understood, several people found the process demoralising. Someone described the Foreign Office as a group of over-achievers struggling to get along. The one-upmanship and chest-thumping hubris of the Chancery meeting typified this. It would have felt a better use of time if Chancery colleagues gained their insight by time outside of the

Embassy, meeting Russian contacts in Moscow and further afield.

In fact, much of the insight was drawn from unclassified media or from diplomats in other Western embassies. It was in this august setting, nine years ago, that I first heard the rumour that Putin's occasional disappearances from public view might be related to a mysterious and terrible illness that could kill him within days. Together with sudden political implosion, imminent death of Putin is one of the popular narratives that you still see today online as Bing.news and Geezer.live cling to any sign that the war in Ukraine might be brought to its end.

A new set of diplomatic telegrams (DipTels) for London was commissioned at each meeting. Every working day, we'd barrel-bomb Whitehall with DipTels about Russia. For particularly significant issues, Tim wrote letters to the Prime Minister or Foreign Secretary, which we'd draft.

As most officers in Chancery couldn't speak Russian, they spent their time cutting and pasting Russian articles into Google Translate.

Of course, the most valuable piece of any diplomatic telegram is the opinion from our man or woman wherever about what it means for the UK's relationship with that country. But again, that relies on diplomats getting out to build a deep understanding of the political landscape. Veteran BBC correspondent Steve Rosenburg has more knowledge and insight on Russia in his big toe than the Foreign Office's finest in Moscow at that time. We might just as well have asked him to sit with Tim and a typist whenever we wanted to send a Telegram; it would certainly have been cheaper.

With his tatty beard and expensively tailored waistcoats, Tim Barrow was like a character from a seventies Catherine Cookson drama. As he seldom used his computer, draft DipTels were presented to him on paper. He'd study the draft, scribble a few notes, then put his feet up and read a novel for a while. He'd scribble more notes before handing the draft back, then go out for an evening function or dinner. His writing was illegible, like a spider had been dropped in ink and allowed to scurry across the manuscript. Whichever poor schmuck had drafted the piece would spend aeons deciphering the writing so amendments could be made. Officers would hang around all night waiting for Tim to return to look at a final draft and approve the partially re-digested piece of third-party journalism that might have started its life on page six of *Izvestia*.

When I arrived in Moscow, officers were exhausted after six months in a Chancery pressure cooker which had been steaming since the onset of the Ukraine crisis. Several staff were unhappy about the crushing long-hours culture. When I visited to look at apartments, Thorhilda "Thorda" Abbott-Watt was camped out in my office. She'd been despatched to talk with staff and make recommendations to London on how to improve morale. Thorda was a Foreign Office legend, having served as Ambassador in a string of embassies across the region. She was the right person to test the temperature and report back to London. With a paper version of her report burning a hole in Tim's in-tray, Martin Harris convened a meeting for Chancery staff to discuss its findings, not long after I arrived.

The conclusion was that "Tim's never going to change."

Tim is a formidable diplomat and can be a lot of fun. But, with a young family, I'd made a conscious choice not to buy into his working practices. I left work by six-thirty most days and seldom later than seven. If I had an evening function to attend, I'd leave the office earlier to see my family. If Tim hadn't cleared my DipTel, it could wait until the morning. Having worked on many of the biggest crises the UK has been involved in since 2001, I have a fairly good feel for what is genuinely urgent, and in those situations, I'd stay as long as I needed to get the job finished. And in fairness to Tim, he never insisted I work unreasonable hours.

But more junior officers were in awe of one of Britain's most senior diplomats, and that was part of the problem. Colleagues would work until eight or nine o'clock each day even if there was no DipTel to send. It gave them a chance to have "Tim time," as he'd often stalk the corridors of Chancery late at night, cracking jokes with the team, who lapped it up. In a big embassy like Moscow, young ambitious officers also want visibility with seniors in London and a regular suck on the career-affirming momma-nipple of policy relevance; you don't get that by spending time outside of the building. So, some Chancery colleagues exhibited a sort of Stockholm syndrome. For as much as they complained about captivity, they loved their captor, wanted desperately for Tim to love them too, and couldn't bear the thought of escape.

Chancery was packed with super-intelligent and talented people, but this was a far cry from William Hague's vision of the 'Best Diplomatic Service in the World;' none of the junior staff saw themselves as diplomats! An exception was the Internal Political Head. She'd taken up figure-skating, a Russian obsession. This had opened a whole world of travel around Russia for skating competitions, through which she'd got a feel for the pulse of the country and a wide circle of friends. When I arrived, she was the only officer in Chancery to have passed her Russian-language exams, furnishing her with written and spoken Russian up to degree level. While I hadn't been able to complete my Russian studies before my posting to Moscow started, I was determined to sit the exams by the end of the following year. I wanted to get out of Moscow as much as possible and acquire first-hand insight into this ginormous, complex country. The British Embassy could surely do better than sending repackaged downstream opinion to Ministers and senior officials in London.

5. UNDER THE FSB MICROSCOPE

Moscow, Russia, August 2014

"Shit on the walls?" I asked.

"The cleaners found the men's changing room plastered in the brown stuff first thing on Monday," my colleague Sandy clarified, with a nervous smile.

"Might have been Eddy," he continued. "He pooed his pants after a night on the drink once and still brags about it."

I sighed.

The changing rooms were around the corner from the Embassy bar. It was standard, whenever anything weird happened at the Embassy, to point a finger at the FSB by default. However, the jury was out on the poo-smeared wall. It wasn't that long ago that someone had shat in the Embassy pool and left it floating.

This mattered to me because I'd agreed to become chair of the Embassy sports and social committee. It's normal for diplomats to take on voluntary roles at overseas embassies and I was keen to start off on the right foot. I thought it would be a doddle.

However, the Embassy bar – the Hammer and Pickle – resembled a Wild West duty-free saloon which stayed open late most nights. Most evenings, "compound kids" tore up and down the long red corridor that connected the apartment and office blocks, hollering like hyenas. And Martin Harris said from the start that he wanted me to crack down on these feral antics. Specifically, he wanted a strict closing time for the bar and rules on the behaviour of children. I knew that would go down like a lead balloon. So, I decided the perfect counterpoint to tougher rules was a free Christmas party for all staff and their families at the Ambassador's Residence. Everyone would love that, right?

"The SO has started an investigation, although I don't think we have CCTV cameras in the swimming pool area," the first colleague went on.

"Ah yes. The SO," I replied.

. . .

"I'll give you a security briefing at two o'clock in the meeting room." A while later, the tall, lumpen shape of the Security Officer or SO for short, blocked all light from the door to my office. As I breathed, it was as if the air turned to ice in my lungs. He stared at me, unblinking, as if his eyelids had been removed in training.

"I have something else on at two. Do you mind if we meet slightly later?"

He glared back at me like Obi-Wan Kenobi finding an Imperial Stormtrooper in his path. "We will meet at two."

"We will meet at two," I replied.

You never say no to the SO. He's the guardian of our secrets and protector against infiltration. He's supported by a team of mostly British ex-military and police security officers who prowl the Embassy 24/7.

All British Diplomats go through a process called Developed Vetting, or DV. Getting DV or having it renewed involves (normally) a retired police officer interrogating you for several hours having checked up on you with people you know. I have agreed not to disclose the specifics of how the process works.[18] But suffice it to say that most staff get a security once-over before they fly to

18 I agreed with the Cabinet Office request to remove a 500-word section of text here.

Moscow, for obvious reasons. DV is normally awarded for several years, before renewal.

Life in the Chancery was akin to membership of a secretive monastic order. The need for a solid wall between East and West was considered unfortunate but inevitable. And of course, the risks were even greater outside of the secure walls of the Embassy.

• • •

"That's my seat," I said.

The scruffy man looked up with an oily smile. "Oh, were you sitting here?" He spoke with a slight English accent, suggesting an expensive education.

We'd been in Moscow for less than a month and decided, as a family, to visit the Anglican Church of St Andrew, close to the Kremlin. A good chance to meet non-Embassy people and enjoy a Sunday service. Built in Victorian times, the neo-Gothic church had been used by the Soviets for various purposes: as a machine-gun tower, a warehouse and, in more recent years, because of the amazing acoustics and its organ, a recording studio. It was handed back to the Anglican church in 1994 during a visit to Russia by Her Majesty the Queen. It's now a major centre of worship not only for expat Brits but also for a community drawn from many countries, including Russia. Until recently, the vicar carried the title of Chaplain to the British Embassy and was afforded diplomatic status – God's Ambassador.

We sat down surrounded by a sea of empty seats as it was the holiday season. St Andrew's was waiting for a new vicar to be issued with his visa, so a lay preacher was holding the service. The kids were bored and cranky, so my wife Katharine took them to an adjacent playroom. I had stepped out to see them, but when I walked back into the nave, this geezer was sitting in my chair. Could have picked any chair. There were over one hundred empty seats all around and the bric-a-brac of personal possessions, toys and hymn books on our seats. No. He'd decided to sit in my chair.

He got up and moved to sit somewhere behind me, though I was aware of his prying porcine eyes on my back. After the service, as I was having coffee, he slimed up and offered a limp handshake.

"So, are you new to Moscow?" he asked.

"Yes, that's right."

"Did you come here to work?"

"Yep."

"Where do you work?"

You know where I work. "At the British Embassy."

"Oh, that's interesting. Do you organise lots of events to promote relationships between our countries?"

"I've just arrived. Still figuring it out."

I turned away, found Katharine and we left with the kids.

This Russian dude at church kept appearing throughout my posting. Whether he was in a suit or in scruffs, his appearance was unmistakable. A greasy, unattractive face with jam-jar glasses, fawning, slightly bent posture and an obsequious manner. I had a handful of "regulars," and he was one.

You might be surprised to learn that the number of British diplomats in Russia is smaller than the number of Russian diplomats in the UK. So, for the FSB, that makes every one of us a high value target. Taking out a single British diplomat from Russia tips the balance even more in their favour. If they get under our skin, we might get fed up and leave. If we are stuck to a honeytrap, the Foreign Office will send us home. If we are turned, we'll be traitors and cursed for all eternity. And maybe end up in jail. We shine as brightly on the SO's radar as on the FSB's. More than any other British Embassy, we are aware of that pressure every day we walk outside of the Embassy walls. Which may help to explain why many officers remained inside. Another victory, to Russia.

It's hard to exaggerate the feeling of being under scrutiny by the intelligence services in Moscow. Unlike any other expat job in the city, as a diplomat, you are constantly under the microscope. At any time, in the most random ways, the FSB can try to intimidate you or, more sinister, obtain "Kompromat."[19]

In 2009, the then UK Deputy Consul General to Ekaterinburg was secretly filmed in a hotel room with two prostitutes. As soon as the video was leaked in the press, he resigned. The media speculated on the role of the FSB in the video's capture. But he didn't appear to be under duress.

It's common practice for the FSB to enter diplomats' apartments while they are not home. When the FSB had been for a visit, it was common to find an unflushed poo in the toilet. I called this "state-sponsored shit." If the agent was a smoker, there might be a cigarette butt on the toilet seat. If it was midwinter, the windows at the apartment might be left open. Mostly, you never saw them. You just knew they had visited. With a couple of high-profile and violent exceptions, the FSB don't usually cause physical harm to foreign diplomats. Low-level harassment is intended to undermine an officer's feeling of security and make them question whether it's in their best interests to stay in Russia. Having served a tour in Helmand Province during the most violent period of the Afghan conflict, soft surveillance never bothered me that much. Katharine and I laughed off the oddities of perfect Russian couples wandering on the street outside our apartment block then appearing at the table next to us in restaurants on the other side of town. We were starting to enjoy family life in Moscow.

When interviewing officers who'd applied to work at the Embassy in Moscow, I asked them to think seriously about whether Moscow was right for them. If they were prepared to come with eyes wide open, ready to laugh off the harassment and perma-surveillance as a bit of a joke, then the chances were they'd be fine. I never felt my family was under threat and we enjoyed our weekends and holidays in Moscow, with its parks, restaurants and attractions.

However, at the back of my mind, I was always wary of being

---

19 Kompromat is a compression of the Russian words for compromising and materials.

compromised. In those circumstances, it's almost impossible to trust anyone completely. But I was determined not to let that stop me having a normal life in Russia and to make friends where possible.

A few days later, I walked into work and steeled myself for the daily battle with the diplomatic police. Yards ahead, I spotted a British colleague holding hands with a female member of the Russian staff. A frown wrinkled my forehead. *This is going to end in tears.*[20]

---

20 It did end in tears. The Cabinet Office insisted that I redact a relevant section of text in a later chapter.

6. FIRST CONTACTS

Moscow, Russia, September 2014

I stared at the untidy pile of whitened satsuma segments on the plate before me. My American counterpart raised an eyebrow. With studied care, Chef had laid on a lunchtime sanctions scrawny satsuma "screw you!" special for the unfriendly Westerners.[21] With its glass barrelled roof and commanding views towards the Kremlin, the White Rabbit restaurant was famed for its fine dining take on Russian classics. At our table in the far corner of the empty dining room, we might as well have been in a working man's canteen in Soviet days.

After Western nations increased sanctions against Russia in late July 2014, relations with the Kremlin deteriorated quickly. Following the collapse of a low-cost airline Dobrolet on 4 August, President Putin said Russia would retaliate. I spent a lot of time with my team assessing the options at Russia's disposal and reporting to London. It was clear that many of the measures considered would cause at least as much economic harm to Russia itself.

Cutting oil and gas exports to Europe would be like playing Russian roulette with a fully loaded gun; there is no evidence that Russia has ever sought to cut energy supplies to Europe to serve a wider political goal. Prior to the war in Ukraine, flag carrier Aeroflot

---

21 I enjoyed many lunches at White Rabbit after this first encounter, without incident.

would have lost a lot of income if Russia banned Western airlines from flying across Siberia en-route to Asia. Stopping sale of rockets to Western space agencies would have advantaged US producers at Russia's expense. So, on 6 August, Prime Minister Medvedev announced a ban on most food and dairy products from Western nations that had imposed sanctions on Russia.

Banning food imports in 2014 represented the toughest economic sanction Russia could impose without significant self-harm to its own economy. Indeed, it opened an economic opportunity: in 2013, Europe exported $12 billion in agricultural goods to Russia; the Kremlin authorised massive state subsidies for domestic producers to plug the gap in food supplies, at least in part. Russian state TV news soon carried images of bulldozers triumphantly crushing piles of Spanish peaches or Polish apples into the black earth of the motherland. Western produce quickly disappeared from supermarket shelves in central Moscow. How do you like them apples? But for the UK, the impact was small at less than £50 million, the main casualties being spuds, mackerel and cheese. For the Americans, the nominal economic cost was lower still.

One aspect of western media commentary on sanctions that gets little coverage is how few retaliatory economic options Russia has as its disposal. Since the war in Ukraine started in February 2022, Russia's economic countermeasures have been tiny when compared to the tidal wave of western sanctions. As the need to retaliate is hard-wired into Russian doctrine, this helps to explain the increasing use of asymmetric tactics since 2014.

I suggested we discuss Russia's shift in focus towards trade and investment with China and other countries. Two-way sanctions had precipitated a juddering transition in which Russia was scrabbling to set up new supply chains and find new sources of lending globally. This threw up tensions. How might deeper relations with China rub up against Russia's established partnerships with Vietnam and India? What would a pivot to China mean for Russia's longer-term political relations with Europe and the US?

We agreed to meet with our respective teams for a deeper and more open discussion. After a lunch that was low in corporeal and intellectual calories, I paid the bill and decorously refused to add a tip. We left the restaurant together and left the building through different exits.

I've worked with some great American colleagues, including in Russia. But in my experience, the Americans are unremittingly transactional and always put their interests first. In the initial phase of the Ukraine crisis, EU and US sanctions against Russia overlapped significantly, with differences of detail around the edges. So, it undoubtedly made sense to talk.

However, I enjoyed a closer relationship with my European colleagues. Wolf, the jovial Bavarian, was one of the first to reach out; he invited me to join a lunch club with like-minded northern European diplomats.[22] The group met throughout my time in Moscow, with old friends departing at the end of their postings and new members joining. It was always a friendly, professional venue to compare insight and gossip. We'd often invite guests, like the IMF and World Bank resident representatives, or well-regarded Russian academics.

Every month, Economic Counsellors from those member states with Embassies in Moscow met at the European delegation office for a round-table. In those early days after my arrival the meetings were often bad-tempered. My Spanish counterpart ranted about the economic damage caused to his country by Russian agricultural sanctions. Southern European nations in particular had significant reservations. I wasn't convinced that the EU consensus on sanctions could hold for long. No one had spelled out what the conditions might be for sanctions removal, and in those early days many people, at least in the EU, seemed to think sanctions would be fairly short-term.

---

22 My counterparts from the Dutch, Finnish, French, German and Swedish Embassies met once a month for lunch, joined by a very nice guy from the Swiss Embassy. We'd later be joined by the economic lead from the Polish Embassy.

. . .

"I'll get a cab from my place and pick you upon the way," Tom, my energy expert, said.

It was a bright September evening when the taxi dropped us outside a Korean restaurant with a view across the river to Gorky Park.

Our host, Ivan Zolotov had been a Soviet, then Russian, diplomat, serving in senior roles including at the Russian Embassy in London. At his dacha, a couple of hours out of Moscow, a framed photo sits in pride of place: a younger, handsome Ivan a few steps behind President Yeltsin and Her Majesty the late Queen during her state visit to St Petersburg in 1994. After retirement, he'd taken a job as head of international relations at Russia's gas giant, Gazprom.

Prior to the Ukraine war, Europe got just over one third of its gas from Russia and for some countries, such as the Baltic states, there was an almost 100% dependency. That undoubtedly gave Russia some leverage. In reality, Russia needs to export its gas, in part to subsidise domestic consumption at discounted rates, a hangover from Soviet days. For a Russian economy that has struggled to diversify, gas exports provide a significant source of foreign reserves and domestic tax receipts. At that time, cutting off gas supplies to Europe would have represented a nuclear option with massive economic costs to Russia itself. And there was practically no evidence that Russia wanted this.

But with a large proportion of Russian gas exports to Europe piped through Ukraine, energy security emerged as a totemic political issue. Ukraine secured significant income – around $3 billion per year – from transit revenues, a fee paid by Russia for the right to export its gas over Ukrainian territory. Ukraine wanted to buy less gas from Russia, moving to import gas via Europe in what was called "reverse flow." But it didn't want to lose the lucrative transit income.

And so Western solidarity with Ukraine over Crimea and the war in the Donbass leaked across into the energy relationship. Nothing characterised this more than Russia's planned underwater gas pipeline. Nordstream II would increase capacity to export gas into Europe by over fifty billion cubic metres per year. With a separate Southstream pipeline[23] planned through Bulgaria, the Ukrainians saw this a major threat to the gas pipeline through their country and the related transit income.

We didn't have much skin in the game. Shell held a 10% stake in Nordstream II. But at that time, the UK got less than 2% of its gas from Russia, importing the largest share from Norway. But Russia's energy relationship with Europe often got policymakers in London hot under the collar. The Americans were set against Nordstream II and Southstream, while seeking to expand their exports of liquified natural gas to Europe. And so, the UK found itself in another policy no-man's land: we didn't import much gas from Russia, but if the Americans were opposed to the project, then we must be so inclined, even though we had little leverage to block it.

Ivan dressed immaculately, with an expensive silk tie and matching handkerchief in the breast pocket of his blazer. After pleasantries, he made a short and formal speech in which he welcomed me to Russia and extended best wishes for my posting. In classic Russian fashion, he offered a toast before we all tossed back our first vodka of the night. *Na zdarovyeh!*

We washed that down with beer and munched on zakuski snacks, as he ordered another round and some food. I learned my first Russian aphorism: vodka without beer is money on the wind. Vodka is Russia's national drink, but it's seldom drunk without a chaser and food, to soften the alcohol. And so, the evening wound on. Earnest discussion of the merits of another Russian gas pipeline to Europe was punctuated by vodka toasts. Heartfelt professions of desire to achieve greater heights of friendship and cooperation

---

23 The Southstream project was scrapped in December 2014, to be replaced by a Turkstream project, in which gas would be piped via Turkey.

were fortified by beer chasers, kimchi and grilled meat.

As the alcoholic fog descended, Ivan and Tom fell into a heated argument about who was at fault for the war in the Donbass. Tom called Ivan out on the self-evident truth of Russian military support to the Ukrainian separatists; Ivan dug in along a line of contact drawn by the West's indifference to the suffering of Russian-speaking communities. It was a graphic illustration of how differently British diplomats and Russians perceive the issues at stake in eastern Ukraine. After going after each other hammer and sickles for a while, it was clear that agreement was impossible, and I was too hammered to go for another vodka toast. So, I suggested we draw a line under the evening. We summoned a cab and offered Ivan a lift home. When we dropped him off, there were hugs, handshakes and fervent drunken promises to meet again soon, with no trace of rancour. As I rubbed my temples in the taxi home and contemplated a big jug of water and paracetamol, I focused on a small flame of understanding through the rapidly closing tunnel of my mental senses: Russian people are fearsome in an argument, but they prefer to settle with no hard feelings and agree to disagree.

· · ·

Across the river, the cream and gold façade of the Grand Kremlin Palace shone under a cornflower sky. I stared out of the large window, past the fluttering Union Flag towards the iron-gated entrance to the British Ambassador's Residence. In addition to my office at the Embassy, a lot of my work took place here, meeting senior Russian contacts at various receptions and dinners, of the type caricatured in Ferrero Rocher adverts.[24]

More than a month into my posting, I'd been on a non-stop roller coaster of meetings. Still early days, but I'd learnt, when dealing with Russian contacts, that you need the conversational confidence

---

24 After you've been to as many as I have, believe me, the excitement wears off.

to get past the sometimes hostile and antagonistic public face. Some people interpret the two-headed Russian eagle as looking both east and west, which I think may be right. But I always had a sense of the private and public faces. If you refuse to talk, or do all your talking via the press, then the public eagle will peck your eyes out.

Of all the senior figures I met, Andrey Kostin was the most outwardly hostile towards the West, at least in public. Kostin is the chair of one of a large state owned bank, VTB, which has been sanctioned since 2014. I'd go to various economic conferences and see him, red in the face, smashing his fist into the table and railing against the Western lackies trying to emasculate Russia. Like a cornered Russian bear, his default was to come out swinging his big paws at the pale-faced Western hunter in plaid.

But he didn't appear obviously to be driven by a deep-rooted enmity towards the UK. He'd known Tim Barrow since the early nineties when Tim had been a Second Secretary at the British Embassy and Kostin had been a junior staffer at the Soviet Ministry of Foreign Affairs. That emotional connection seemed to matter to Kostin. Many top-level Russians avoided receptions at the British Ambassador's Residence like the plague, but Kostin would often show up. When he wasn't playing to the public galleries, he could be jovial and good-natured, talking in more conciliatory terms, despite huge differences in viewpoint on many issues, including Ukraine. Like a diplomat, Kostin was not averse to exploring the scope for common ground, as if he believed deep down that with a bit of effort and mutual understanding, we could be friends.

• • •

Moscow was enjoying a warm September and I decided to walk home after an evening reception. I wandered along the riverbank, the illuminated turrets and defensive walls of the Kremlin on the opposite bank. Walking across the wrought-iron Patriarch's Bridge, I admired the Orthodox Cathedral of Christ the Saviour, which was rebuilt in the nineties with oligarch funding, having been destroyed in the thirties by the godless Soviets. If anyone was following me, I didn't notice, and frankly didn't care, as it was a gorgeous evening. Across the road to the tree-lined Gogol Boulevard. Then left up Gagarin Lane, a stone's throw from Sivtsev Vrazhek, through whose desolate slums Pierre Bezukhov had wandered in Tolstoy's *War and Peace*. Much like my daily walk from Waterloo Station to the Foreign Office at King Charles Street, it was a small tour of some of the capital's most beautiful sights.

• • •

"Do you consider Russia your enemy?" the lecturer asked.

Students shifted in their seats. I looked at him. *What a surprising question.*

I didn't then and I don't today consider Russia or Russian people my enemy. I don't agree with Russia's government on many issues, especially on Ukraine, but I'd arrived in Moscow hoping to improve relationships through honest dialogue.

On my first visit to Plekhanov, Russia's oldest economic university, I aimed to start a process of understanding how young Russians thought about the world around them. I enjoyed a tour and gave a speech on the link between trade and relationships: the European Union had become a success because it dismantled walls between previously warring countries through commerce. A focus on dysfunctional processes and regulation normally missed that bigger picture.

It's seldom a good idea to take a short-term view of politics. On Christmas Day in 1989, the President of Romania, Nicolae Ceauşescu, was summarily machine gunned with his wife as the Warsaw Pact imploded. No one at that time would have believed it possible to drive to Romania without border controls, as it is today. In those early days of my posting, I considered that a more open economic relationship with Russia had a greater chance of earning peace than chest-thumping political posturing. Ministers and Colleagues in London invariably saw it from the other end of the telescope: that Russia needed to make political concessions before the UK would engage economically. However, nine years after the start of the Ukraine crisis, that approach has simply inflamed resentment and prompted increasingly dangerous tactics by Russia in response. The risk that our political leaders, unable or unwilling to engage in dialogue, will allow us to sleepwalk into the devastation of war with Russia appears greater than ever.

Wandering through the beautifully columned building afterwards, I pulled up to stare at a large, framed photograph. Realising it wasn't a modern-day Tsar Nicholas II, I focused on the stern visage of Prince Michael of Kent, a regular visitor to Russia and supporter of the Russo-British Chamber of Commerce.

My host, Ruslan Agarunovich Abramov, ushered me into his office for tea. I glanced at the oversized face of Prime Minister Dmitry Medvedev woven into a carpet that hung from the wall. Grappling for small talk, it was clear he was sizing me up with some sort of sincerity-ometer.[25] Glancing at a Land Rover plaque on the wall, I ventured that I'd purchased a Range Rover Evoque that would soon be delivered to Moscow.

He looked at me, puzzled, before whispering to my Russian colleague from the Embassy, "But that is woman's car!"

A few weeks later, my lady wagon was delivered to Moscow. Having trixied it up with baby seats and pink fluffy dice, I took the family for a drive. As I swept along the riverbank towards the Embassy a big-boy Range Rover screeched out in front of me, jammed on its brakes and backed me up to two other vehicles behind. Boxed in, we drove in a procession back to our apartment on Money Lane.

---

25 As it turned out, Ruslam Abramov would become one of my dearest friends in Russia, helping me secure a platform for Boris Johnson to speak when he visited Moscow in 2017.

7. GIVE US YOUR MONEY

Moscow, Russia, September 2014

Out of nowhere, a remarkable image flashed onto my computer screen. A beautiful, naked lady, legs akimbo, the photo displaying a smooth hardwood floor and other perfectly apportioned features. *Blimey, the Firewalls aren't working well today!* I wondered whether it might be kebabs for dinner.

"Ian, can I get your advice, please?" My colleague Amy hovered at the door to my office.

I glanced quizzically at the sheet of paper clutched to her body. "Sure, what's up?"

"I want your opinion on whether I should put this on the wall downstairs?"

As she turned the paper, I stared at the schoolgirl capital letters in blue biro: "CENSORSHIP"!

Chancery staff were in uproar. Three separate sketches of a woman's leg in stockings, rendered in pastel colours, had been removed from the first-floor corridor, near the bar. They were part of the Government Art Collection.[26] In fancy restaurants around Moscow, it wasn't uncommon to see artistically photographed or

---

26 The British government holds a collection of art that is displayed in UK government buildings, including in British Embassies and Diplomatic Missions. The Foreign Office doesn't own any of the art in its Embassies and needs to consult the Government Art Collection if it wants to make any changes to the art on display.

painted boobs and bums in toilets. Only the most sexually repressed could see anything remotely erotic in these two-dimensional, identikit drawings of a leg.

However, to one colleague's wife, they were tantamount to hardcore porn. The recent arrival of a new Corporate Services Manager in Mike opened a new avenue for her campaign against wickedness. She'd separately cornered Mike and the Ambassador's wife to denounce the stockinged legs as a flagrant insult to the virtue and chastity of Britannia.

No one else at the Embassy cared about the stockinged legs. However, when Tim had his ear bent by his wife about the filth on the Embassy walls, he took the line of least resistance and ordered the art removed. Bursting with pride that Tim was taking an interest in his work for the first (and probably only) time, Mike tore the art from the walls with the passion of a Taliban fighter riddling the Bamiyan Buddhas with high explosives.

"Where exactly are you going to put that sign?" I asked.

"I'm going to stick it on the wall where the art was."

It was all patently ridiculous. But what should I tell her? She was not the only Chancery colleague fed up with the almost Monty Pythonesque security culture.

"Do it when lots of people are moving around the building, so your movements don't attract attention. Be surreptitious and place it as you walk by. And do try to stay out of CCTV."

Stockinggate, as it became known in Chancery, was a turning point. I'd spent too much time inside the Embassy building, talking to London about Doomsday scenarios with Russia's economy. With Chancery colleagues recycling BBC Monitoring reports and fretting about artwork, it was time to break out.

DO YOU WANT TO travel coupe? I think it's really nice." Amy was looking at tickets on the Russian Railways website to help me organise my first trip to St Petersburg.

Just before midnight, I walked along the platform at Leningradsky Station. Railway terminals in Russia are named after the destination at the end of the line. Though Leningrad was renamed St Petersburg after the downfall of the Soviet Union, the station name wasn't changed.[27] A long line of polished scarlet carriages, with the words *Krasnaya Strela* painted in gold Cyrillic, stretched into the distance. Each carriage has a *provodnik*, an official who takes care of the passengers – and they were lined up along the platform in their smart grey uniforms, checking tickets and passports. Inside, a corridor ran down one side of the carriage, with a red carpet and gold curtains at the windows. Everything was spotlessly clean.

There were two other occupants of my cabin, a man and a woman, sitting opposite each other on the sofas. Self-consciously, I took a seat, wondering what to do next. Both passengers ignored me and, dead on time, the train rolled away from the station. I jumped into the top bunk and settled down for the night.

St Petersburg, Russia, September 2014
Precisely on time again (Russian trains are almost never late) the train rolled to a halt at St Petersburg's Moskovsky terminal. As I wandered down the platform, my spirits were uplifted by the lilting movement of Reinhold Glière's 'Hymn to the Great City' – St Petersburg's anthem – which is played to mark the arrival and departure of every Red Arrow train. It felt like the perfect way to arrive in Russia's gateway to Europe for the first time.

'Leningrad Hero City' is written in big Cyrillic lettering on a building opposite the terminal, to remind those arriving of the life-and-death struggle for survival during the two-and-a-half-year siege in the Second World War. The driver from the Consulate General was waiting for me, and as we drove through St Petersburg, it looked and felt so different from Moscow, with its series of concentric ring roads pulsing out from the Kremlin. Beyond the

---

27 The region which neighbours the city of St Petersburg is still called Leningrad.

heart of the capital, there is a mix of Soviet constructivism, opulent pre-revolutionary styles and those wooden buildings that survived the burning of Moscow in 1812, when Napoleon's forces overran the city. In St Petersburg, meanwhile, the architecture is a mix of pre-revolutionary styles, from the gothic through to the neo-classical. The streets are narrower. Everything in the historic centre flows from the Nevsky Prospekt, which runs in an almost straight line from the rail station to the Winter Palace. And there are so many canals, hence the city's moniker, the Venice of the North. Everywhere you look there is another beautiful building, canal, cathedral or garden to admire. I was in love with this city from the first.

The Consulate General occupied an attractive early twentieth-century mansion with pleasant gardens at the back. The top floor housed the Residence, with beautifully appointed rooms for entertaining guests, and separate living quarters. I showered in the small visitor flat and changed into a suit before going up for breakfast with Keith Allan, Her Majesty's Consul General. A mahogany table had been set for two, with silver cutlery and porcelain tableware. An inviting bowl of berries and cream sat at each place setting.

Keith was midway through his posting and before St Petersburg had been UK Ambassador to the weird and really-not-wonderful dictatorship of Turkmenistan. He was welcoming, serious, enthusiastic about his diplomatic vocation. Over breakfast, we chatted about his work in the north-west of Russia. The St Petersburg operation was tiny compared to Moscow's: there were just two British diplomats supported by a handful of Russian staff. But they were covering lots of territory: making connections with regional governments, businesses and universities; linking up UK companies with potential partners; and supporting impressive collaboration on shared military history, which was largely focused on commemorating the Arctic convoys. Between 1941 and 1945, convoys of British and allied vessels sailed through Arctic seas to deliver much-needed military supplies through the Soviet ports of

Murmansk and Archangelsk and suffered heavy losses at the hands of German U-boats.[28] It amazed me that Keith and his team were doing ten times the amount of diplomatic engagement undertaken by the Embassy in Moscow, which had ten times the staff. I thought it must be possible to unleash the potential of the Moscow team to do more.

Accompanied by Keith's PA, I enjoyed two days of visits and meetings, ran a discussion and question-and-answer session on sanctions for a group of British business contacts and had lunch with a mixed group of academics. I didn't garner earth-shattering insight from a two-day visit, but I made one good contact who remains a friend. Maxim Bouev, Oxford-educated, a former vice-president at Royal Bank of Scotland, with a passion for mountaineering, was Head of Economics at the European University in St Petersburg. The European University was one of very few private universities in Russia which was achieving good results from its teaching and research programmes. The funding it received from foreign students, would cause it no end of problems throughout my posting.

Having travelled overnight to St Petersburg on a historic train, I returned to Moscow on the high-speed *Sapsan*[29] service, which takes just four hours. A lot had been happening while I was away.

Moscow, Russia

On 17 September 2014, oligarch Vladimir Yevtushenkov was placed under house arrest, charged with stealing shares and money laundering. The arrest sent shockwaves through Russia's markets; Yevtushenkov had played by Putin's rules and stayed out of politics, and yet here he was stuck in his mansion with an electronic bracelet

28 Eighty-five merchant vessels and sixteen Royal Navy ships were lost during the Arctic convoys. Putin presented medals to surviving veterans of the convoys in 10 Downing Street during his visit to London for the 2012 Olympics.

29 The *Sapsan* (in English, peregrine falcon), a joint venture with the German company Siemens, was one of the first high-profile investment projects to be completed after Putin came to power.

around his ankle. Several prominent Russian businesspeople and Russia's Economy Minister, Alexei Ulyukaev, leapt to his defence. The case centred on the original privatisation of mid-sized oil company Bashneft in the early noughties, which was alleged to have been fraudulent. Yevtushenkov's Sistema[30] group now controlled Bashneft, which it had purchased in 2009. Bashneft was hastily renationalised a few days after Yevtushenkov's arrest.

After the Soviet Union collapsed, there were no rules or legal framework to manage the bone-crunching transition from communism to a mixed-market economy. Lawlessness ruled across the Russian Federation, and commercial disputes were more often settled by shoot-out than by subpoena. Within this deadly legal vacuum, some smart-minded Russians conjured up schemes to get rich quick: they monetised the Soviet system of credits[31] to grab hundreds of millions of dollars out of thin air, bought up privatisation vouchers[32] from clueless citizens and conned those citizens with pyramid schemes that always collapsed. Vast profits were used to buy ever-larger stakes in Russia's lucrative oil, gas and mineral companies. Surfing this raging torrent of venality were the new oligarchs, who became multi-millionaires almost overnight. After Russia defaulted in 1998, the oligarchs emerged triumphant as billionaires at the summit of Russia's industrial complex, lifted up by a shady loans-for-shares deal with the ailing Yeltsin.

Russian opportunists had pulled off the biggest daylight robbery

---

30 Sistema is a large Russian conglomerate with most of its investments in consumer service companies, including Russia's largest mobile phone operator, MTS. Vladimir Yevtushenkov holds a majority stake and Lord Mandelson was a member of the Sistema board.

31 Soviet industry was funded by a system of credits through which one factory could obtain goods and services from another without the need for cash transactions. No money changed hands. Mikhail Khodorkovsky persuaded foreign banks to recognise credits managed by his bank on behalf of the Russian Finance Ministry as hard currency.

32 In the early nineties, thousands of state-owned enterprises in Russia were privatised by the mass issuance of vouchers to every Russian citizen. Each voucher wasn't worth much and as most people didn't understand what to do with them anyway, they practically gave them away in the millions for inconsequential amounts.

in human history. Some argue that the actions of certain oligarchs were immoral but not necessarily illegal in the absence of appropriate competition laws. But such arguments are a convenient confection; for example, the auctioning of a packet of shares in Yukos by Mikhail Khodorkovsky's bank Menatep to a company owned by Khodorkovsky, in a process which excluded most of the competition, would be struck down in most countries, including modern-day Russia.

During my time in Russia, Western business practices and good corporate governance had started to take root in a growing number of Russia's regions, underpinned by a stronger legal framework and political leadership. But the challenge was enormous. No region beyond the Urals[33] has ever made it into Russia's top ten investment destinations. Far from Moscow, local officials, police chiefs, FSB hoods, and business honchos divide the spoils in dysfunctional regional fiefdoms. Endemic corruption, economic underdevelopment and grinding social problems are often the norm in the more isolated cities. The idea that an omnipotent Putin watches over his new Russian empire with the eye of Sauron is a fiction; his power is heavily circumscribed by distance and Russia's eleven time zones.

Blaming the West for what happened in the nineties is a popular narrative in Russia today, used partly to dampen the appetite for liberal reforms to Russia's sluggish economy. In turn, the UK has had a schizophrenic relationship with the oligarchs. On one hand, we bemoan the flood of corrupt Russian capital into London. On the other, we have a painful history of giving refuge to oligarchs, many of whom gained their enormous wealth through plunder, and elevating them as paragons of Western liberal values against a hostile and corrupt system under Putin. Russians have a saying

---

33 The Ural Mountains, less than a quarter of the way across Russia's gigantic landmass, mark the dividing line between the European and Asian continents. It is also the area where much of the Soviet industrial complex was moved, lock, stock and barrel, to avoid capture by the onrushing Nazi forces during World War II. It remains a heavily industrialised belt, before the endless forest and steppe beyond, into Siberia and Russia's far east.

that money doesn't smell – *dyengi nye pakhnut*. For decades there was an odour of double standards from UK politicians and officials in attitudes towards rich Russians in the UK and the Russian state.

After Russia invaded Ukraine in February 2022, Liz Truss was determined for the UK to issue more sanctions than any other country. In a flurry of breathless emails, her Private Secretary made it clear that she was desperate to close *Londongrad!* It seemed to me that she thought it was an actual suburb where the likes of Abramovich, Fridman and Usmanov hung out in the hottest mansions and spent millions on their refurbishment.

The media can't get enough of London's reputation as the epicentre of dodgy Russian loot. Politicians on both sides huff and puff, EU policymakers flick peas at us and, much to my annoyance, so do the Yanks, jealous about London's status as the premier global financial centre. It clearly stems from the Nineties era of bandit capitalism that followed the Soviet Union's collapse. The UK now has a moderate-sized Russian population (approximately 150,000), most of whom are living their lives and paying their way. However, during my time in Moscow, the UK had become a mid-sized player in the world of Russian finances. By a Mediterranean mile, Cyprus is the most popular destination for Russian money, which sloshes in and out in vast quantities each day. Russian stock in Cyprus amounted to seventeen times the size of Cyprus's GDP. The British Virgin Islands, Ireland, Luxembourg and the Netherlands housed more Russian capital than the UK.[34] While expensive properties in *Londongrad* make for big headlines in *The Sun*, they represent small change in the multi-billion-dollar world of Russian capital flows.

With the advent of unexplained wealth orders[35] and greater due diligence by banks on flows of foreign capital, it's now harder for London to be used as a centre for money laundering. Much to

---

34 Recent years have seen an outflow of Russian capital from the Netherlands as the Dutch have sought to clamp down.

35 Unexplained wealth orders were introduced by the Criminal Finances Act 2017 and compel a target to disclose the source of their unexplained wealth.

their discomfiture, the Russian trade delegation in London even had its bank account frozen in 2017 and had to make alternative arrangements. The Russian Embassy tried to pin the blame on us, of course, although their claims were baseless.

In December 2014, Yevtushenkov was released without charge, and his company was later awarded damages from the shell company that had sold on Bashneft. But, given the timing, many people in Russia saw this as a fig leaf for a takeover of Bashneft by Igor Sechin, the shark-faced ex-KGB head of Russia's state-owned oil giant Rosneft. Yevtushenkov had been subject to a humiliating shakedown, and that wouldn't be the end of the matter.

The Bashneft affair was another signal that oligarchs held onto their assets at the whim of the Kremlin, which could expropriate their wealth at any time. This uncertainty fuelled huge capital flight from Russia. Billions of dollars of foreign investment from Western companies in Russia were small change against the flood of Russian capital that was parked in offshore banks each year. In the years following the 2009 global financial crisis, the net flow of capital out of Russia was greater than the annual output of Sweden's economy.

Exporting countries invest their earnings overseas and Russia is one of the top three global exporters, along with Germany and China. However, only a small proportion of the capital flowing out of Russia constituted legitimate investment. Until very recently, when Russia's Central Bank clamped down, one third of Russian capital moving offshore was made up of fraudulent and fictitious transactions. Some Russian oligarchs domiciled their companies offshore and moved capital back and forth to Russia for cashflow purposes. Some shuffled their money constantly around the globe through complex structures, with the intention of evading taxes. In the early days of the Ukraine crisis, oligarchs weren't won over by the Kremlin promise of an amnesty if they repatriated their capital to Russia, and Yevtushenkov's arrest made them more suspicious.

In any case, much bigger forces were coming into play which would reduce the stream of Russian capital to a trickle.

8. STRAT COMMS, SCANDALS AND SKILLS

Bangkok, Thailand, 2007

My colleague leaned closer to the Met Police officers and said, "Now, imagine the chaos if a small explosive device went off in here."

I waved the mamasan away when she appeared to ask if we "wanted meet nice lady, have good time."

We'd picked a crowded go-go bar for the final stage of a walking tour of the bombing route for a thwarted 2003 terrorist attack on Bangkok. Nana Plaza occupies a three-storey rectangular courtyard with a single, narrow entry road in and out. Most nights it would be packed with hundreds of tourists, mostly male, looking for bar girls to turn their clock back forty years in a pay-by-the-hour hotel. The attack would have borne similarities to the October 2002 Bali bombing. Small device explodes in a bar, panic ensues, everyone rushes to flee the scene. The narrow exit from Nana would quickly jam up. At the end of the road, a pick-up truck loaded with explosive would detonate, causing countless deaths and injuries and damage to buildings across a whole block.

The two officers sipped their beers and stared ahead thoughtfully at the neon-lit stage in the centre of the bar, crammed with bikini-clad dancers. Jammed together on a bright-red couch, with short hair and a tendency to button-down shirts, the four of us stuck out like steaks at a vegan stag night.

Before they turned their minds to other explosive trouser events, we moved on to get a drink somewhere else.

My four-year posting to Thailand ended explosively for me, in quite a different way. In May 2007, in my final weeks at the Embassy, a Thai friend at an English-language newspaper suggested I wrote a blog offering personal reflections from my posting. The blog was extremely complimentary about Thailand and Thai people. But it was quickly seized upon by disgruntled expats; as a senior Embassy diplomat, I became a lightning rod for grievances about failed attempts to secure visas for their (normally much younger) Thai girlfriends. I almost never got involved with visas and I seldom spent time with expats, as most of my friends were Thai. The comments on my blog quickly snowballed and soon all sorts of increasingly seedy claims were made about my alleged antics in the red-light district.

Blogging, and indeed strategic communications, was still in its infancy. Anyone could post a comment using any name, without registering. I didn't realise there was a problem until a stringer from Associated Press called me for a comment. My error was in not researching the mechanics of the blogosphere beforehand. And in not understanding my audience. I had thought my homespun tales of positivity were aimed at Thai people. But in fact, I was talking about Thailand to a less hospitable, expat audience.

Towards the end of my posting, I was in a steady relationship. I'll admit that I enjoyed being single early in my posting, but as I speak fluent Thai it was easy to date women on the Embassy circuit. The trolling was malicious and unfair, but also proof that in life, sometimes, shit happens.

The incident also served as a reminder that the Foreign Office will hang you out to dry if you make the mistake of airing dirty laundry. My Ambassador, David Fall, backed me up and I will always appreciate that kindness. But Human Resources wanted rid of me; my career was in tatters. I was drinking and smoking heavily and suffering from stress. A retired US special forces friend had an idea to set up a marriage bureau for Vietnam vets. As part of the experience, we'd take them up to Laos or Cambodia for a nostalgic ride in a Huey helicopter with a belt of M60 ammo to fire out the side. That venture never took off.

Then, I learned my mum was terminally ill with cancer. I returned to the UK and moved in with my parents to help Dad care for Mum. It was one of the best life choices I ever made. I stopped drinking on worknights – a sort of alcoholism lite – and commuted to London every day, hoping someone would give me a decent job. I tried to set up a business so I could leave the Foreign Office, but the global financial crisis intervened and that collapsed.

My mum passed in December 2008, despite my futile efforts to give her CPR on the floor of my parents' bedroom. Not exactly the tragically poignant farewell that I might have imagined, if I'd ever thought about it; my beloved mum, Sheila Proud, was just 67 years old when she died. On the worst day of my life, I couldn't give monkey's about failing in my career. But my parents were incredibly proud of me, supported me come what may, and my biggest regret was of letting them down and causing untold worry.

Some Diplomatic Service colleagues who knew me were unbelievably kind and helped me get back on my feet. My boss Janet, a trained coach, invested a lot of effort in helping me rebuild my confidence, with no expectation of reward herself. I found her generosity profoundly moving.

When you screw up in life, however much help you get from other people, your ability to recover ultimately depends on the choices you make and the effort you put in. I focused on the things I could control: learning from my mistakes, doing every job to the best of my ability, while developing my skills and knowledge.

But I also determined to help other colleagues too. Despite everything that happened, I had a wealth of experience that I could share with junior colleagues to help them improve in their careers. My passion for learning and development was ignited at the lowest point of my career.

London – October 2014

In 2010, an email from an internal brainstorming session about a visit by the Pope was leaked. It contained colourful suggestions for the visit, including Pope-branded condoms, the blessing of a gay marriage and a duet between the Pope and Her Majesty the Queen. The press had a feeding frenzy. And, as had happened with me after my blog, the Foreign Office closed its shutters and waited for the news cycle to move on.

Four years on, the arrival of a new Foreign Secretary in the shape of Philip Hammond had heralded a shift in the tone of UK foreign policy. Not a statesman in the mould of William Hague, spreadsheet Phil didn't want to engage with Soviet Sergei Lavrov about a resolution to the conflict in Ukraine (although the door had mostly closed on that).[36] Russia was an enemy to be countered, not a nuclear-armed regional power to be negotiated with. So ministerial communication with Russia was effectively severed.

From that point on, the UK Ministers engaged with Russia principally via the press. In November 2014, I bumped into veteran BBC correspondent John Simpson who came to an event at the Residence having visited Moscow where, among other things, he interviewed Putin's spokesman, Dmitry Peskov[37]. The six-minute interview, which you can find online, is essential viewing for anyone who wants to see how Russia's position on the origins of the Ukraine crisis hasn't changed since 2014. This is the type

---

36 David Cameron squeezed into a place at the table for a Normandy Group lunch at the Asia-Europe Meeting in Milan on 17 October 2014, together with the Italian Prime Minister. It was clear that the main Normandy participants, including Germany and France, had no investment in giving the UK a permanent seat at the table. Later that day, Putin, Merkel, Hollande and Poroshenko met for substantive talks in a hotel. It marked the final closing of the door on UK influence on the peace process in Ukraine.

37 The only time I ever recall Peskov meeting the Embassy was when he met Laurie Bristow; he was doing the Embassy a favour as we had helped sort out a visa problem for his daughter. Reciprocity!

of conversation the UK should have been having with Russia, to understand better our respective positions, and to mitigate risks. Hammond saw disagreement as an opportunity to talk less, not more. He wanted the Foreign Office to take on Russia in the propaganda sphere and Ministers were crawling over themselves for ideas on how to score points against the Kremlin. Step forward Deepak, who had been caught up in the internal fall-out from Popegate. Flamboyant, over-confident and looking to make a career comeback, Deepak arrived to establish a strategic communications team; targeting Russia's flagging economy offered an easy opportunity to bank some credit. In a storm of bad economic news, the strengthening of Western sanctions against Russia in July 2014 coincided with the end of a four-year run of high oil prices.

The world was awash with more oil than it needed. Laden tankers lay at anchor, unable to deliver shipments of oil to storage dumps that were already full. Hydraulic fracturing and horizontal drilling sucked ever-increasing volumes of oil and gas out of shale formations in North Dakota, Texas and New Mexico. For the first time since 1949, the US was staring down the pipe towards oil and gas self-sufficiency and income from energy exports.

Russia exported $283 billion of oil and oil products in 2013. So, when the price per barrel of the black stuff inevitably fell below $100, the rouble sagged; having traded at 30–35 to the US dollar for several years, it broke through the 35 mark and started a slow climb.

Adding two plus two to make seven, Deepak saw an easily digestible recipe to score propaganda points.

Russian involvement in Ukraine = sanctions = rouble weakening

In his view, if the rouble sank to 40 to the dollar, it would represent an economic earthquake, shaking Russian confidence in its economy to the core. He wanted ministers to celebrate this putative victory for Western sanctions through tweets and newspaper articles.

However, I considered the UK would look fatuous if British

ministers took to the press to crow about the rouble's decline. Why would the UK want to claim credit for this? If Russia faced economic decline because of a fall in commodity prices, then Russia would need to become less dependent on the export of fossil fuels. We might as well have said to the Russian people, "Don't blame your own government, it's our fault."

It wasn't that I had particular sympathies towards Russia. But I did believe UK policy and statements towards Russia should be grounded in evidence and solid analysis. Unfortunately, few colleagues in London appeared interested in the economics. This spoke to a deep level of economic illiteracy in His Majesty's Diplomatic Service. Most British diplomats prefer to live in the world of "sexy" politics. Partly this is cultural. One job of the diplomat is to make sense of how the political systems of foreign countries work. However, with globalisation and in an era of sanctions, the need for politico-economic analysis has expanded, and the Foreign Office hasn't kept pace.[38]

So, for Deepak it was easy to push a bad economic story in London. People became misty-eyed at the impending prospect of the rouble roaring into the forties against the dollar. Having lost the Russia Director over the summer, a temporary stand-in arrived with no Russia experience and even less interest in economics. Any mention of the dismal science would render him, like Billy Bunter of Greyfriars, silent and indifferent, as if in a lecture by Mr Quelch.

It didn't seem to matter that sanctions policy was the main lever the West was using against Russia following events in Ukraine. Sanctions were valued primarily for the political signal they sent. Even today, internal assessments of the impact of sanctions don't seem to focus on whether they are materially affecting Russian behaviour or promoting a resolution of the conflict in Ukraine.

---

38 This has started to change with the 2020 merger of the FCO and the Department for International Development, as the latter placed much greater emphasis on deep subject-matter expertise in economics, data, evidence and analysis.

I was asked constantly for proposals on new sanctions against Russia, by colleagues who didn't understand or really want to know how existing sanctions were working. Economic analysis requires actual study. You don't need qualifications to say what Ministers want to hear on sanctions.

So, I blocked several attempts by colleagues in London to make public statements on the rouble's decline, removing each reference to sanctions in draft speeches, op-eds and tweets. Colleagues in London didn't understand why I was being so difficult. What harm could it do? For the first time, I became aware that I was the misfit in Moscow, unwilling to follow the economically illiterate groupthink of the London policy establishment.

The rouble breached the 40 mark in mid-October 2014, a moment that passed largely unnoticed; it still had a very long way to climb. Deepak was too ambitious to stick around doing a communications job for long and soon moved on to other things. The early forays into the propaganda sphere didn't deliver any major successes. But they were a harbinger of a new trend in the way in the UK conducted its communications towards Russia, which would become magnified over time. In wanting to tweet about a weak rouble, Deepak wasn't thinking about a Russian audience; he was talking about Russia to other countries.

• • •

All this augured poorly for UK relations with Russia. David Cameron excluded the UK from the Ukraine peace process because of his fixation on a lush Luxembourger. Philip Hammond preferred to talk about Russia rather than engage directly, destroying all scope to influence events on the ground. Economic illiteracy and amateurish efforts to take on Russia through our messaging spoke to a two-decade disinvestment in skills and tradecraft at the Foreign Office.

The dumbing down of diplomacy started under New Labour,

seduced by the notion that modern diplomats needed little more than a laptop. Language skills? Look 'em up online. Even today, digital learning is only starting to make a positive contribution to the development of skills and the acquisition of knowledge in the Foreign Office. But diplomacy is primarily a people business. While there used to be specific political courses in the Foreign Office, these were nixed in the noughties.

This generational disinvestment in skills results in diplomats in Moscow sending regurgitated press insight to ministers through the medium of Google Translate. William Hague's Diplomatic Excellence campaign, "the biggest drive to enhance the cutting-edge abilities and diplomatic skills of the Foreign Office the department has ever seen," slowly withered on the vine after his departure[39]. In a complete reversal, Philip Hammond made not talking to people a central tenet of Britain's diplomacy. We were reduced, trembling, avoiding eye contact and potential social awkwardness, to a form of diplomatic Asperger's.

The Foreign Office still has a considerable well of experience that it could draw on better to help the younger generation develop their skills and cut their teeth. But it hasn't yet reaped the potential reward from Hague's vision for a modern and expert organisation. Over time, a future generation of Britain's externally appointed Ambassadors will have reached the top having received no training and having had no senior mentors to guide them. The Foreign Office doesn't have a long-term plan to equip itself for diplomacy in the modern era. Accomplished diplomats like Tim Barrow, and also experienced misfits like me, are a dying breed. In the 70–20–10 model of learning, the Foreign Office is fast approaching a triple zero of incapability: no training, no experience, no senior mentorship. That all adds up to no impact overseas at a time the world is facing an unprecedented set of challenges.

---

39 Driven by the ex-DfID policy profession, this is also slowly starting to change, although it will take years to rebuild policy capabilities in the new FCDO.

9. CASH, CRASH AND KOALAS

Moscow, Russia, December 2014

" I sold nineteen cars today, for cash!" The chief executive of Bentley in Russia was clearly delighted with himself. Customers had turned up with bags stuffed with loot. Audi had enjoyed a stellar run on its sporty R8 as well. All over Moscow, high-end stores were rammed with shoppers. Apple had temporarily ceased the sale of iPhones. Shoppers bought TVs, fridges and other white goods they didn't need.

This wasn't Black Friday. It was Black Tuesday. On 16 December 2014, the rouble was in freefall. At one point, it crashed to 79 roubles to the dollar, less than half its value three months previously.

Russians were putting roubles into purchases that might hold their value better than cash. It was mildly evocative of 1998, when Russia took a bailout from the IMF after its economy imploded under a huge pile of unserviceable debt. I'd seen queues at streetside currency exchanges, with people waiting in the cold to trade their increasingly worthless roubles for US dollars. It proved the adage that when the going gets tough, Russians get shopping.

• • •

Three months earlier, the regional chief executive from Christie's had invited me for breakfast in the grand surrounds of the Hotel

National. After the Russian Revolution, the hotel became the seat of the first Soviet government and for a while housed Lenin while the nearby Kremlin was repaired. Having fallen into dilapidation, it was renovated as a hotel for visiting dignitaries in the early thirties and filled with priceless artifacts from the Romanov palaces.

Christies wanted to open a new office in Moscow as demand was booming, and the chief wanted to hear my thoughts on the state of Russia's economy after sanctions. I was mildly intrigued. Why was the enthusiasm for high-value goods at auction growing in Russia now of all times? Over beautifully prepared eggs Benedict and coffee, I opined that as art wasn't sanctioned, I couldn't see a problem if Christie's thought the market was strong enough to reopen in Moscow. Even if Russia's economy was slowing rapidly in the face of an oil price decline and sanctions, the wealthy still had considerable capital to burn. And therein lay the answer.

In times of economic stress, Russian people often put their money in assets that may hold or even increase their value over time, compared to the value of keeping money in the bank or under the bed. The classic flight to value. And what better place to store one's value, or indeed launder money, than in fine art and rare collectibles? Wealthy Russians were losing faith in the rouble and worried about a possible economic storm on the horizon.

• • •

"Look, I'm going to shirt-front Mr Putin. You bet you are. You bet I am." In Australian sporting parlance, shirt-fronting means to charge into an opponent and knock them to the ground or shake them roughly by the shirt. Aussie journalists weren't clear which variant PM Tony Abbott was intending when Vladimir Putin turned up at the 2014 G20 summit in Brisbane. And, very obviously, Abbott looked like a complete knob when, with hilarious inevitability, he was pictured cuddling koalas with judo master Putin.

Throughout my time in Moscow, I got to know Russia's G20

Sherpa well. Svetlana "Lana" Lukash sits behind Putin at the negotiating table, keeping him up to speed with Russia's policy lines
on whatever's being discussed. Unfussy and with a mop of blonde
hair, I always found her open and engaging.

Where there was a firm Russian policy position, Lana would
set it out without sugar-coating. But otherwise, she was open to
exploring ways to strengthen collaboration with the UK on G20
policy where it made sense to do so.

Tax transparency, including bearing down on tax evasion
through offshore banks, was an area where UK and Russian policy
priorities most closely coincided. Russia had launched a programme
of de-offshorisation, offering tax breaks to oligarchs with billions
in capital ferreted in offshore tax havens such as Cyprus and the
British Virgin Islands. But here, UK policymakers in London could
never get past the tendency to see de-offshorisation as an effort
by the Kremlin to plunder private sector assets.

David Cameron had his final meeting with Putin at the Brisbane
G20, which the British press seized on but which in terms of
substance was a non-event. Cameron pressed on Ukraine but got
nowhere. Russia saw fellow Normandy Group members Germany
and France as the main European players on Ukraine policy. And
Merkel and Hollande saw no more reason than Putin to open the
door to UK involvement. It was the decisive moment when UK
efforts to influence talks between Russia and Ukraine fizzled out,
not that they'd ever really existed. Within two months, a new
UK strategy towards Russia would be agreed that took a wholly
different tack.

• • •

Ominous storm clouds were looming over the rouble. By early
November 2014, it had already slipped to 43 to the dollar. Russia's
Central Bank was bringing forward plans to free-float the currency.
The alternative would have been to watch the oil price continue

to slide while trying to hold the rouble at its historical trend. At a time of greater economic uncertainty, Russia wanted monetary policy to manage inflation, which remained high at around 8%.

A free-floating currency would ensure rouble-denominated income from Russian oil exports remained relatively stable, as a weaker currency helped to offset reductions in dollar prices. When the market challenged Central Bank resolve by selling roubles and driving down its price below 47, the Central Bank Governor Elvira Nabiullina held her nerve and the rouble stabilised.

But on 27 November, the Organization for Petroleum Exporting Countries and Russia met in Vienna and agreed not to cut oil production. Big states like Saudi Arabia decided to let oil prices fall rather than lose market share to the US. Their short-term gamble was that small US shale producers would go out of business before they stopped pumping from conventional fields. So, the gun fired on a race to the bottom and oil prices immediately took a nosedive. From a 2014 peak of $112 in June, the price of Brent crude tumbled to $62 in December.

In London, colleagues fixated on the magical break-even price of oil: the price per barrel at which Russia could turn a profit from the oil it exported. $100 to the barrel was a simple figure that colleagues at the Foreign Office could digest, so $62 oil caused much excitement in King Charles Street. With a fixed rouble, Russia would lose significant income at this oil price. However, like the oil price, the rouble was also falling like a stone, partially offsetting any losses.

I had lunch with David Campbell, President of BP in Russia, and he took a pragmatic view: the oil industry focused on the long term and able to surf cyclical peaks and troughs in pricing. He pressed me on the need for the UK government to understand Russian motivations better than it did. In that regard, he would be the first of many British businesspeople gently to express concern about UK foreign policy objectives cutting across UK commercial objectives in Russia. It was a theme President Putin would return to often.

In the short term, at least, it was clear to me that Russia's largely state-owned oil industry wasn't going to fold any time soon. In the face of rapidly falling oil prices, economic conservatives piled pressure on the Central Bank to step in again to protect the rouble. Facing a huge drop in demand for roubles on the foreign exchange markets,[40] Governor Nabiullina found herself atop a rouble roller-coaster on the precipice of a hair-raising descent. Having faced down the currency markets in mid-November, she buckled under the pressure of domestic criticism two weeks later. Russia's Central Bank opened the taps and hosed $100 billion of foreign exchange reserves into the money markets in the hope of propping up an ever-weakening rouble. It was never going to work.

• • •

Russia's Black Tuesday coincided with the British Ambassador's Christmas reception at the Residence. Waiters in white jackets edged through the crush of people in the White and Gold Room with trays of canapés and drinks.[41] Through the hubbub, guests checked phones nervously. Earlier at the Embassy, I'd watched the numbers on Bloomberg moving faster than the dials on a slot machine. Having been excited in September about the rouble hitting 40, colleagues in London were now more excited about the rouble hitting 80 in December. Predictably, they wanted to know if this was a moment to illustrate the link between the rouble's decline and the imposition of sanctions. It was clear to me that some event in the foreign exchange market had sparked the run.

---

40 As oil is traded in US dollars, receipts from Russian oil exports are converted into roubles on the foreign exchange markets. As the quantum of dollars falls, so the demand for roubles falls, causing a drop in the value of the currency.

41 The Ambassador's Christmas reception is one of three major events that the British Embassy hosts each year in Moscow. The other two are the Old New Year reception in mid-January, to commemorate Orthodox Russian New Year, and the monarch's birthday party in June, when British Embassies around the world celebrate the Sovereign's official birthday.

Opinions vary on what prompted Black Tuesday. Former Finance Minister Alexei Kudrin fanned the flames by blaming state-owned oil company Rosneft, which had issued a $10 billion domestic bond to shore up its sanctions-affected finances. Rosneft's chief, Igor Sechin, responded furiously, decrying "these people, these Navalnys, Nemtsovs, and Kudrins," who served others' (i.e., the West's) goals.

Lumping Kudrin into the same grouping as Kremlin nemesis Alexei Navalny and political critic Boris Nemtsov was a remarkable statement. It laid bare the fault-line in Russia between the so-called *siloviki*, the KGB old guard, and the economically liberal wing of the state, both of whom vied for Putin's favour. Sechin was adding economic liberals to the list of groups in Russia seen as craven to Western influence. It was a reminder that the direction of economic policy in Russia often teeters between those who hanker after a return to Soviet-style central control and those who would integrate Russia more closely into the global economy. I made a note to meet Kudrin.

President Putin went on the rampage to blame currency speculators and international organisations for precipitating the rouble's collapse. It was a fork-in-the-road moment, and I was fascinated to see where the state would land on what to do next. Late on the night of 16 December 2014, Russia's Monetary Policy Committee met and agreed to hike interest rates from 10.5% to 17%. The Central Bank could no longer keep spraying foreign exchange reserves at the money markets to no effect. Economic nationalists were furious, repeating calls for Nabiullina to be hauled in front of Russia's state Parliament, the Duma, to explain herself.

Putin backed her decision in public, siding with the economic liberals over the old guard, in this fight. And Nabiullina remains the Central Bank Governor to this day. Russia's Finance Minister, Anton Siluanov, has occupied his role since 2011. Together, they have steered the Russian economy through a nine-year period of major external economic shocks, including volatile energy prices and COVID. This stability in fiscal and monetary policy making had undoubtedly helped Russia manage the economic impact of sanctions.

I contributed to a memo for the Foreign Secretary, setting out the crash in neutral terms. To the extent to which the Rosneft bond precipitated the rouble's collapse, it is fair to say that sanctions contributed indirectly. But when the dust had settled on Black Tuesday, it was clear that the rouble was tracking the oil price, while being bolstered by foreign investments attracted by higher interest rates. A new phase of Russian monetary policy had begun.

· · ·

The Residence's general fixer glared at me as if I'd pissed on the parquet. The Ambassador's wife wanted me to get rid of the stash of left-over Christmas party booze in the scullery. Well, that was the reason for my visit.

I've never watched *Downton Abbey*, but standing in the basement I felt every bit the Edwardian servant. She wasn't the first Ambassador's spouse I'd met who thought the Residence was their personal estate. I wasn't sure if the issue was that the servants' wine was still in the scullery twelve hours after the staff party or that the plebs had been allowed to have a party at all. I packed the wine into my car and crawled home through the sleet and the rush-hour Moscow logjam.

It had been a glorious staff party. Colleagues and their guests, dressed to the nines, toured the Residence, pausing for photographs by the giant Christmas tree. For many, particularly for Russian staff, it was their first visit to this historic building. I joined a small Embassy group on the stairs to sing a traditional Russian festive song (*Malenkoy Yolochkye* – 'Little Christmas Tree'). With impeccable timing, Tim Barrow arrived to extend his Christmas wishes as I was making a thank-you speech. He even took a turn serving drinks.

Moscow's International Choir performed Christmas carols. Staff got a free salsa lesson and we boogied to Russian and Western hits until after midnight.

Since I'd taken over the Social Committee, the Embassy was opening its doors to diplomats from other embassies for social events, including a packed-out James Bond quiz and casino night. Social events brought in extra cash that I intended to use for a free Christmas Party for all staff at the Embassy. I contributed £100 of my own money towards the party, and other members of the Embassy senior leadership team were contributing too, including Tim.

But a vocal minority of British staff, primarily those who lived inside the Embassy compound, hated the idea of a free party. In a curious twist of irony, the oil price collapse had seen prices at the bar double. So, in their minds, I became like allegorical Lenin, stealing their riches to give to the proletarian Russians. It was all ridiculous, for British staff who raked in £2-3000 extra each month in tax-free allowances. The tuxedo and cocktail dress-clad guests who came to our Embassy parties were neither shaken nor stirred by the 150 rouble cocktails. However, even my most ardent critics seemed to enjoy the party. Though the entente cordiale wouldn't last for long.

The snow arrived on 25 December. Having decided to spend our first Christmas in Russia, we enjoyed a counter-sanctions-affected Christmas lunch of skinny duck in our super-warm Moscow apartment on Money Lane. I reflected that UK–Russia relations remained as cold as the streets outside. I'd try to warm things up in 2015.

10. MINSK

Moscow, Russia, January 2015

Sasha prowled the changing room, bollock naked. The retired Russian Air Force colonel had enjoyed a workout in the Embassy gym and a shower. He spotted me pulling on my pants and padded across.

"Ah, Ian, how was your workout?"

"Yes, it was good, thanks," I replied, absolutely determined to maintain eye contact.

He put one foot on the bench beside me and stretched, taking time to air-dry his undercarriage.

"Have you been to Russian banya yet?"

I replied that no, I hadn't been to the Russian sauna yet. In cold countries like Russia, the Scandis and the Nordics, saunas are extremely popular, particularly during the winter. But I'm from southern England, where a chilly winter amounts to a couple of days of sub-zero temps before the rain sets in again. Stripping off with your mates, steaming up and getting beaten with birch sticks didn't appeal. It was a level of cultural immersion that I never felt ready for.

"Fancy doing some snow angels, Sasha?" I asked, as we came to the end of a workout a few days later. "Yes, sure Ian, great idea," he grinned. We stripped down to our pants, ran out onto the tennis court and leapt into the two foot blanket of snow. Diplomacy: it's all about compromise.

...

I rolled over in bed, pulled back the curtain and peered at the neon Cyrillic letters. The train had stopped at Smolensk, close to the fictional estate of Bald Hills from Tolstoy's *War and Peace*. Besides 1812 and the fight against Napoleon, the city has seen other ferocious battles through Russian history. In July 1941, the rapid Nazi advance was halted here for two months by a series of Soviet counter-offensives. It bought time for the defence of Moscow and earned Smolensk the title Hero City. I wasn't about to get out to explore at 2 a.m. This was just a brief stop before crossing the border into Belarus.

My colleague snored gently on the other bunk. I'd persuaded a member of the Embassy political team to join the trip. Soon, the Belarusian Railways train rolled away from the station, and I nodded off to the gentle ker-klunk, ker-klunk of wheels on track.

Minsk, Belarus, January 2015

Upon arrival in Minsk, there were no border controls or checks. When the Soviet Union collapsed, Russia and Belarus created a union state, a loose federation aimed at economic, defence and intelligence cooperation, with separate heads of state. In 2015, the border between the two countries was completely open, as it is in the EU. A modern glass-fronted railway station let out onto well-ordered, clean roads, along which passed a spotless public bus. It might easily have been Lithuania or another modernising EU country. At least on the surface. Having been flattened by the Nazis, Minsk rose phoenix-like out of the devastation, a model Soviet city. You can't help but be impressed by the grandeur of the buildings and boulevards, apparently designed to drive armies of tanks through in the event of war in Europe.

The taxi soon delivered us to the front door of the British Embassy. After a couple of rings, the Ambassador popped his head out of the top-floor window, still in a dressing gown, and said he'd be right down. His Residence, a large flat above the "shop" was alive with the sizzle and smell of bacon on the fryer as his wife prepared breakfast.

Bruce Bucknell was larger than life. An experienced British diplomat, he'd invited me to Minsk not long after I arrived in Moscow, to look at the Belarusian economy. The Embassy had only three diplomatic staff and no one with economic experience.

British Embassy Minsk is a classic example of what we call Very Small Embassies and Posts (VSEP), outposts in lower-priority countries where the British government wants to keep a light finger on the pulse. Belarus was considered an anachronistic Soviet throwback, its strongman leader, Alexander Lukashenko, labelled Europe's last dictator by the Americans. Its location, sitting between Europe and Russia, made it important enough to have an Embassy, which included a team of dedicated Belarusian staff. In 2013, the EU lifted sanctions against President Lukashenko. As a member of the EU's Eastern Partnership, Belarus was taking small steps to strengthen economic links with Europe, from a low base.

So, for two days, we toured Minsk in the flag car for meetings[42] with Belarusian government officials, companies and foreign diplomats. Bruce's effusive bonhomie and half-decent Russian helped him set meetings off on a positive note. Much like Keith Allan at the British Consulate in St Petersburg, Bruce and team were working the diplomatic circuit hard. As Belarus was not a policy priority, it was hard work to generate the barest flicker of interest among policy desk officers in London, let alone with British ministers.

There were reasons to feel mildly optimistic about Belarus. While it isn't a member of the World Trade Organization (WTO)[43],

---

42 A flag car is the term used to describe the vehicle used by an ambassador, which carries that national flag when the Ambassador is a passenger, travelling on diplomatic business.

43 Belarus started a process to join the WTO in 1993 which is still ongoing.

its exports had been growing steadily. The Belarusian education system is strong in STEM subjects, a legacy of the Soviet era. The emptying out of labour markets in places like Poland[44] had generated demand for high-skilled workers from Belarus and other former Soviet countries, including Ukraine; a Polish diplomat I met spoke of a programme to award work visas to Belarusians in certain economic sectors. With the help of heavily subsidised Russian oil, Belarus was exporting electricity into the EU; Rosatom had started construction of a nuclear power plant near the Lithuanian border.

However, most exports were of wood and raw materials. The rump of Belarus's economy was state controlled, and real economic reform appeared to be moving at a glacial pace. And the country was starved of foreign exchange. Running a trade deficit with the EU and Russia, and lacking any major source of foreign investment, Belarusian FX reserves bounced along the bottom of an empty barrel. As in Soviet days, the Kremlin was the banker of last resort, and Belarusian sovereign debt to Russia grew yearly. This undoubtedly gives Russia considerable power over its much smaller neighbour.

Western commentators focus on Russia's putative efforts to recreate the Soviet Union by stealth. However, Belarus is the only remaining former-Soviet where Russia exerts considerable influence, such that absorption may be even a remote possibility. More realistic, Belarus acts as a dysfunctional yet compliant buffer between Russia and NATO.

It's easy to overstate the surface similarities between the two countries, including the Russian language.[45] Prior to the war in Ukraine, Russia had made progress in becoming an investment

---

44 The noughties saw significant labour migration from countries like Poland to the UK, as talented workers sought higher salaries, even at the expense of undertaking lower-skilled work. As Poland's affluence has grown, and on the back of Brexit, this trend has gone into reverse.

45 During my four and a half years in Moscow, it was interesting to observe the slow trend towards greater use of the Belarusian language.

destination for western companies, particularly west of the Urals. Major companies could look around the EU and Russia and see much lower risk and greater potential reward in setting up a factory there than in Belarus, which is essentially a police state. Speeding up membership of the WTO and diversifying its export sector seemed an easier win, in the short term.

The other challenge was the recently created Eurasian Economic Union, which included a customs union that Belarus was a party to. Belarus would benefit from liberalising its trade with the EU but could only do so in the context of EU negotiations with the Eurasian Union. The scope for Belarus getting caught in a trade policy ménage à trois was high.

• • •

Sugar n Spice bar might as well have been called Sugar Daddy, given the impossibly attractive Belarusian women flanking the UN Resident Coordinator on the leatherette sofa. The Sri Lankan UN staffer was louche, with the good humour and hubris of someone getting paid too much to do too little.

His companions were locally recruited staff from the UN Office in Minsk. Bored by his attentions, one moved to sit opposite me, and we fell into conversation. She had a PhD, long, lustrous hair and oversized round glasses that accentuated her perfect face.

"We don't need people in Europe to lecture us about how to live our lives," she chided, leaning forward so far, I could smell her perfume through the clouds of cigarette smoke. Why did the West treat Belarusians like country bumpkins because they didn't actively embrace gay rights in public culture?

I hadn't been in Russia, or indeed Belarus, long enough yet to have a clear position on LGBT rights. However, I made the point that in the West we considered everyone should be free to decide how to live their lives irrespective of issues such as sexuality. I quickly found the conversation tedious, so palmed her off on my political colleague.

I grabbed my vodka martini and moved across to chat with the Resident Rep. He couldn't really explain what his office did in Belarus, although I got the distinct impression it wasn't very much. With an inebriated grin, he asked in a loud voice what a British diplomat from Moscow was doing visiting Belarus. He offered a patronising lecture on how the West was being too tough on Russia with its sanctions. Aside from the cocktails, meeting the UN felt like a crushing waste of time. It was getting late, so I called it a night and, with my colleague, wandered through the empty streets back to the British Embassy, tailed by a couple of hoods..

I had mixed feelings about Minsk. We'd enjoyed the city, eating European cheeses banned in Russia and joking about the wonderful Belarusian scallops and prawns.[46] But the perfectly clean streets were a fig leaf. Alexander Lukashenko majored on offering his citizens security and stability in his regular four-hour drone-fest state-of-the-union speeches. But the city reminded me of the Hollywood movie *The Truman Show*, in which comedian Jim Carrey lives in an idyllic, confected world, yet his every move is scrutinised by a state that ultimately controls his destiny. The big question was whether the snail-paced steps to liberalise Belarus's economy would be quick enough to satisfy the needs of a growing group of young, well-educated citizens with aspirations. I was sceptical.

Bruce invited the diplomatic set to his Residence on my final evening, and I gave a talk about EU sanctions against Russia and their economic impact. Towards the end of a vigorous question-and-answer session, as we veered into more social topics, the Finnish Ambassador piped up. "Have you had a chance to try the Russian banya yet? It is a wonderful way to relax."

---

46 After Russia banned the import of food from Western countries, a range of Belarusian-labelled products appeared, including various types of seafood; Belarus is landlocked. Russia would soon clamp down on Belarus's role as a transit route for contraband Western foods.

"Not yet[47]," I replied, with a smile.

A week or so later, on 11 February, President Putin arrived in Minsk to meet Presidents Hollande and Poroshenko and Chancellor Merkel. Minsk had become the place where negotiations to end the bloodshed in the Donbass took place. A Minsk Protocol was signed on 5 September 2014 by Russia and Ukraine, the Organization for Security and Co-operation in Europe and representatives from the breakaway provinces of Luhansk and Donetsk. This allowed for the temporary decentralisation of power in parts of Luhansk and Donetsk, exchange of prisoners, a demilitarised zone and a one-week ceasefire. A follow-up memorandum two weeks later included a permanent end to military operations.[48] However, the ceasefire provisions had never held because of a lack of progress on decentralisation of some local government powers to the separatists, and control over the territorial border between Russia and Ukraine. So, by January 2015 the Minsk Protocol had all but collapsed.

The Minsk II agreement that emerged was a more detailed version of the Minsk Protocol from September 2014.[49] Much greater emphasis was placed on constitutional reform in Ukraine, "the key element of which is decentralisation". A ceasefire would start on 15 February 2015, and ahead of that a massive separatist offensive pushed Ukrainian forces out of the strategically important railroad town of Debaltseve. From that point on, the line of contact between Ukraine and the separatist areas of eastern Ukraine barely shifted until Russia invaded Ukraine in early 2022. Regular breaches of the ceasefire took place from both sides. Progress towards some form of decentralisation or special status for parts of the Donbass had run into the sand come the summer of 2015; it was clear that Ukraine would not follow through with this provision. For its part,

47 Or ever!

48 Parts of both Luhansk and Donetsk have remained under Ukrainian government control throughout the conflict.

49 The original Minsk Protocol was a more detailed version of a peace plan first put forward by President Poroshenko in June 2014.

Russia made little attempt to hold up its end of the bargain either. The lack of progress on decentralisation and the continued low-intensity warfare rendered Minsk II dead in the water soon after its birth.

· · ·

Moscow, Russia

We enjoyed vodka with lard on black bread at a Ukrainian restaurant close to Russia's Foreign Ministry. Jaz was visiting from London, having been parachuted into the Russia team as its head. The UK government needed to rethink its strategy towards Russia, and he was seen as the right technocrat to do so; he had been involved in negotiating EU sanctions against Russia at the start of the Ukraine crisis.

In terms of crafting a UK strategy towards Russia, he didn't have much to play with. The UK had been in self-inflicted exile from mediation in the Ukraine conflict from the beginning. The old sweats of the research establishment in London thought any diplomatic engagement with Russia would show weakness rather than resolve. The centre of gravity in UK policy was shifting towards hard deterrence and disruption of Russian behaviour.

I argued continually for economic and cultural engagement to remain a core part of UK strategy towards Russia. And in fairness to Jaz, they were included, at least on paper. But word had got out across government that no one should touch Russia, even with a bargepole. The Department for International Trade had started cutting trade promotion jobs at the Embassy. The Department for Business had started a process to nix the buyout of a low-grade North Sea oil and gas field by Mikhail Fridman's LetterOne Group, essentially to avoid upsetting the Americans. The Department for the Environment, Food and Rural Affairs asked nervously whether it was still OK to sell Scottish seed potatoes to Russia.

On the flip side, there were plenty of agencies of government queuing up to take on Russia. With Philip Hammond not interested in dialogue, the diplomats had handed over the Russia strategy keys to the die-hards. And any wording on positive engagement in the strategy was heavily caveated with Soviet-style slogans such as "not giving Russia a blank cheque to act," "exacting a price from Russia for her actions" and "no return to business as usual."

The latter phrase would act like a millstone round the neck of efforts to engage Russia in a dialogue towards peace in Ukraine. Not returning to "business as usual" was consistently cited as the reason British ministers should not talk to their Russian counterparts at all. All the major EU nations kept high-level political channels open with Russia, as did the US and Japan. The UK was the only major state effectively refusing to talk to Russia at a senior level. Rather, we continued to talk to other countries about Russia.

But the most debilitating phrase was that there could be no relief from sanctions against Russia unless the Minsk agreement was implemented in full. An agreement which, at the very least, required as much action by Ukraine. Were Ukraine to fulfil its end of the bargain and drive forward with decentralisation in the Donbass, there would be greater pressure on Russia to secure Ukraine's territorial border and to withdraw its troops. And there would be greater legitimacy to the maintenance of sanctions against Russia.

A clearly laid out set of conditions might pave the way towards some sanctions relief for Russia in the event of compliance; but these were never articulated. Minsk implementation was described in binary terms; it either was or was not implemented in full. This might make sense on a tightly edited Foreign Office draft strategy in King Charles Street. However, it was unrealistic in a complex insurgency with state and non-state forces fighting on both sides of a line of contact that stretched for hundreds of miles.

De facto, Minsk conditionality would give Ukraine the casting vote; inaction on their part would lock in sanctions against Russia, so why would they engage with the separatists in the Donbass?

Officials in London weren't interested in the risks and started to push EU Member States to support this approach.

11. MANCHURIA, MANDARIN AND MODERATES

Manzhouli, China, March 2015

"**A**re you Russian?" the taxi driver asked.

"*Da, kanyeshna!*" I replied.

He studied me in the rear-view mirror before focusing on the road ahead. We drove past a Russian-themed wedding palace, the Institute of Russian Language in the shape of one of Moscow's Seven Sisters, and shopping centres with onion domes à la St Basil's. At the border crossing, I stepped out of the warm taxi and thrust my hands in my pockets to spare them the bitter winter winds; the weather had been milder in Beijing. I gazed at the brightly painted Russian matryoshka doll, the size of a house, and briefly contemplated buying a T-shirt with Putin cuddling a panda. The seller seemed the only other person around; a train wasn't due to pass any time soon.

The Trans-Siberian Railway enters China through the city of Manzhouli, on a line constructed at the dawn of the twentieth century to shorten the journey from Moscow to Vladivostok. In 1929, the final act of a brief military conflict between the USSR and China played out here over control of the railway. In 1949, Mao Zedong boarded a train in Manzhouli to cross into the Soviet Union for his first visit. Today, it's a gaudy border town and tourist stop-off, its shop signs painted with Chinese and Russian characters. The locals often addressed me in Russian, and I didn't get the impression they saw many Brits.

The identikit buildings and boulevards of the city centre create a sterile, soulless urban landscape. However, one can't help but marvel at China's ability to throw up buildings, roads and rail networks. A massive investment binge has transformed China into the world's second-largest economy in three decades. Year in, year out, investment accounts for over 40% of Chinese GDP. During my time in Moscow, the comparative Russian figure hovered around 22%, not much higher than advanced European economies with better infrastructure like Germany or the Netherlands. A fundamental economic difference between two of the UN Security Council's permanent five members is that where China invests and its citizens save, Russia consumes, and her citizens spend. Therein lies one reason why Russia struggles to grow at the rates of fast-developing Asian economies.

Beijing, China

I'd travelled east to consider Russia's so-called pivot to China, which had a small following among policymakers in the UK. I'd spent three days in Beijing with a colleague from the political team.[50]

Beijing is a fascinating city in which modernity crashes against tradition in a choking cacophony of commerce, construction and smog. A stone's throw from our high-rise steel and glass hotel was the British Embassy, a two-storey nineteenth century building in the leafy diplomatic quarter. Stern Chinese sentries stood to attention on plinths outside the Embassy, but inside the security culture felt less repressive than in Moscow. Sure, there were classified and unclassified parts of the building. But sensible security precautions

---

50 The China visit would be my last of two visits with political colleagues; the new political chief thought visits outside of Moscow were a distraction from time spent trawling BBC Monitoring reports.

didn't seem set up to wring the joy from day-to-day life, which sometimes felt the case in Moscow.

More notably, most Chancery staff in Beijing had an operational level of spoken and written Mandarin, and their use of language as a tool of tradecraft was impressive. It was more than translation. The quality of their spoken Mandarin made a noticeable difference in meetings, where culturally specific routines played out to prevent Chinese guests losing face.

One evening, we visited Beijing's remaining old-town hutongs, narrow cobbled alleys now smartened up for the tourists. We enjoyed spectacular Uyghur street food, and craft beer in a hipster bar, mostly populated by loud gap-year foreigners. "Wow, they have craft beer in China too, dudes." Afterwards, we hailed a cab and our colleague jotted down the instructions for our hotel in Mandarin script. Impressive!

In Moscow, only two staff in Chancery had operational Russian, and that was thanks to the recent arrival of a second speaker on posting. I suppose we could say there had been a 100% improvement in attainment.

Colleagues in Beijing set up meetings with contacts in the economic sphere, highly formalised affairs often conducted over meals, with weak beer and wonderful food. I was interested in the developing energy relationship, following Gazprom's announcement of a 2,500-mile gas pipeline to China called "the Power of Siberia". In May 2014, Russia and China signed a thirty-year gas supply deal worth an estimated $400 billion. Putin launched construction of the pipeline that September with the Chinese Deputy Premier, Zhang Gaoli.

Despite signs that its investment splurge was running out of steam, Chinese growth was still motoring, with demand for energy growing year on year. From the Chinese perspective, Russia was one of many countries helping to meet this demand. Qatar and central Asian states like Kazakhstan and Turkmenistan export significant volumes of gas each year. China has been trying over several years to invest in an energy corridor through Myanmar to Yunnan Province as part of its Belt and Road Initiative. Australia and the USA have more recently made huge deals for LNG exports to China.

In the context of Western energy sanctions, a big deal was being made of Russia's proposed new gas pipeline. Some in London poo-pooed the Power of Siberia as an unprofitable vanity project, but the arguments for Russia to diversify her energy relationships were clear. Indeed, since the outbreak of war in Ukraine, Russian energy exports to China have boomed, having already risen faster than expected.

On a wider political and economic front, both countries work together through the G20, BRICS and other international fora. China and Russia share near-identical positions on weakening US hegemony to create a multi-polar world. But I had no sense that China had a misty-eyed, sentimental attachment to its relations with Russia. Chinese contacts seemed acutely aware that their economy is more than nine times larger than Russia's and their population ten times larger.

Russia and China have had an on/off relationship over the past century. A larger military conflict erupted between them in 1949 over a disputed border area in the east of Manchuria. A split emerged in 1969 as both countries battled for intellectual supremacy over the direction of global communism. Russia has longer-standing, more enduring partnerships with India and Vietnam, countries with similarly troubled relations with China. And Russian and Chinese interests collide uncomfortably in the former Soviet States of central Asia.

Alliances change, of course. Much airtime is given to the strength of Xi Jinping's relationship with Vladimir Putin. Russia no doubt wants to have a more stable relationship with China at a time when her relationships with the West are in their worst state since the Cold War. However, Putin works as hard to maintain a close relationship with Narendra Modi, to ensure strategic balance in the sometimes-difficult set of relationships between Russia, India and China. Real diplomacy seeks to balance competing interests to prevent conflict.

Of course, policymakers in London worry what a Sino-Russian alliance might mean for global security with a muscular China now exerting its influence in the South China Sea. But the people I met west of the Urals, where most Russians live, had a sense of their country having one foot as firmly in Europe, as in Asia. There's a risk of overstating the geo-strategic importance of Russia–China. Continued hostility between Russia and the West will continue to make Putin look east. But that is, in part, out of Russia's longer-term desire for self-preservation.

As I stared across the border from Manzhouli into the vast rolling plains of Russia, I was struck by one thing: emptiness. Russia's landmass is almost twice that of China's and the further east you travel, the lower the population density becomes; in large swathes of land, there is less than one person per square kilometre. In Russia's far east, the state has set up a giveaway programme in which citizens can claim a hectare of land to use for any purpose.[51] However, more than three times as many hectares are now owned or leased by Chinese farmers, using Chinese workers to grow crops for Chinese consumers.

Many in Russia worry about the loss of its far east to China. In a nightmare scenario in which Russia ended up in a full-blown military conflict with the West over Ukraine, I don't get the sense China would rush to her defence. A Russia exhausted by conflict with the West would struggle to defend her vast open spaces.

Moscow, Russia

I was a little late, and the Ambassador's flag car was outside the building. Security let me through without fuss and ushered me

---

51 Almost 100,000 people have claimed their free hectare so far, although these figures are tiny in an area considerably larger than Europe.

into a small, wood-panelled conference room. Tim glanced up before introducing me to Alexei Kudrin, who sat across the table. I'd made it a priority to meet Kudrin on the back of Black Tuesday; he smiled, and we shook hands.

Kudrin is quietly spoken and there's a largeness about him. He's not excessively tall, at six foot or so, nor overweight, but has a heavy frame, big hands and a large, rounded nose on which spectacles perch. Kudrin was Finance Minister for eleven years, during which time the bulk of Russia's external debt was paid off and two rainy-day reserve funds were established to help manage external shocks. He established a strong international reputation as a liberal, winning *Euromoney*'s Finance Minister of the Year award in 2010.

It all came crashing down in September 2011. With Putin expected to return as President in 2012, Kudrin announced that he wouldn't serve in the new government if stand-in President Dmitry Medvedev became Prime Minister. Medvedev asked him to resign that day and Kudrin duly obliged, moving into academia at St Petersburg State University. He continued to maintain a high-profile role from the outside, arguing for liberal economic reform, including privatisation, and for Russia to improve its relations with the West. It's fair to say that Medvedev and Kudrin aren't friends and probably don't spend their downtime beating each other with sticks in the banya.

By early 2015, Russia's economy had tipped into a grinding recession on the back of the oil price collapse and sanctions. However, economic growth was already slowing before 2014 and while oil prices remained over $100. And while the Finance Ministry and Central Bank were doing a decent job of macro-financial policy, it was less clear there was a plan for economic policy. Prime Minister Medvedev – who is a lawyer, not an economist – seemed largely powerless to chart a way forward. The Economy Minister, Aleksei Ulyukaev, only ever seemed to say that the economic situation would improve soon, except that it never did.

The Prime Minister's pitch at the January Gaidar Economic forum – one of two set-piece economic events he fronts each year – was underwhelming. I found the lack of a clear economic policy baffling.

The conversation with Kudrin flowed easily. Tim conducted the meeting in Russian; his fluency wasn't great, but that didn't deter him, though he drifted into English when faced with a phrase that was beyond his vocabulary. In my experience, Russian contacts appreciated someone who went out of their way to speak to them in broken Russian rather than English. Trying to understand the local culture goes a long way in most countries.

It was a useful run over familiar economic ground, but Kudrin was clearly keeping his cards close to his chest. Speculation was whirling, not for the first or the last time, that Kudrin might be called in as Prime Minister in a shake-up, to get the economy firing on all cylinders again. That all depended on the strength of his relationship with Putin.

• • •

The camera panned to Kudrin, who offered his characteristic Mona Lisa smile.

Putin had taken some initial questions from callers and Kudrin was invited to ask a question from the studio audience.

Every spring, Putin has a televised 'direct-line' phone-in. It's one of two set-piece opportunities he has in which to engage directly with Russian people on issues from the global to the local.

Is this going to be it, I wondered? Some sort of big reveal of a dazzling strategy for the economy?

Kudrin boiled his question down to a simple comparison. In Putin's first term, Russia's economy had grown by 7% per year, while oil was $30 to the barrel. For the foreseeable future, it would grow by 1.5% per year – less than the global average – with oil at $65 to the barrel.

"The old economic system has exhausted its potential, and nothing new has been proposed so far. What can you do to help us create a new growth model?" he concluded.

Kudrin had either nailed the best and most audacious interview question for a new job or committed career suicide. Another way to read his question was "When I was Finance Minister, Russia grew at 7% with low oil, yet under dad-dancing Dmitry, it's hardly growing, with still fairly high oil." He had trashed the Russian government's economic policy live to an audience of millions on TV in front of the President.

Putin was emollient, referring to Kudrin as almost a friend and not directly disagreeing with anything he said. However, there was an undertone of rebuke. "To shape economic policy competently, a brain is needed. But if we want people to trust us, we need a heart, too. And feel how ordinary people live and how this affects them."

The lawlessness and economic collapse of the nineties is a theme Putin draws on often in any debate about economic reform. Indeed, it's normally used as a reason reform shouldn't happen more quickly. Putin seems publicly to acknowledge the textbook remedies that would help Russia's economy to perform more strongly. Yet fear of plunging more citizens into poverty is held up as justification for the inertia.

During the three-hour marathon of questioning, Putin would receive pleas from World War II veterans waiting for state housing and an anxious mum worried about free medication for her child with cancer. He was enjoined to order a retired army officer to let his wife have a dog, and a four-year-old boy asked how he could become President. It was a classic example of Putin playing the role of Tsar. Sitting above the government, he can be petitioned directly by his people to intervene when government policy fails them. It is extremely rare for citizens publicly to criticise Putin [52]for the weak state of Russia's economy. I always thought, in that regard, that it didn't matter whether Medvedev had a credible

---

52 Even during the remarkable mutiny of June 2023, Yevgeny Prigozhin avoided publicly directing his answer at Putin personally.

plan for the economy or not. The point was that he was a loyal and convenient scapegoat.

I liked Kudrin because he was an outspoken misfit. And throughout my time in Russia, economic debate – unlike political debate – appeared genuinely vibrant and open. I thought that for Putin, having Kudrin inside government was less useful than having him outside, trumpeting the need for change. I also wondered whether, despite his evident thirst for government high office, Kudrin felt the same. The big question was whether he'd be Prime Minister in June, when I'd be in St Petersburg for Putin's yearly International Economic Forum.

12. IN MEMORIAM

Kabul, Afghanistan, 2010

The US Army Black Hawk scudded across a leaden sky over the grimy suburbs of Kabul. Side doors open, machine guns pointed out to return fire if necessary. The air was chill, but with my adrenaline pumping, it didn't bother me.

Two days before, the largest joint NATO military operation in Afghanistan had commenced in Helmand Province. Operation Moshtarak sought to clear the remaining Taliban stronghold in the towns of Marjah and Nad Ali. I needed to get to the UK-led Provincial Reconstruction Team (PRT) in Helmand as soon as possible, to work on strategic communications. On arrival at the Embassy in Kabul, I'd been told that I might need to wait a few days before I could fly south. Every available military air asset was tied up in the operation.

A British Army Lt Colonel based at the Embassy gave me a billet for the night at his house in the Green Zone. At around midnight, he banged on my door; the Americans had offered to take me, but I had to be out the door at 6 a.m. Earlier in the day – Valentine's Day – a NATO rocket had destroyed a house in Nad Ali, killing twelve civilians. General McChrystal, commander of NATO forces, was flying south to apologise at a shura[53] of tribal elders. His team had offered me a lift.

When the helicopter settled on the tarmac at Bagram Airbase, I stepped out and hauled my thirty-kilo rucksack onto my shoulders. I then followed the American soldiers in a line up the ramp into the belly of a US Air Force C-130. The flight to Helmand and the sprawling UK military logistics base at Camp Bastion took around an hour.

Helmand Province, Afghanistan

After a smooth landing, we bimbled down the loading ramp and into bright sunshine. The military buildings and tents in a dun desert landscape contrasted starkly with Kabul.

"We're goin' someplace else, buddy, and will need to leave you here." The Americans wandered off towards a couple of V-22 Ospreys on the other side of the runway.

I'd left my British Embassy ID card at NATO headquarters in Kabul and didn't have body armour or a helmet. Looking like a middle-aged backpacker with short hair and olive drab, I wandered off the airstrip pondering what to do next.

An RAF air specialist has his head under the open bonnet of a truck at the airfield fire station, so I wandered across.

"Hello, mate, don't suppose you can help? I'm from the Diplomatic Service in London. I just arrived with the Americans and need to get across to Lashkar Gah as soon as possible."

He looked me up and down suspiciously before ushering me to a nearby tea hut with a TV showing Sky News. He disappeared to consult his boss and, I presume, phone calls were made to Kabul. After an hour or so, I was taken to meet the group captain who ran the airstrip. A friendly wing commander then took me for lunch at a giant mess tent, where he not-so-subtly probed me for

---

53 Shuras are consultative meetings that can happen at all tiers of society and government. NATO forces in Afghanistan made a practice of attending village shuras to engage with tribal elders and discuss areas of mutual concern.

information on my role at the PRT. Lunch done, I borrowed a spare set of body armour and a helmet from the quartermaster and was soon walking into an RAF Merlin. After take-off, a loadie[54] sat at the edge of the open ramp pointing a machine gun out. I was fascinated by the shadows of the second helicopter bouncing off the buildings below as we came in to land.

A couple of days later, boots stamped in the dust and shoulders straightened on the parade square a stone's throw from my office. British troops came to attention, smart in their sand and tan desert camouflage and delineated by coloured regimental berets and tam-o'-shanters. Flags fluttered quietly on the dry Afghan breeze. The army chaplain, black stole draped around his shoulders, stood on the low dais to lead the service of remembrance to the five soldiers who had died fighting the Taliban during the previous week.

Four hundred and fifty-seven British service personnel died in Afghanistan between 2001 and 2020. Almost sixty of those died between February and June 2010 during military operations that took place while I was in Helmand. You always knew when a soldier had died, because the camp would go into communications lockdown until relatives had received the devastating news.

I attended every memorial service while I was there. Having grown up in an army family, I associated myself with the sense of duty to Queen and country and found the prayers of the relatives deeply moving. Of my two great-uncles who served in World War II – working-class lads raised in pit villages in the north-east – one didn't come home.

While he was in the British Army, my dad would often quote Rudyard Kipling's poem 'Tommy,' in which the squaddie Tommy Atkins is patronised by polite society until the time they need him to fight a war. Well, the band was certainly playing in Helmand while I was there.

---

54 Loadie is short for loadmaster, the crew member responsible for loading cargo on and off the aircraft.

For every serviceman or woman killed in Afghanistan, an honour guard awaited them on their return to the UK. A Union flag draped over their coffins, the hearses would process through crowds lining the streets of Royal Wootton Bassett, near to the RAF base. Royal Legion flags were lowered, and flowers laid on the vehicles. It was a fitting return for those who paid the ultimate price for their country. We will always remember them.

Moscow, Russia, May 2015

My four-year-old son gripped my forehead excitedly, his legs astride my shoulders, as the tanks and missile carriers of the Russian Army thundered along New Arbat Street. Crowds three-deep roared their approval, waving Russian flags.

Victory Day, 9 May, is the moment Russia commemorates the enormous sacrifices made in the defeat of the Nazis. Estimates vary, but Russia suffered around seven million military deaths and a similar number of civilian deaths during World War II.[55] That's a level of devastation incomprehensible today, following an era of relative peace.

The world is awash with pundits on all sides eager to reinterpret the Second World War. Historians in the West focus on the Soviet Union's alliance with Germany and the cruel division of Poland in the two years before Operation Barbarossa. Russian historians crow that Soviet forces did most of the fighting while the West made up its mind about opening a second front. For ordinary people in Russia and the UK, the sacrifices made by family members in defeating Hitler are a source of pride and remembrance. In the same way that the British recall the Battle of Britain, El Alamein and the Dambusters, so Russians recount the great victories in Stalingrad and Kursk and breaking the siege of Leningrad.

2015 marked the 70th anniversary of the defeat of Nazi Germany. It was a public holiday in Russia and the Embassy was closed. In

---

55 Total military and civilian deaths throughout the Soviet Union are estimated to be more than 25 million.

the morning, I visited the Foreign Ministry – as I lived just around the corner – to deliver a copy of the official message from Her Majesty Queen Elizabeth II.[56] It was a short message – the Foreign Office had worked hard to boil it down as much as possible to avoid praising Russia too much. But it was right that the British head of state should mark the occasion and extend her best wishes to the Russian people at a time of remembrance.

Several Western countries, including the US, had boycotted Victory Day celebrations in Moscow. France's Foreign Minister, Laurent Fabius, attended on 9 May, though he didn't join the parade on Red Square. He said, "We are playing a very important role in trying to find a solution in Ukraine. We hold discussions with the Russians; we are not going to talk one day and not be there the next." German Chancellor Angela Merkel found a neat compromise by visiting Moscow on 10 May, the day after Victory Day, to lay a wreath.

I felt the UK should be represented at ministerial level. The defeat of Nazi Germany is part of our shared history and at a time when the UK–Russia relationship was in a deep trough, it offered a rare opportunity to reflect a more positive spirit of conciliation. Not showing up would just accentuate the ongoing sense of alienation from Russia with no obvious benefit.

However, it was clear that Philip Hammond would never visit Moscow, let alone celebrate a historic military victory with Russia. Nor was he about to sanction UK ministerial involvement, even at junior levels. Policymakers in London were tripping over their logic about the risk of endorsing Russia's military in the modern era. The Defence Section in Moscow had hatched a plan to bring an army band to deliver a performance around Victory Day, but the idea of British guardsmen in Moscow made Hammond see red. In the end, working through 10 Downing Street, where Prime Minister David Cameron was more open-minded on engagement with Russia, Tim Barrow pulled a rabbit out of the diplomatic hat.

---

56 The original, signed, letter would arrive in the diplomatic bag a few days later.

Sir Nicholas Soames, Member of Parliament, former British Army officer and, most importantly, grandson of Sir Winston Churchill, agreed to travel to Moscow for Victory Day. It was a brilliant compromise. He had no status in government, but his relationship to Britain's wartime leader, who had visited Moscow during the war, would resonate in Russia. Ahead of travelling, he said, "I am honoured to represent the British government at the commemorations in Moscow to mark the 70th anniversary of the end of the Second World War. We share in this Victory Day, as Britain and Russia stood together with our allies against the Nazis." Tim gleefully recounted the grudging admiration at the Kremlin reception about the "typical bloody Brits" and their clever idea. It was a small victory for diplomacy over gesture politics.

Smartly polished ranks of troops marched through Red Square, heads angled, arms swinging, rifles sloped. "Don't fuck with us" was the clear message.

After Russia's lacklustre performance in the five-day war with Georgia in 2008, a massive rearmament programme started. Sustained yearly increases in defence spending from 2011 aimed to improve salaries and conditions for soldiers, professionalise the army, including through training and exercise, and modernise and increase the stock of military equipment. Of course, we know from Russia's experience in Ukraine that a large army isn't a guarantee of modern and decisive leadership on the battlefield. And there remained question marks over the modernisation itself; the super hi-tech T-14 Armata main battle tank – "better than anything in the West" – broke down during rehearsals for the parade.[57]

Russia's military industrial complex was going flat out to create analogues of hi-tech components that were no longer available from the West. The state-owned defence manufacturing conglomerate Rostec, run by long-term Putin ally Sergey Chemezov, was a big winner in the massive subsidies that poured into the programme

57 The T-14 has yet to enter active service, including in Ukraine.

of import substitution.

After the military parade finished, tens of thousands of ordinary people processed through central Moscow, holding aloft photographs of relatives who died in the war, in a vast "immortal regiment." It's a moving way to remember loved ones who served their country. The Embassy posted a photo of Sir Nicholas holding a photo of Winston Churchill, another well-chosen statement of common cause.

At the entrance to Red Square, the military and civilian parades passed the monument to World War II hero Marshal Zhukov, astride his white steed.[58] There is also a museum dedicated to the defeat of Napoleon in 1812. Struggle and sacrifice to defeat an invading foreign enemy are concepts hard-wired in the Russian psyche. Over the centuries, that enemy has included the Germans, French, Poles, Lithuanians, Swedes and Mongols, among others. There appears an underlying belief that Russia's willingness to endure more suffering than her enemy in a fight to the death is key to eventual victory.

When Russia expresses alarm at perceived NATO encroachment on her borders, it isn't only out of a restatement of short-term grievances about the deterioration of relations with the West since the downfall of the Soviet Union; it is out of this deeply historical sense of foreign threat. Western journalists and armchair generals make a grave mistake in dismissing these concerns entirely as Putin's and, more generally, Russians' paranoia.

Hard-wired into Russian doctrine is also a determination to punch harder to win a fight. In the diplomatic manoeuvrings that still lay ahead, I observed Russia repeatedly overmatching Western diplomatic responses, in a bid to test the energy of their opponent.

---

58 Marshal Zhukov, who masterminded Soviet victories including at Stalingrad and the liberation of Leningrad, rode a white horse at the head of the first Victory Day parade in Red Square on 24 June 1945.

Helmand Province, Afghanistan, 2010

Prime Minister Gordon Brown stood on the dais in the parade square and proceeded to make a speech in which he emphasised his support for UK efforts in Helmand. Some army mates had joked about parking a couple of Snatch Land Rovers[59] nearby as a form of political protest. As it turned out, two enormous US Marine Corps Super Stallion helicopters took off nearby, rendering him completely inaudible.[60] Just a few weeks later, he would be voted out of office at the UK general election. He was replaced by David Cameron, heading up the Tory–Liberal Democrat coalition.

There is a saying in Afghanistan: "You have the watches, but we have the time." The well-equipped NATO and before them Soviet armies might succeed in controlling Afghanistan but would eventually give up the stomach to fight and leave. Eight years on from toppling the Taliban, Western military doctrine had largely focused on mowing the grass: large military operations would clear towns and cities of insurgents, only for them to return as soon as NATO forces had withdrawn to base. Post 9/11, we followed the Americans in with one goal and no strategy, leading to mission creep.

While I was in Helmand, the concept of stabilisation was finally taking root, with an impressively joined-up effort to support political, social and economic regeneration in towns liberated from Taliban control. I saw the type of cooperation between military, police and a wide array of government departments that often seems impossible in Whitehall itself. I led a team that comprised colleagues from the British Army, RAF, US Marine Corps, US Army and State Department, and we worked and ate together as one team.

But the strategy of promoting stabilisation through a rich mix of development assistance, political, military and security support

---

59 The Snatch Land Rover, originally designed for use in Northern Ireland, was dubbed a mobile coffin by critics in the press thanks to the low level of protection it offered British service personnel. Thirty-seven service personnel were killed in Snatch Land Rovers in Iraq and Afghanistan.

60 Gurning away, Gordon battled on with his speech regardless.

would need a good decade to begin to prove itself. The changing of the guard in 10 Downing Street led, inevitably, to a slow shift in UK policy towards Afghanistan. At just the moment we were starting to figure out an effective way to support Afghan stabilisation, the seeds were being sown for the UK's withdrawal. Having followed the US in, in 2002, we inevitably followed them out, in 2021, in a disorderly fashion.

At the end of my time in Helmand, a Royal Navy Sea King awaited me on the helicopter landing square. As I humped on my rucksack and clambered aboard, I was excited about going home.

Halfway across to Camp Bastion, the engine note changed to a scream as we pitched into a gut-wrenching climb before spinning into a sharp dive. The old, riveted airframe juddered violently as the infra-red countermeasures system kicked out hundreds of flares. I gripped my body armour and enjoyed the roller-coaster, with new and improved "possibility-of-death" perception. *Farrrrkin' 'ell!*

During a break in the UK in April, halfway through my time in Afghanistan, I'd proposed marriage. I'd met Katharine four months after my mum died, at the Civil Service ballroom dancing club in Westminster.[61] She was a civil servant at the Department for Education at the time. I quickly realised Katharine, a devout Christian, was a far better person than I could ever be, and I was uplifted by her goodness. I'm not sure what she saw in me, though I wonder if I brought her out of herself somewhat, with my grizzled war stories and adventurous spirit. Her family must have thought she was crazy to get lumbered with me. But I worked hard to be a better person and good enough for her. For the first time in a very long time, I was settled, I was deeply in love and, while less important in the grand scheme, my career went from strength to strength.

The last thing I wanted, therefore, was to end up wounded and left on Afghanistan's plains, waiting for the women to come and

---

61 I'd taken up ballroom dancing in Thailand, and after Mum died, I decided to go to the after-work club one night per week to give me a break from spending all my time with Dad at home in Southampton.

cut up what remains. Mercifully, I made it home.[62]

Modern Western society has rightly become sensitive to military losses in faraway lands. Losing four to five British soldiers each week was considered an intolerably high price to pay. Just seventy-five years previously, the whole of Europe was engulfed in the flames of total warfare that extinguished the lives of tens of thousands each day. Today, war again rages in Europe, with the death toll far higher than anything I witnessed in Afghanistan. Estimates vary greatly, but at least one-hundred-thousand Russian and Ukrainians have been killed since the start of the war in February 2022. That's more than US losses in the Korean and Vietnam wars combined. And a similar number to those killed during the ten years of bloody conflict in the Balkans.

What I see is a Conservative government that has been, at first inadvertently but later deliberately, disengaged from efforts towards peace in Ukraine since 2014. Rather, there has been an encouragement of Ukraine in its aspiration for eventual NATO membership, knowing - from the experience of Georgia in 2008 - that Russia would sooner invade Ukraine than let that happen. At the same time, there has been an explicit determination not to deploy British Tommies to fight in a war made more likely by British foreign policy towards Russia. Another irresponsible absence of vision and strategy.

---

62 From Rudyard Kipling's 'The Young British Soldier':
When you're wounded and left on Afghanistan's plains,
And the women come out to cut up what remains,
Jest roll to your rifle and blow out your brains
An' go to your Gawd like a soldier.

13. MURDERING BASTARDS

Ufa, Bashkortostan, Russia, May 2015

"Murdering bastard," I muttered under my breath. We walked past the statue of Felix Dzerzhinsky[63] in the centre of Ufa, the capital of the Republic of Bashkortostan. I was keen to look around the city. The President of China, together with those of Brazil, India and South Africa, would land here on 9 July for the BRICS summit. After Russia was evicted from the G8, Putin placed more emphasis on the value of BRICS as a counterpoint for political and economic collaboration. You see this specifically on the issues of sanctions and international financial architecture.[64]

For the Bashkirs, it was their moment in the global spotlight as they sought to emulate the success of Tatarstan; the neighbouring, also largely Muslim, republic had raced to the top of Russia's

---

63 Felix Dzerzhinsky established the Bolshevik Secret Police, nicknamed the Cheka, in 1917. He was responsible for combating internal threats. The Cheka became notorious for egregious and widespread crimes against humanity, including the summary executions of thousands of prisoners in the basements of prisons and in public places. Dzerzhinsky once said, "We represent in ourselves organised terror."

64 The Ufa Declaration, issued at the end of the BRICS summit, pushes back against the adoption [read, by the West] of unilateral sanctions and emphasises the need for new global financial architecture to move away from reliance on the [Western-dominated] Bretton Woods institutions. You see exactly these themes adopted by BRICS since the outbreak of war in Ukraine, as part of the drive against what China and Russia call a Unipolar (i.e., US dominated) world.

investment ratings by using its oil and gas wealth to invest and attract foreign companies to set up factories. Bashkortostan has significant wealth from oil and gas exploration and wanted to become more appealing to investors. Hosting a major international summit would give Ufa global media coverage for two days. A lot of investment had been made in the city in the run-up to the event, with a couple of major hotel chains having opened new venues.

This was my first visit to the Urals. The arrival of British diplomats in sleepy Ufa, a few weeks before BRICS, grabbed the attention of Iron Felix's modern-day soulmates in the FSB. As far as they were concerned, it was like Christmas and their birthday had come at once. On the basis that every summit is a major intelligence-gathering opportunity, our arrival offered a perfect dress rehearsal.

I flew in from Moscow with Cally from the International Trade team. We were collected from the airport by a couple of "guides" who made awkward small talk on the ride into town. At the hotel, someone filmed our arrival on an iPad. There always seemed to be someone lurking near my bedroom. Good job I packed clean skids.

Jeff Shipman, the Acting Consul General in Ekaterinburg, arrived by car with a Russian colleague Yelena. That evening, we enjoyed drinks and feasted on horse meat and honey[65] in the hotel bar. Guys in their early thirties sat at all the tables around ours, each one nursing a glass of beer all night, their smartphones face up on the table. I felt incredibly well taken care of, as I sipped my drink and puffed on a shisha pipe. Yelena took a photo of me which Jeff named "two whiskies and a hookah."

The following day, the Economic Development and Finance Ministers of the Bashkir government welcomed us at their grand offices. Our guides sat sullenly at the back of the cavernous meeting room, wearing headphones. Deloitte had helped pull together a glossy investment pack and it was clear they had big plans. In

---

65 Bashkortostan is renowned for both and is Russia's largest honey-producing region.

addition to their oil and gas wealth, they wanted to improve power infrastructure, urban development and transport links. This would help them branch out into new areas, such as eco-tourism. They were keen for Ufa to be a training base camp during the FIFA 2018 World Cup in Russia.[66]

Ufa city centre was pleasant enough, with a mix of pre- and post-revolutionary low-rise architecture common in provincial Russian cities spared the ravages of Nazi bombs. We visited the state university, where I flirted gently with the interpreter (I didn't need interpretation, but Jeff did), only to find she was an academic's wife. The other academics were pleased with my visit and talked of their hopes to establish a collaboration with a British university; their efforts to that point had been fruitless. In the nicest possible way, it wasn't obvious why people would want to visit this place especially when Russia has many other more easily accessible, destinations. The statue of Russia's first Chekist outside the former KGB HQ building underlined the issue; the FSB leapt out more than any USP. I could see the theoretical potential to invest in this republic. But I wasn't feeling the love.

After a pleasant Caucasian meal, we strolled the city, followed all the while by a friendly Felix. Jeff and I fell into the habit of stopping and turning to admire particularly interesting features, like an attractive leaf, or a stone on the path. At every stop, our follower would dash into cover, even if that meant jumping behind a bush.

Cally had found details of a Scottish-themed pub. Sure enough, on Karl Marx Street was the McHighlander. With a decent selection of whiskies and Scottish mementos on the wall (from tourist trips, I assumed) it looked every bit the part. The kilted bartender and his lissom assistant in a flowing white dress with tartan sash appeared like supporting actors from *Braveheart*. He beamed at our compliments on the authenticity of the pub and seemed pleased to receive British visitors. I saw time and again that Russians are great

---

66 They weren't successful in their bid.

hobbyists; when they find a particular interest, they will pursue it with passion and determination.

Between drinks I'd pop out of the pub from time to time. On the other side of the road, our friend would duck into a side alley whenever I appeared. I could see that our visit was huge training opportunity, so I was supporting his professional development. I can just imagine the briefing at FSB HQ Ufa before our visit.

"Felix Vladimirovich, just make sure they don't see you when they're in the pub."

"Fuck your mother! I'm well good at this covert surveillance shit."

Cally flew back to Moscow, but I joined Jeff and his team for the eight-hour drive back to Yekaterinburg. The landscape undulated gently across the four hundred miles or so. Gennady, the Consulate driver, had clearly fancied a career in Formula One, as we hurtled along single-carriageway roads, kicking up dirt with each hair-raising overtake. It was another reminder of the basic state of road infrastructure across most of the world's largest country, and the need for investment. The towns, when they appeared, were often wooden and rural. Outside of the bigger cities, Russia is far from being an advanced economy (mind you, you could say the same about the US).

I was planning my first big speech in Russian at the Ural Federal University in Ekaterinburg the following day. Having criticised Chancery colleagues for their low level of Russian, I had written the speech hastily in English and put it through Google. *Arrggghhh!*

Yelena in the back seat spent a good while tutting and taking the mickey about the poor-quality Russian translation. It was the last time I would take this shortcut.[67]

While Ufa was overcast and damp, Ekaterinburg was warm and sunny. Sitting on the border between Europe and Asia, the blue

---

67 Writing speeches in the language you are using is far easier than writing them in English then retrofitting them, particularly when the language is very different from English.

sky appeared infinite. The hotel sat beside a small reservoir and from my window I could see the onion dome of the Church on the Blood in the distance. The following day, Yelena took me to visit the church. Until 1977, when Boris Yeltsin ordered its demolition, the Ipatiev House had occupied the site. On 17 July 1918, Tsar Nicholas II of Russia was summarily murdered by the Bolsheviks with his family and servants in a small basement room. The execution was messy and took around twenty to thirty minutes to complete. In 2003 this beautiful church was built, and Tsar Day remembrance events take place every July. Outside the church stands a monument to the royal martyrs: a cross, around which curl twenty-three steps, signifying the imperial family's final descent into the basement of Ipatiev House. The seven royal martyrs face outwards. Their remains now lie at rest in the Fortress of St Peter and St Paul in St Petersburg. I found the site incredibly moving.

I was able to meet representatives of both the Ekaterinburg and the wider Sverdlovsk governments during my visit. The Minister for Economic Development hosted me for talks at the fine Governor's Residence by the waterside and was enthusiastic to explore the potential for collaboration. Sverdlovsk has a large industrial complex which dates to World War II, when the Soviets moved most of their wartime manufacturing east in the teeth of the Nazi advance. It is also rich in precious metals, which meant that Western companies including Airbus and Boeing set up facilities for parts manufacturing. The Ekaterinburg government was also keen to deepen links with the UK, with a particular interest in collaboration around the supply chain for the 2018 World Cup.[68]

It struck me that the Ekaterinburg Consulate operation was working hard across this part of Russia. With only two diplomats and a handful of Russian staff, it was a tiny outpost, and there had been all manner of problems. A previous Deputy Consul General was famously caught on camera with call girls. Another

---

68 Ekaterinburg hosted four group games during the World Cup.

diplomat had dipped a tad too often into the delights of inter-cultural relationship building. Jeff Shipman was the perfect guy to steady the ship, as it were: experienced, settled in his family life and short-term enough to be trusted not to shit either his bed or anyone else's. Even though I was technically the more senior, I let him lead on meetings and he was great at the representational side of the work: down to earth, engaging, avoiding potholes and dead ends in conversation.

While the city is remarkably pleasant, there were still considerable challenges. I didn't notice anything like the attention that I received in Ufa, but Yelena was starting to hit what would become quite unacceptable harassment. A nationalist blogger had already started a campaign of nasty, spiteful posts calling her a spy and a traitor for working with the British. It would only get worse.

The Ural Federal University, a nondescript concrete campus in the city centre, laid on a warm welcome for the final act of my visit. I delivered my Russian speech, much improved by Yelena and Sveta, to an interested audience of academics and students who asked lots of questions, not only about the economics but about my personal reflections on Russia (I stuck to the positives). Almost ten months into my posting, I'd boiled my economic assessment of Russia's challenges down to a four-step analysis.

First, sanctions had impacted Russia's economy by limiting flows of capital. This was affecting Russia's ability to invest and diversify its economy away from an over-reliance on fossil fuels. However, it was already clear that with huge stocks of Russian capital parked offshore, a major repatriation of assets was taking place to offset the loss of foreign capital. And Russia had low levels of investment in any case, compared to high-performing Asian economies like China and Vietnam. Banning investment in offshore, Arctic and shale oil exploration hadn't yet had a major impact, as the huge drop in oil prices had reduced the profitability of these ventures, at least in the short term. Russian oil production hadn't been affected by energy sanctions (and would continue to rise).

So, sanctions made a small contribution to the drop in Russian economic growth that had started in 2014.

Second, shale production in the US and a drop in global demand for oil had led to the rouble more than halving in value. This mattered, because it had driven up inflation in Russia and caused a shift in Russia's monetary policy towards inflation targeting, through high interest rates. Ordinary Russians were facing higher prices in the shops, a decline in real earnings and a rise in the cost of serving domestic debts. Poverty was on the increase as a result.

Third, spending in the economy fell. Not only did households have less money, but the federal government also saw a drop in tax revenues, principally caused by the lower oil price; prior to the collapse, tax receipts from oil and gas accounted for almost a quarter of total tax revenue. This general depression in spending made a huge contribution to the recession that followed the oil price collapse. Privatisation of inefficient state-owned assets was moving at a snail's pace.

Finally, sentiment, which is Russia's biggest obstacle to attracting foreign investment. Despite the good work happening in some parts of the federal and regional system, operating in Russia was still considered a risky venture in many boardrooms, especially in Western countries. Events in Ukraine had a chilling effect on investor sentiment. And it wasn't only Ukraine.

Three months earlier, the funeral had taken place in Moscow for Boris Nemtsov, who was assassinated on 27 February 2015. The former Deputy Prime Minister and critic of Russian policy in Ukraine was shot in the back four times while walking across Moskvoretsky Bridge near Red Square with his Ukrainian girlfriend. He was killed on the eve of a protest march he'd planned against Russia's military involvement in Ukraine. The murder met with international condemnation and growing concern in Russia's small opposition movement about the consequences of speaking out against the Russian state.

Opposition figure Alexei Navalny, who at the time was serving a period under arrest, was not given dispensation to attend the funeral. For the UK, former Prime Minister John Major attended, having met Nemtsov during his period in office. Orchestrated by Tim Barrow, it was an ingenious way to show UK support without formal representation by the government of the day. Several other foreign dignitaries attended, although there was an outcry from Brussels when Moscow blocked visas for two politicians from Poland and Latvia. In the EU camp, Poland and the former Soviet states of Latvia, Lithuania and Estonia were conventionally the most hawkish about Russia, alongside the UK.

While Russian state participation in the funeral was limited to an official representative of the President, several high-profile liberals paid their respects. It was another visible sign of the tensions between the outward-facing liberals and the refashioned fat-cat Felixes.

Five Chechen men were later arrested and subsequently convicted of the murder. Shortly after their arrest, Ramzan Kadyrov, the head of the Chechen Republic, took to Instagram; he declared the leader, Zaur Dadayev, a "true patriot," suggesting his devotion to Russia could not be questioned even if he was convicted of murder.

Russia has spent centuries trying to bring to heel restive Muslim clans in the North Caucasus. Kadyrov rose to prominence in the decade-long second Chechen war between 1999 and 2009. He led the Kadyrovtsy militia[69] that supported the Russian armed forces in their battle with Chechen separatists. Aged just twenty-seven, he entered politics in 2004 after his father's assassination, rising to the very top three years later. He enjoys almost complete authority in Chechnya, in return for his allegiance to Russia. That brings with it risks. In the words of Anna Politkovskaya, the journalist who was murdered in 2006 by five Chechen men, "the Kremlin fosters a baby dragon, which it then has to feed to stop him from setting

---

69 That same militia has come to prominence more recently, fighting alongside Russian forces in the war in Ukraine.

everything on fire". Other baby dragons have come to prominence more recently, such as Yevgeny Prigozhin.

The Wagner Group was already active in Libya and Syria prior to my arrival in Russia. It played a prominent role in the war in Ukraine until Prigozhin orchestrated the failed military mutiny in June 2023 that briefly threatened to reach Moscow. The difference between Kadyrov and Prigozhin was that while the former has a clearly defined geographical and ethnic boundary to his power base, the latter only had free rein to fish in the cesspools of society. That undoubtedly made it easier for the Kremlin to neutralise Prigozhin in the short-term, as we have now witnessed. But as Russia increasingly falls back on non-state actors in its hybrid war against the west, Prigozhin was also a reminder that the biggest risk to Putin's authority longer-term is the growth in other would-be warlords. Ekaterinburg provided a healthy reminder of what happened to the last Tsar who didn't indulge his dragons with sufficient care.

14. CRUNCH TIME FOR SANCTIONS

St Petersburg, Russia, June 2015

I ignored the zone markers directing Western diplomats to sit at the back of the cavernous convention hall and sat among the Russian high rollers near the stage. Three men soon occupied seats in the row before mine. Ramzan Kadyrov, aforementioned head of the Chechen Republic, sat directly in front of me, between strapping bodyguards. Shorter, at around five foot nine, and in a leather jacket blinged-up with gold stitching, he was stocky, no doubt from the workouts he often posted online from his gym. Here was the man who had eulogised the prime suspect in the murder of Boris Nemtsov four months previously.

For very different reasons, we'd found ourselves in the same spot to listen to Vladimir Putin's annual keynote address. The St Petersburg International Economic Forum was in its nineteenth year, a chance for Russia to open its doors to the world for business and economic discussion. Everyone who was anyone from the Russian government, presidential administration or business sector sat attentively in the front rows to hear the words of the oracle on the state of Russia's economy. Every major Western company in Russia was represented at senior levels.

Since the oil price collapse of November 2014 and the sharp hike in interest rates the following month, Russia's economy had entered a recession. With a currency that had halved in value, the cost of imports had correspondingly doubled. Supply chains were shifting away from reliance on EU agricultural products, putting a short-term dent in supplies of key foods. Taken together, inflation was over 15% year on year; ordinary Russians had less spending power and faced higher interest rates on lending. By the end of 2015, an estimated three million Russians would have fallen below the poverty line. And the Russian state had fewer resources with which to offer support, having entered its first fiscal deficit since 1998 because of a sharp reduction in taxes from oil exports. In this "second phase" of Russian economic and monetary policy, privatisation of state-owned assets was seen as the key vehicle for narrowing the fiscal gap, but little progress had been made.

Uncharacteristically on time,[70] Vladimir Putin walked into the auditorium to thunderous applause from the mostly Russian audience. Already on stage sat a carefully selected group of "safe" panel members, including a Chinese Vice-President and an on-message head of a German electrical company.

In his speech, Putin elevated such positive economic factoids as existed. He didn't highlight the underlying weakness in Russia's economy laid bare by the oil price decline, specifically the lack of diversification away from fossil fuels. He laboured through prepared notes undoubtedly written by a committee of staffers in Staraya Square. But it quickly became clear that setting out a credible plan for Russia's economic future was not the key aim of the event. After each panel member had delivered an on-message speech, an elderly and decidedly mid-rate American journalist, Charlie Rose, put questions to Putin for a full hour.

The main topic in town was, of course, Ukraine. Returning to an already familiar narrative, Putin put the blame firmly in the lap of the US and its Western allies. Russia had not caused the crisis in Ukraine. It had started with a "coup d'état" that saw the overthrow

---

70 Vladimir Putin is famous for being late for functions, on one occasion keeping the Pope waiting two hours for a scheduled meeting.

of Yanukovych. The Minsk agreements must be implemented in full, but Russia could not do that in isolation from the authorities in Kyiv. Key would be the requirements in the Minsk agreements for constitutional reform, including decentralisation in the Donbass. Direct dialogue between Donetsk, Luhansk and the Ukrainian authorities needed to take place, and this hadn't happened.

In what some might have seen as a thinly veiled repudiation of Ukraine's right to statehood, Putin said that the common cultural and spiritual foundations connecting Russia and Ukraine meant both countries were destined for a common security. "We are one people."

Underlying Putin's remarks, a clear message that the separatist forces in the Donbass would continue to receive arms and military support in the absence of political progress. "Where there's conflict, arms will follow."

Across a broad swathe of issues, Putin tried to position Russia as a responsible international player, keen to reach political solutions to global challenges. He railed against the US trying to impose its decisions within a unipolar world created by the downfall of the Soviet Union – interfering in the internal politics of Russia, financing NGOs etc. At that time, Russia had already started to clamp down on what it deemed "foreign agents," placing restrictions on foreign funding of everything from universities to charitable groups and limiting foreign ownership of media outlets.

After a pedestrian walk over economic topics, this was a more confident Putin talking on themes that were familiar to him. For those of us listening, there was nothing that we hadn't heard before. It was what Western policymakers often describe as Putin repeating historical grievances and embedding the narrative of Russia protecting her interests against a hostile West. Few policy-makers in the West ask whether, on some issues, Putin may have a legitimate point.

Four months after the Minsk II agreement was signed, there had been no progress on the Ukrainian side of the bargain in terms of moving forward consultations on some form of devolution. Such proposals faced widespread political resistance in Ukraine, out of a not illegitimate fear of giving an inch only for Russia to seek another mile. Very obviously, Russia wasn't holding to its commitments either, in particular to secure Ukraine's territorial border and withdraw its troops. Russian military personnel, supposedly "on leave," were supporting the separatists in the Donbass with equipment and advice.

The difference was that in a decision by the European Council of March 2015, the duration of sanctions against Russia was linked to the "full implementation of the Minsk Agreements". The UK government had succeeded in its efforts to insert this conditionality into EU-wide sanctions policy towards Russia.

However, Russia had no intention of putting pressure on the separatists to meet their obligations under Minsk II without engagement by Kyiv. And there was little incentive for Kyiv to meet its obligations, as this would lead to sanctions relief for Russia. Putin, in his specific way, was seeking to illuminate what he saw as the poverty and injustice of the Western position.

It was clever politics by Putin to take extended questions from a Western journalist, watched by Western diplomats and business-people. It's hard to think of a UK Prime Minister letting themselves be interviewed at a large business event by a Russian journalist; they just wouldn't take the risk. But it was also clear that I, as a Western diplomat, was not Putin's main audience. I didn't hear anything I wasn't already aware of or couldn't figure out for myself. The main audience for this event was domestic.

Charlie Rose was tamer than a drugged tiger at a circus photo stall. Time and again, Putin batted off his questions with confident responses that drew rounds of applause from the largely partisan crowd. For the Russian onlooker, here was Putin courageously pitting his wits against a credible journalist with a Midwestern drawl. I wondered what Ramzan Kadyrov was thinking directly in front of me. I should imagine, in part, that President Putin reinforced what he already believed was the case, in terms of Russia's difficult relationship with the West, i.e., that it was the West's fault. For the ranks of Deputy Prime Ministers and ministers sat directly in front of Putin, it was a clear signal that Russian policy was correct and justified. And for the babushki and dedushki dialling in from Siberia, it was a reminder that Tsar Vladimir Vladimirovich was in control and protecting Mother Russia, and thus their interests.

After two and a half hours in a hard plastic seat and starting to feel the pinch on my bladder, I tried not to get too excited about the other main event at this plenary session.

Sat near the front of the stage, nodding like an ornamental dog on a taxi dashboard in Corfu, was Alexis Tsipras, Prime Minister of Greece. The Hellenic Republic was in the middle of a debt crisis. The global financial crisis of 2008 had tipped Greece into an economic depression and illuminated the country's fundamental lack of competitiveness and lax fiscal policy. Bailouts by the Eurozone and IMF in 2010 and 2012 worth €216 billion had been agreed. However, a final payment on the second programme was faltering on Greece's repeated failure to meet its austerity commitments and implement market reforms.

Greece had therefore swung to the hard-left Syriza party at a snap election in January 2015, with Tsipras promising an end to austerity and a commitment to play hardball with the Eurozone. By mid-June, negotiations with the European Central Bank and Eurozone Finance Ministers were gridlocked, meaning Greece was staring down the barrel of a sovereign default. The other looming deadline was the rollover of European sanctions against Russia.

And therein lay the reason for Tsipras's visit to Russia. During a visit to Moscow two months previously, he had said that his government "openly disapproved of sanctions." Colleagues in London were having kittens about the prospect of Greece breaking EU consensus on sanctions; to be extended, EU sanctions required unanimity by all twenty-eight members. Senior British diplomats shuttled around the EU lobbying their counterparts to hold the sanctions line and to encourage the Greeks to do so too. Southern

European countries were also wavering on continued sanctions against Russia, given their exposure to Russia's ban on agricultural goods. A small debt bailout of Greece by Russia could see the sanctions house of cards collapse overnight.

And so, after Charlie Rose had finished his questioning, Tsipras was invited onto the stage. He shook Putin's hand on the way to the podium before commenting to the audience, "You are probably wondering why I'm here," as if it wasn't blindingly obvious.

Tsipras offered a rambling and indescribably pompous speech in which he spoke of Greece's problem being Europe's problem, and how Greece could help build bridges between Russia and Europe. He offered a vague mention of Minsk and avoided the more direct criticism of sanctions that he'd made during his April visit. The video feed panned to Russian ministers like Sergey Lavrov making eyes and joking with each other as if to say, "What the fuck is this all about?" When his fifteen-minute speech finished, Tsipras turned on his heel and strode off the stage without acknowledging anyone, including a bemused-looking Putin.

As the marathon plenary ended, I filed out of my seat without bidding farewell to Ramzan Kadyrov. In the distance, I spotted Tim Barrow coming down from the cheap seats and we walked out together, sharing a car back to the British Consulate General.

It had been an interesting two days at the forum. A couple of non-EU governments had lobbied the UK and other European countries to boycott the event, and we had declined to do so. A low-key visit by Tim, me, Consul General Keith Allan and a member of my team had been agreed by London, who scrutinised suggestions for attendance at any Russian-hosted events. The Ukrainian Embassy had been in touch with me beforehand, wanting details of how large our delegation to St Petersburg would be.

It was right that we attend. The event offered not only a rare opportunity to see Putin in action but also a chance to read the mood music in the room. Plus, some big UK companies were still in Russia, including the likes of BP and HSBC, allowing Tim to meet them all in one place and hear their concerns.

I saw VTB chair Andrey Kostin at one discussion session, red-faced and thumping the table about the interference of Western lackeys trying to put a straitjacket on Russia. Anatoly Chubais, the side-lined but still prominent protagonist of the disastrous loans-for-shares scheme of the nineties, stuck to a similar narrative in his bid to sail close to the Kremlin walls. There was an awful lot of back-slapping and playing to the Russian galleries. But the Russian state was also putting on the charm offensive to Western fat cats and getting their message across about Russia being open for business despite the difficult politics (in their words, caused by the West).

A raft of Western academics merrily joined panel discussions on a range of economic topics. Former Prime Minister Tony Blair made an appearance fresh from a visit to Kyiv, where he'd offered his services as a peace envoy. He joined a panel discussion with Alexei Kudrin – who had not been made Prime Minister - and Herman Gref, the chair of state-owned bank Sberbank. They discussed policy reform in government and Blair didn't touch on Ukraine at all. I assume he was handsomely paid.

After my ill-fated visit to Ufa in May, the Deputy Prime Minister of Bashkortostan invited me to meet for a further discussion of potential UK economic collaboration. He presented me with a gift bag containing an enormous pot of Bashkir honey, a stone bottle of balsam and a litre of vodka. We had a good-natured discussion which piqued my interest in a return visit. Like him, I was keen to see how Bashkortostan had fared in the soon-to-be-released results of the yearly Russian Investment Climate Rating index. Bashkortostan was desperate to break into the top ten Russian regions. In the end, they slipped down to eighteenth place and the Deputy Prime Minister was sacked the following day. I hope meeting me didn't seal his fate. My thin interest in the Bashkir Republic promptly fizzled out. In any case, my travel plan was already filling up for the coming six months.

Tim collected his bags from the Consulate and headed for the train to Moscow, while I spent an hour bashing out a telegram for London summarising key insights. Still weighed down by my five-kilogram bag of Bashkir swag, I jumped into a taxi and headed into the city centre.

I had a dinner date with my Swedish and Dutch counterparts, Eva and Wendela, with whom I'd built a nice working relationship through our northern European lunch club. We were joined by two officials from the Dutch Economic Ministry in a gloriously packed-out Georgian restaurant behind Kazan Cathedral. Over khachapuri, shashlik and cold Russian beer, we shared our experiences from the forum, joking about Tsipras's bizarre speech.

Midsummer in St Petersburg is referred to as the "white nights," as night-time doesn't fall completely on the Venice of the North, and a cerulean light lingers in the sky. It was always my favourite time to visit this magical city. Indeed, as I enjoyed my food, my team member Sandy proposed to his girlfriend Tasha by one of the canals.

As I made my way to my hotel in the twilight hours, it was clear to me that if he had wanted to, Putin could have offered Greece a small bailout loan in a deal to break sanctions. Despite the macro-challenges buffeting Russia after the oil price collapse, the country possessed still generous foreign exchange reserves, which were valued at above $400 billion. But Tsipras left Russia empty-handed.

With the renewal of Russia sanctions on the immediate horizon, Tsipras was clearly playing the Eurozone to drive progress in negotiations on a third bailout package. The benefits of taking a sticking plaster pay-out from Putin were, I suspect, far outweighed by the risks to Greece's economy of burning bridges with the EU. While Greece defaulted on a small IMF payment at the end of June, a third Eurozone bailout package was nonetheless agreed on 12 July 2015 worth €86 billion.

Three days after Tsipras's visit, on 22 June 2015, EU sanctions against Russia were extended; from that moment, they were effectively set in stone.

Linking the extension of EU sanctions to Russia's full implementation of the Minsk agreements was a mistake. The agreements were useful as a basis for peace negotiations and confidence-building measures between Russia and Ukraine. But Ukraine was never going to meet its commitments on devolution, so the notion of "full implementation" was, at best, fanciful. On this basis, the domestic political risk to Putin from offering major concessions towards peace in Ukraine with nothing in return would be too high.

And he'd probably made the judgement that Russia could manage economically. Russia was going through its own recession, but the Central Bank and Finance Ministry had stabilised the economy. More than sanctions, the big variable remained the oil price. The fact of sanctions was helpful to Putin in bolstering his domestic narrative that the West was bent on bringing Russia to heel rather than solving the situation in Ukraine. That narrative has barely changed to this day.

My first year in Moscow had been characterised by relative stability in which Russia and the UK maintained a barely functioning diplomatic relationship underpinned by deep foundations of mutual hostility. The summer of 2015 marked the point in time from which the possibility of a durable peace agreement in Ukraine evaporated, and the risk of all-out war grew, first slowly, then at an increasingly worrying speed.

PART TWO

15. THE NIGHT TRAIN TO KYIV

Moscow, Russia, October 2015

The conductor sidled up to me in the corridor. "The next cabin is empty if you want to be together tonight," she said, with a coquettish glint, twirling her bottle-blond hair in her finger. Amy had settled into her cabin with another young female traveller. She blushed and appeared horrified at the prospect of kipping down with me for the night.

"Err, that's OK, thanks," I said. "She's my colleague."

"It's fine, no one needs to know about it," the *provodnitsa* continued, leaning conspiratorially against the door jamb, generous bosom threatening to burst out of over-tight blouse.

I skulked back down the corridor to my cabin. My companions for the overnight service to Kyiv from Moscow were two stocky gentlemen in sweatpants and vests. Probably called Serhii and Oleksii, or Sergei and Aleksey; I wasn't entirely sure if they were Ukrainian or Russian. Nor whether the evening for them was social or business.

The previous week, direct air travel had been cancelled between Russia and Ukraine. With sanctions against Russia now set in concrete and the Minsk agreements dead in the Pripet marshes, relations had soured further. So, the only direct transport route to Ukraine's capital was by train, from Kievskiy Station in central Moscow.

Every arrangement had been made to ensure the Ukrainian Railways service was as inconvenient as possible. I'd queued for an hour, but when I was within touching distance of the counter, the stony-faced ticket lady pulled the shutters down and went for a tea break. Thankfully, Amy paid a gypsy to print out tickets from the impossible-to-fathom komputerised machine. We had boarded the train with barely a minute to spare. There was no restaurant car, nor associated alcohol to dull the misery. The carriage was sweltering inside.

Serhii and Oleksii made up my bed, stored my carry-on bag beneath theirs and couldn't do enough to make me feel looked after – or over. I settled down for the night on the top bunk, to the now-familiar ker-klunk, ker-klunk of slow-moving wheels on track. Travel by overnight rail service had become a guilty pleasure for me in Russia. Passport checks and cabin searches were carried out on both the Russian and the Ukrainian sides of the border, which made for a disrupted sleep.

Kyiv, Ukraine

In the early morning, the train ground to a stop in a chilly Kyiv.

This was my first of several visits to the capital of Ukraine, the centre of which is strikingly beautiful. The British Embassy sits atop wooded hills above the river Dnieper in an especially pretty part of the city. It's a stone's throw from the Mikhailovskiy Monastery, whose gold onion domes have provided a backdrop to BBC news coverage of the war. In the other direction, the Andriivskyi Descent, a cobbled alley of shops and restaurants, winds down the steep hill to the historic Podil district. Down this hill strode Volodymir Zelenskiy and Boris Johnson during the latter's first visit to Kyiv after war broke out.

My visit had been prompted by a regional residential training school for staff from the twelve embassies across Eastern Europe and central Asia. The recently established Foreign Office Diplomatic

Academy had created a qualification that all staff[71] – diplomatic and country-based – could complete. The qualification, while at a basic level, offers a vital introduction to most aspects of the Foreign Office's work, and should be mandatory for all new staff who join (but somehow isn't).

Keen to seize the initiative, the Directorate set up residential schools to bring together staff from as far afield as Chisinau and Bishkek for a burst of learning. Senior colleagues from across the Directorate descended on Kyiv to deliver talks on a range of topics. I gave a lecture on UK policy in Afghanistan since 2001 and, separately, on Foreign Office protocol, having worked on a range of major summits including the G8. Bruce Bucknell made the short trip from Minsk, and it was nice to catch up with him again.

The Embassy, which didn't have its own in-house economic expert, laid on a programme which included meetings with Deputy Ministers and Central Bank Governors. I was interested in three issues.

Eighteen months on from the onset of the Ukraine crisis, the country's economy was being kept afloat with the aid of foreign assistance. In early 2015, foreign exchange reserves had dropped to a perilously low $5 billion, insufficient to cover two months of imports. With the help of the IMF and the European Union, macro-financial bailout packages were helping the National Bank of Ukraine rebuild its reserves. In the short-term, external debt repayments had to be met and businesses needed to pay for imports with foreign currency. Devaluing the national currency wasn't a palatable choice, as that would make it almost impossible for Ukraine to service its debt, which in 2015 was close to 130% of GDP.

And Ukraine still owed debt repayments to Russia. A $3 billion Eurobond purchased from Russia was due to be repaid in late 2015. This bond was the down payment made to Viktor Yanukovych ahead of his decision not to sign an association agreement with the

---

71 My association with the Diplomatic Academy and with the Foundation Qualification would continue to grow over the remainder of my career.

EU at the 2013 Eastern Partnership summit. Other international creditors had agreed a debt restructuring deal with Ukraine which involved a write-down of 20% of debt owed and a revised payment schedule. Russia wanted more favourable terms – repayment in three tranches of $1 billion between 2016 and 2018 – but in the politically charged nature of the relationship, a deal could not be reached. Arseniy Yatsenyuk, America's choice as Ukrainian PM, then declared a moratorium on repayment of the Russian bond. He was supported by Ukraine's Finance Minister at that time, a former US State Department Official, Natalie Jaresko.

Fundamentally, the long-term economic challenge for Ukraine was to enact economic reform to make the country more competitive, more able to boost foreign exports and attract foreign direct investment. Easier said than done in the midst of a conflict in which Russia had annexed Crimea and supported a separatist insurgency in the Donbass. However, despite the injustices Ukraine felt about Russian actions, refusing to meet its international debt obligations was an unhelpful move which threatened wider restructuring efforts.

Arguments about debt led into the second major topic that dominated my discussions: Russian gas. Since the mid-noughties, Russia and Ukraine had had several disputes over gas supplies, centred around two issues: debts owed by Ukraine for Russian gas supplied and allegations that Ukraine had diverted gas intended for Europe for its domestic use. Since the outbreak of the conflict, Ukraine had again fallen behind on paying for gas supplied from Russia. Russia had therefore scrapped a generous discount, hiking the price of new gas supplies by $200 per 1,000 cubic metres, to $485. The two sides entered international arbitration over their disputes, and Ukraine started to receive gas from the European Union, in what some people called "reverse flow."

Throughout these disputes, Russia continued to pipe around 60% of natural gas supplied to Europe across Ukrainian territory. This generated transit revenues for Ukraine of around $3 billion per year. It was clear from the discussions I had in Kyiv that retaining the lucrative transit revenue was a key priority of the Ukrainian state. In short, Ukraine didn't want to buy Russian gas, but still wanted to benefit financially from its delivery to Europe. And so, new Russian pipeline projects were in Ukrainian and US crosshairs, particularly a second Nordstream gas pipeline to Germany. A proposed Southstream pipeline through Bulgaria had been cancelled following pressure from the Americans and replaced by a project through Turkey. American efforts to prevent new Russian pipelines appeared as much about supporting Ukraine as they were about boosting American LNG exports to Europe.

Throughout my time in Moscow, the UK was never a leading player within Europe on issues related to Russian energy, principally because we received such a small proportion of our gas and oil from Russia. Germany was by far the biggest player on Nordstream II, but the UK positioned itself to press for conditionality by insisting that Russia continue to pipe a proportion of its gas via Ukraine. I always found this a ludicrous proposition. Russia's energy relationship with Ukraine had been fraught since long before the onset of recent hostilities; it made commercial and political sense for Russia to seek alternative routes. But in circular discussions with London, colleagues would respond, "Well, Russia doesn't need to build other pipelines because it can transport gas through Ukraine." We'd ended up in the bizarre position of British civil servants adjudicating on how Russia should and should not transport its natural gas.

The third issue was corruption. Ukraine was still battling with endemic corruption through all tiers of politics, business and society. Partly this was a hangover from the Soviet period. Much corruption, including the petty rent-seeking by the police, health workers, government officials and university professors etc., shared similarities with the type of corruption still common in Russia. However, deeper corruption in Ukraine resembled the Wild West, in which the most powerful groups were in permanent competition for resources, including schemes to divvy up the state budget. In

Russia, the oligarchs had been cowed by Putin, political power was carefully regulated by the Kremlin, and access to resources was increasingly directed through a network of state-owned firms controlled by Putin-friendly cronies, like Sechin and Chemezov etc.

Corruption remains by far the biggest obstacle Ukraine will need to overcome if it is to realise the ambition one day of securing European Union membership. It has a very long way to go. I wonder how much progress would have been made on governance reform in Ukraine without the distraction of the UK and the US actively stoking an antagonistic relationship with Russia.

However, I left Kyiv optimistic about Ukraine's future, although acutely aware of the challenges. It was clear that younger generations were desperate for change and reform, although less clear how soon the government could deliver this. Despite its not inconsiderable size as a country, I was reminded at every turn how fragile Ukraine was compared to Russia. Notwithstanding the impact of the oil price collapse of November 2014 and sanctions, Russia remained a country with considerable foreign reserves and relatively low debt, the opposite to Ukraine.

Ukraine was a much larger version of Belarus in many ways, with the one key difference that it wanted to make a change for the better, with the aim of securing the type of prosperity that neighbouring Poland had achieved. It had lived in a state of economic dependency on Russia for over ninety years: dependent on cheap gas, dependent on handouts and loans to keep its national accounts from collapsing. That represented a status quo that it was not in Russia's interest to change. I really admired that aspiration and hoped Ukraine would succeed. But at the back of my mind, I still considered that in the long term, success would be more likely if Western countries were also promoting a positive and healthy economic relationship between Ukraine and Russia, rather than encouraging Ukraine to make a binary choice. Six months after my visit, Arseniy Yatseniuk resigned as Prime Minister of Ukraine, his government plagued by a string of corruption allegations.

. . .

Being in Ukraine as a British diplomat felt markedly different from operating in Moscow. From the happy greeting at the hotel to meetings with ministers and senior officials, people were generally pleased to meet me. The warmth of the reception reflected the UK relationship. UK ministers from across Whitehall were engaging with their Ukrainian counterparts on a regular basis. The UK should support Ukraine in reforming its economy and putting in place stronger governance, on the road to greater EU integration.

In stark contrast, the UK had practically no ministerial relationship with Russia, especially while Philip Hammond was Foreign Secretary. That terrible phrase "no return to business as usual" cropped up whenever Ministerial dialogue was suggested to colleagues in London. Engagement with Russia was to be doled out like sweeties in response to improved Russian behaviour, on a scale that no one had articulated. Except the Russians didn't see that they were completely to blame. If one purpose of diplomacy is to improve relationships between states and reduce the risk of conflict, then not talking to Russia would only, it seemed to me, achieve the opposite. You can't be friends with everyone, but real diplomacy involves talking to those people you disagree with the most in a search – however challenging – for common ground.

And there was a wider problem. Diplomats use influence and gather insight: they influence decision makers in the countries where they operate in the search for common ground; they gather insight into what's happening in those countries, to advise their ministers on policy. In Ukraine, the UK had influence and gained insight constantly from having access to meetings at all levels of government; in Russia, the UK had no influence, and this made it much harder to garner insight.

This placed an added premium on British diplomats in Moscow using their skills to the maximum, in the constant struggle to find anyone useful to talk to. The standard wheeze at the Ministry of Foreign Affairs was to field officers for meetings more junior than the British diplomat they were meeting. It was all incredibly tedious, but as the Economic Counsellor, I could also engage with academics and businesspeople. For colleagues in the Political Section, it meant reading Russian newspapers through Google Translate.

I decided not to repeat the rail journey back to Moscow but instead took a connecting flight via Chisinau, the capital of Moldova. This tiny, former Soviet state between Ukraine and Romania is the poorest country in Europe. It is also host to Transnistria, another forgotten frozen conflict precipitated by the downfall of the USSR. I determined to return later.

During my brief stop in Chisinau, a British colleague was dragged off the train service from Kyiv at Bryansk station in Russia by FSB border guards. Despite carrying a diplomatic passport, he was threatened with immediate deportation. Mercifully, Amy had been on the same train and got off with him to provide support; she could speak some Russian, whereas he could not. Panicked phone calls were made to the Embassy and, eventually, he was released from custody, free to travel back to Moscow. The timing didn't feel entirely coincidental.

Moscow, Russia

I scribbled furiously on my notepad, took a deep breath, looked up and repeated in English what the examiner had said to me in Russian. The British colleague who'd been dragged off the train at Bryansk, said something in English. I thought about it and replied in Russian.

So proceeded the simultaneous interpretation part of my spoken Russian examination.[72] As the Foreign Office had gone to great expense to train me in Russian prior to my arrival in Moscow, I decided to reach for my target-level attainment of C1

---

72 The speaking exam consisted of a presentation, a one-to-one dialogue with the examiner on a subject of their choosing and a simultaneous interpretation exercise.

(the equivalent of a bachelor's degree).[73] Over a year after my arrival in Moscow, no one in my team had passed the exam, despite having been in Russia for much longer than me. They reflected the established pattern at the Embassy: British officers would arrive in Moscow having not completed their Russian qualifications and slowly watch their language skills go down the toilet.

That pattern remains unchanged to this day. And unfortunately, when the top officials at the Embassy don't put in the effort to reach the required standard of Russian, it sends a signal to everyone else that they don't need to either. The list of excuses for why officers don't hit their attainment mark is long, from having laryngitis when taking the (never re-taken) spoken exam to just being too busy. One chap fell behind with his Russian recently because he'd been asked by a Director General to prioritise work on an FCDO cookbook; Liz Truss had made food a foreign policy priority given the disgraceful state of British cheese exports. My favourite was when officers said their Russian skills had gone downhill since they arrived in Moscow because they didn't have opportunities to practice.

In a country where public officials routinely conduct meetings with Western diplomats in Russian, a working command of the language is absolutely essential. A good contact at the Eurasian Economic Commission who had formerly served at the Russian Embassy in London always spoke in machine-gun Russian when we met; he'd then turn up at British Embassy receptions speaking better English than me. And for officers travelling around Russia – not that many did – language skills were vital.

I passed my C1 exam at the first attempt. However, Russian is such a complex language, grammatically, that I consider C1 remarkably inadequate. While I could discuss quantitative easing or macro-financial assistance with great aplomb, I still struggled

---

73 There were three parts to the exam: speaking, reading and listening, and you had to pass all three with an average of at least 70% to qualify.

with day-to-day Russian, for example, asking for the correct things in a supermarket.

But language skills are as much about creating opportunities for human connection as they are about developing skills for discussing technical subjects. Someone told me once that "Americans are soft on outside, hard on inside. But Russians, we are hard on outside, soft on inside." Within that sweeping generalisation was a small grain of truth. My get-out-of-jail trick with the stoniest-faced supermarket babushka was to clock their name badge and thank them in Russian by name. Nine times out of ten, they would break out into a warm smile. Russians are sometimes considered awkward and hard-headed, with a tendency to cut off their nose to spite their face. However, if you can find an emotional connection, then in my experience, Russian people can be warm and friendly to an excess that the taciturn Englishman may find unsettling. The reason *War and Peace* is such a compelling novel is its insight that Russian people approach battle and love with the same all-in emotion.

Another benefit of studying any language in depth is the opportunity it presents to understand why people from different countries think and behave the way they do; not necessarily to agree, but at least to understand and know how to respond. The Foreign Office's longstanding poor performance in Russian speaks to a much deeper lack of understanding of the country itself, I fear. And there is a link between that deficiency in understanding and the dreadful state of UK-Russia relations which preceded, and arguably helped to precipitate, the war in Ukraine.

I never fully understood why the Foreign Office continues to perform so poorly in Russian language attainment. It isn't just a case of easy languages performing better, given the quality of the Mandarin training programme. The Eastern Europe and Central Asia Directorate which is responsible for Russian languages has never gripped the skills deficit; there is a pressing need collectively for people to stop making excuses, pull on their big boy and girl pants, and try harder.

16. TIM BLASTS OFF

Sochi, Russia, October 2015

D mitry Medvedev avoided my gaze like a bartender in Wetherspoons servicing a crowd of drunken flirty women on a hen night. My arms strained above my head like a spotty-faced swot, but to no avail.

I was at the Olympic media centre, in the lea of a mountain range where winter sportspeople duked it out for medals in 2014. Where the St Petersburg Forum was Putin's set-piece economic event, Prime Minister Medvedev fronted this "international investment forum" in the Black Sea resort of Sochi.[74] While Putin let a has-been American journalist pose tame questions for an hour, Medvedev opened the floor to the assembled audience for questions.

I was once more sat near the stage. The crowd was less high-profile than in St Petersburg. The questions, if you could call them that, were safe and pre-planned. "Oh, Prime Minister, are you really five foot four? You look so much bigger." In truth, they were more probing than that. But not much more.

And in fairness, Medvedev's speech wasn't bad. Where Putin's event was really an opportunity to talk about international politics, the Prime Minister spoke to real-world economic challenges. He

---

74 Strictly speaking, the site of the 2014 Winter Olympics was in the town of Adler, an hour up the road from Sochi itself.

produced the standard lines about Western efforts to isolate Russia. But the overall tone was liberal. Russia needed to move on from the "fossil fuel ice age." Attracting foreign investment was key and Russian industries needed to seize the opportunity of a historically weak rouble to boost their competitiveness. I didn't disagree.

Medvedev cut an isolated figure among a low-calorie crowd, and this didn't seem like the place where big decisions were made. Sochi felt a distant two-hour flight from Moscow. And this glitzy pageant simply wasn't that "international."[75] As a direct consequence of sanctions, foreign investment in Russia had largely – but not completely – dried up. However, this drop was offset by a steady repatriation of Russian investments from overseas, mostly back into the banking sector. Russia had seen massive capital flight of $130 billion in 2014, largely caused by the repayment of foreign debt that was not renewed. But by 2015, net capital flight had returned to pre-crisis levels, effectively cancelling out the sanctions effect on economic growth from reduced lending.

It was clear then, as it is clear today, that Russia's Central Bank Governor and Finance Minister have been effective in steering Russia's macro-economic policy through the myriad external pressures. So even with the added hit from low oil prices, sanctions weren't having a sufficient impact to affect Russian policy in Ukraine. Rather, they were promoting resentment towards the West in the Kremlin and a drive to economic nationalism and self-sufficiency. Big subsidies for import substitution, particularly in agriculture and tech components, and an accretion of power in the state-owned behemoths were observable consequences of sanctions. Friends of Putin, like Sergey Chemezov at Rostec, were gaining the most. Pointing this out to London met with stony silence. Sanctions had become an end in themselves, rather than a means to effect change or improvement.

---

75 The event has since been renamed the Russia Investment Forum, given the lack of international interest and engagement.

There was another effect too. In opening his speech, Medvedev remarked that "even when countries are going through a rough patch, business should be above politics, bringing countries and markets closer together." Herein lay the fault-line between mainstream EU policy towards Russia and that of the UK and USA. Despite the supposedly free-market credentials of the Tories, the Brits stuck to the position that economic engagement should be a prize to be handed out for good behaviour, a bit like cheap teddies or goldfish at a funfair. This was partly the result of a Foreign Office that was turned off by economics in general. It was also a result of UK ministers' and officials' desire to remain in lockstep with the Americans, who had limited economic ties with Russia. Economic engagement in any form was looked on suspiciously as a ruse to circumvent the purpose of sanctions, even though that purpose wasn't explicit.

The Europeans tended to separate economic from political engagement, although each member state took a different line – Poland and the Baltic States were always at the tougher end of the spectrum, for obvious reasons. In any case, with sanctions baked in and progress towards peace in Ukraine stalled, many EU countries had started a process of reengagement on trade and economic matters. European agricultural exporters were swallowing the loss of Russian business while European sanctions were having a negligible political and economic effect on Russia, and no one had the energy to shift the sanctions status quo.

St Petersburg, Russia, November 2015

In early November, with the days short and gloomy, spent a week in St Petersburg. The previous week, in the early hours of 31 October, Russian Metrojet flight 9268 crashed in the Sinai Desert shortly after take-off from Sharm El Sheikh Airport. All 224 persons on board were killed by this terrorist act.[76]

I decided to visit Palace Square to pay my respects and look at the flowers, teddies, photographs and messages left in remembrance of those who died. I should imagine similar tributes were left in those countries who lost people when MH17 was shot down over eastern Ukraine. They reminded me of the walls of remembrance that appeared in southern Thailand after the 2004 tsunami, which killed over 6,000 people, including 3,000 tourists. And, indeed, the various shrines of remembrance to those innocent civilians needlessly being killed in Ukraine every day now. They all spoke of love for people whose blameless lives were ripped away in the most sudden and violent circumstances. I found the pictures of children especially heart-breaking.

That was my fifth visit to St Petersburg in 2015. In June, we'd enjoyed a family holiday with our kids in the Venice of the North. Staying in an apartment just off Nevsky Prospekt, we tried every type of transport with the kids, including tram, bus, trolleybus, tour bus, canal boat and Metro train. Most fun was a hydrofoil boat ride across the sparkling Bay of Finland to visit the Peterhof Palace gardens, dubbed the Russian Versailles. We found some fabulous, child-friendly places to eat, our favourite being a restaurant called Teplo, tucked away in a side street near St Isaac's Cathedral. My dad visited again over the summer, so I'd taken him for a trip to St Petersburg; as he's a train buff, we returned to Moscow on the overnight Red Arrow sleeper service.

Moscow, Russia

Tim Barrow was an ambassador who always tried hard and whom some found trying. He was also an ambassador appointed by William Hague, a Foreign Secretary who despite his failures on Ukraine policy in 2014 was always focused on the need for stronger

---

76 The Islamic State claimed responsibility for the downing of the aircraft, although no one has been held to account for this terrible act.

UK diplomacy. In Tim's final two months in the job, he shuttled back and forth between Moscow and London, meeting David Cameron and Philip Hammond in a bid to inject more life into UK engagement with Russia. While Hammond was the archetypal hawk, Cameron remained more pragmatic, which prevented a complete flatlining of the UK policy pulse.

Tim pulled off some small diplomatic successes in 2015 with John Major's visit for the Boris Nemtsov funeral and Sir Nicholas Soames's attendance at Victory Day. He still got good levels of access to senior Russian decision-makers. In a final blast of engagement, the UK was whipped into a frenzy by the exploits of another Tim: Major Tim Peake was set to join a mission to the International Space Station. Tim Barrow was packed off to the Baikonur cosmodrome in Kazakhstan to watch his namesake launched into orbit.

His final act as Ambassador was to welcome Foreign Office Minister David Lidington to Moscow for an official visit. Compared to the amount of ministerial engagement the Americans, French and Germans were carrying out, it was a small, yet positive, step. The UK's isolation from Ukraine policy also made it small beer. However, agreement was reached to mark 2016 as UK–Russia Year of Language and Literature.

Tim is a formidable diplomat and was tireless in his efforts to improve UK–Russia relations. Despite his nineteenth-century work practices, I admired him. However, following two decades in which the Foreign Office has seen its influence steadily eroded by successive governments, he also showed that even the best Ambassadors will struggle to move the Whitehall elephant uphill.

The annual Christmas reception doubled as Tim's farewell party. I spotted Andrey Kostin striding into the White and Gold Room to bid him a personal farewell. Despite the considerable disagreements between the UK and Russia, their personal relationship, built over many years, still mattered. I wondered how bad it might be if the British Ambassador had no friends in Moscow.

• • •

Moscow, Russia, January 2016

"Deputy Prime Minister, may I introduce you to the new British Ambassador," I said in Russian to Olga Golodets after I tapped her shoulder in the crowded room.

"Yes, of course," she replied, her sharp eyes taking in the slight man with slate-grey hair stood nervously at my shoulder.

Laurie Bristow stiffly expressed his pleasure and hopes for a formal meeting soon before we all shuffled into the large plenary room to hear from Dmitry Medvedev.

My abiding memories of Laurie Bristow include him wandering round the Embassy on International Women's Day handing out flowers to female staff, which was a nice touch. And seeing him dress up as a *Harry Potter* character at the Embassy awayday not long after his arrival. He didn't have Tim's charisma, but he made more of an effort to show an interest in the work of staff outside Chancery. Around Chancery, he was the opposite to Tim Barrow and brought greater professionalism to his conduct of business. Officers no longer stalked the corridors late at night waiting for the Ambassador to finish reading his novel before finalising a telegram. Laurie looked at drafts sent to him by email and replied by email; it was a remarkable leap into the twentieth century!

Someone told me that Laurie was the smartest person they'd ever met, but as I got to know Laurie, I wondered whether he'd told them that. I worry about people who tell you that after two months in their previous job they already knew more than all their staff. He had an excellent command of Russian, though he sounded like C3PO, if Russian was one of the protocol droid's six million forms of communication. So, he was shy about using his language skills and often dropped into English.

There and then, Philip Hammond's appointee as British Ambassador was making his first public appearance at the annual Gaidar Economic Forum on the outskirts of Moscow. The event was held in the dilapidated grounds of the Russian Academy of National Economy and Public Administration, run by prominent academic Vladimir Mau. This was the other big yearly event in which Medvedev would make a keynote address, although it was very much Mau's event; the focus was firmly on academic discussion rather than investment promotion.

I'd met Mau a couple of times for lunch with Tim. I personally found him a sinecured academic who never strayed too far from the Kremlin's core script. However, he is also an authoritative figure on economic history, including in the UK. Indeed, he made the most insightful observation throughout my whole time in Russia, that Russia's economy in the tens was in the same position as the UK economy of the late seventies: staring at the need for the creative destruction of its complete economic model yet, unlike the UK, unwilling yet to take the difficult decisions needed to do so. The sheer geographical scale and complexity of post-Soviet Russia made the task of economic reform for leaders like Putin far harder than it was for Thatcher. Of course, that can oft be used as an excuse for inertia. However, it is also true that the north–south scars from the UK's shift away from heavy manufacturing and export to a service-based economy can still be seen forty years on.

What was clear while Laurie and I were waiting for Medvedev to speak was that the economic path his government had set was fast running out of paving. The high-interest, inflation-targeting monetary policy agreed one year previously was helping to reduce inflation. But it wasn't filling the gap in state-tax revenues caused by lower oil prices, it was making it larger.[77] And in January 2016, oil prices hit a new low, bottoming out at just under $28.

---

77 The weakness of the rouble following the November 2014 oil price collapse grabbed lots of headlines. However, the short-term flows of hot money chasing high Russian interest rates from December 2014 onwards meant the rouble was protected somewhat from the full effect of a falling oil price. Where the rouble price of a barrel of oil had for a long time hovered around the 3,500 mark, by January 2016 it had started to dip below 2,000 roubles. This had huge consequences for the volume of Russian government tax receipts from oil exports.

Critics of the December 2014 decision to allow a free-floating rouble were appearing once more from the woodwork. Until that time, economic liberals such as Central Bank Governor Elvira Nabiullina and Finance Minister Anton Siluanov, supported by the likes of Alexei Kudrin and the Sberbank chief, Herman Gref, had held the upper hand in debate about economic reform. Russian monetary policy was predicated on the privatisation of state-owned assets to fill the gap in fiscal revenues and inject new forms of life into the economy. But this was simply not happening. A consequence of the growing economic nationalism in Russia was a resistance among the bloated heads of Russia's state-owned enterprises to see their assets sold off to Western bidders.

So, Medvedev faced a massive economic policy headache as he stepped onto the stage to deliver his speech. His script offered nothing new beyond what he had said three months previously in Sochi. Rather than stay to take questions, he hastily scuttled off the stage. The barricades needed to be put up against a *siloviki* keen to regain control of the heights of economic policymaking.

17. KEEP CALM AND CARRY ON

Krabi, Thailand, 28 December 2004

t was pandemonium. Everywhere you went, beds were lined up three and four deep in the corridors. It had taken me fifty hours to reach Krabi Hospital after the tsunami struck. I was supported by Neill, a Vice Consul, a Thai colleague named Tanida and a British colleague from our Embassy in Nepal who had been on holiday in the area and offered to help. The Hospital was doing an amazing job, but resources were stretched to breaking point. Doctors, nurses and volunteers were being bussed in from unaffected areas of southern Thailand.

I managed to locate the young woman on one of the wards. Her dad was one of the lucky ones able to get through to the Embassy[78], and someone had passed the information to me. Thankfully, I found a mobile phone signal [79] so she could finally talk to Dad. As a parent, I can only imagine his anxiety and concern during that period of not knowing.

Following an emotional reunion, the young lady told me her story. She'd been in a group of six girl friends on a trip to Thailand.

---

78 The Foreign Office phone line was quickly overwhelmed with worried callers, most of whom could not get through for several days.

79 Because of damage to infrastructure and the huge number of people wanting to use the mobile phone network, access was extremely patchy during the first week after the tsunami.

They had all been swept up by the giant wave when it struck Phi Phi Island. Of their group, three had been evacuated to Phuket and another was in Krabi hospital. She told me how she'd seen the sixth member of the group pulled under the water and drowned. I took down the details of the missing young woman and undertook to do all I could to help. [80]

Much of Britain was asleep when the Indian Ocean tsunami hit the Andaman Sea coast of Thailand on the morning of Boxing Day 2004. I was in Bangkok and rushed to the Embassy as soon as the news came through. Many staff were on leave, and the Ambassador, David Fall, was mulling what to do. The airports in the south were closed to civilian traffic as the Thai military supported the disaster recovery effort. I told David we should get in the car and drive south immediately. The British public would want to know their man in Thailand was moving without delay.

The British Embassy in Jakarta took two days to deploy staff to Bali after the bombing of Paddy's Bar on 12 October 2002; in comparison, the Australian government had a plane loaded with emergency response staff within hours of the blast. Twenty-three Brits were killed in Bali, and the UK government was rightly hammered by the press for its inaction.[81]

By late morning on the day of the Tsunami, the death toll already counted in the hundreds and rose by the hour. David agreed with me. I went home to pack a carry-on bag and we were soon on the road. It seems incredible now, but our Thai colleague, Amnat had a cardboard box full of charged Nokia mobile handsets. David, Amnat and I were on the phones non-stop with the Embassy, Thai government officials, journalists and anyone trying to get in touch

---

80 I was in Krabi from 28 to 30 December and with my two colleagues ensured all the British casualties at the hospital were evacuated, except for one young lady who wanted to stay to search for her friend.

81 As a result of the poor UK response to the Bali bombing, the Foreign Office established its first Rapid Deployment Teams: highly trained staff who could deploy to disaster zones at the drop of a hat.

to find out what was happening. When one handset ran out of charge, we'd swap our SIMs into a new one.

The Royal Thai Police provided a police escort for the full 900-kilometre drive south; it was incredible. As we passed from one province into another, a different police car, red light flashing on the roof, would be waiting for us at the side of the road. We stopped once for fuel and refreshment. Late in the evening, the Thai Ministry of Foreign Affairs laid on a flight for foreign officials; three other Embassy colleagues landed shortly before the Ambassador's car crossed the bridge onto Phuket Island around midnight.

We acted decisively, reaching the disaster zone on day zero. To cover a coastline of several hundred kilometres, we had me and David, the amazing Amnat, three consular staff and a driver.[82] Our office was a deserted furniture showroom that an expat let us use for free. I sent everyone out to find affected people and get a feel for the situation on the ground. They came back around 4 a.m. and slept on the floor, David wearing his British Airways pyjamas. I stayed up, glued to the phone, scrabbling around desperately for extra resources.

I'd worked non-stop for almost forty hours by the time I got some sleep at midnight on 27 December. I knew by then that London wasn't sending help.

Paris, February 2016

Several tables across from me in the hotel restaurant, I watched the three mildly overweight white gentlemen dressed in similarly monochrome M&S suits. Team "fifty shades of beige" stuck out like bratwursts at a bar mitzvah and might as well have had "Old Bill" stamped on their foreheads.

I pushed my empty breakfast plate away and wandered across.

---

82 Two hours after we arrived in Phuket, the British Defence Attaché arrived in Khao Lak with his Assistant Defence Attaché, a Thai fixer and a driver. Two hours after that, at around 4 a.m., a comms technician arrived at our base in Phuket, with a Thai member of staff and a third driver. Total staff on day one: fourteen.

"You must be the police team? Hi, I'm Ian from the British Embassy in Moscow." I sat down in the spare seat without being asked.

They shuffled in their seats anxiously before the obviously senior one, looking irked, replied, "Yeah, what are you doing 'ere then?"

"I'm chair of the crisis management committee for the Russia network. Here to check out preparations for the 2016 Euros."

Mark Roberts, then Assistant Chief Constable of the Cheshire Constabulary[83] and head of the UK Football Policing Unit, relaxed a little. In his nasal Mancunian accent, like a chubby grey-haired Gary Neville, he went on, "We're really pleased to be participating. But you'll find I don't have the airs and graces of you diplomats and will tell it exactly as I find it."

After 9/11, the Foreign Office worked hard to learn lessons from mistakes made after every crisis response. The Twin Towers attacks confirmed the need for a 24-hour crisis response centre; the first Bali bombing, the need for rapid deployment teams; the 2004 tsunami, the need for regional rapid deployment teams. The Arab Spring crises and the Fukushima disaster confirmed the need for a bigger crisis centre and better London crisis capability to handle both simultaneous and concurrent crises. A rigorous approach to crisis training and exercising has underpinned the gradual improvement in the Foreign Office's performance since 2001.

I'd worked on many of the big consular operations since 2001 and was one of the most experienced crisis operators in the Foreign Office. Shortly after my arrival in Moscow, I took over chairmanship of the Russia Crisis Committee. Thinking ahead to the FIFA 2018 World Cup in Russia and the potential arrival of thousands of British football fans, I was on a mission. I would apply all my experience to ensure the UK network in Russia[84] was better prepared than any British diplomatic mission had been previously for a global

---

83 Mark is now Chief Constable in Cheshire, having been Deputy Chief in South Yorkshire from 2017 to 2021.

84 The British Embassy in Moscow together with the British Consulates General in St Petersburg and Ekaterinburg.

sporting event.

I wanted to see the Paris Embassy put through its paces in a semi-live crisis exercise[85] ahead of the Euro 2016 football tournament in France. With me was the British Consul from Moscow, Christophe. He would be central to my plans to get the Embassy firing on all cylinders.

My mates from the fuzz were also joining in. British football hooligans have a dark history of bringing shame on our nation overseas. However, in recent years the UK police has stepped up to the task of ensuring the majority of travelling fans enjoy overseas football tournaments in a fun and peaceful way. It's far less common these days to see news reports of drunken English yobbos scrapping in historic European cities. Partly that's about deterrence: banning known football hooligans temporarily from travel. It's also about working with police forces in the countries where football tournaments are happening to share intelligence and spot troublemakers who may have slipped through the net.

The semi-live exercise was fun to watch. The Embassy did an OK but not brilliant job. I recall there was a multi-site terrorist event with, at one point, fictional crowds of British football fans stuck at Gare du Nord not sure if they would get home before being immolated by jihadis. The excellent Kara Owen,[86] Deputy Ambassador, met an angry mob of pretend football fans to be given hell about the lack of Embassy support. Being of a thespian tendency, Christophe proceeded to heckle Kara, repeatedly yelling the word "refund," pressing the Embassy to refund expenses caused by having to leave France in a hurry. She looked noticeably pissed off.

A dedicated operations room had been set up in the Embassy with the crisis team at their desks waiting for the bomb to go off. It

---

85 A semi-live exercise is an expanded desk-top training exercise, in which the London crisis centre is switched on to make the simulated crisis event feel as realistic as possible to the participants. The idea is to put an Embassy under maximum pressure to see if their crisis structures will cope.

86 Kara is currently British High Commissioner to Singapore.

didn't feel that realistic. As the FCO crisis management team rained down bedlam and stress, the Paris crisis manager flagged under the pressure. The British Ambassador, Julian "Karaoke" King, kept out of it. Smiling beatifically, he'd occasionally pop his head round the door to witness the chaos and then slink away; he was smart enough to spot the risk of looking an idiot in front of his staff by getting involved. However, Kara led from the front and was good, providing a calming influence throughout.

But overall, it was an underwhelming performance. There were many areas where the Moscow Embassy could do better. The key weakness was that insufficient staff in Paris appeared involved; they obviously had their core team, but the level of crisis skills appeared low. And more importantly, when these guys and gals were exhausted, who would take over? My golden test is to ask everyone you meet in the office what their role is in a crisis and see how many of them know. I suspected that in Paris the reality was "very few." I was determined to ensure that in Moscow it would be "most."

Truth was, there was less pressure in Paris to be on top of their game. London could have scores of staff on planes or the Eurostar within a couple of hours should something happen in France. The UK–Russia relationship was so difficult that we had to assume it could take at least a week to issue Russian visas to British staff in the event of a major event. We could be on our own for quite some time and needed the resilience to cope.

I joined the wash-up session after the exercise, chaired by Kara. Assistant Chief Constable Mark Roberts helpfully presaged his, frankly scathing, feedback by saying, "Well, you'll find I don't have the airs and graces of you diplomats and will tell it exactly as I find it." Being an incredibly smart diplomat, Kara took one look at me and pronounced, "Well, Ian's an expert in all this, so let's just focus on getting feedback from Paris staff," swerving the opportunity for me to lay into her team, and implicitly her, for a lacklustre performance.

A few weeks later, I landed in Hong Kong to take part in refresher crisis manager training. I didn't learn much on the technical aspects of crisis management. It was helpful to do some media interview practice, specifically, how to get our message across to the often hostile press scrum that chases every mass casualty event. It was good to meet a legend like Sarah Pilbeam, with whom I'd spent many an hour in the crisis centre during the 2011 Arab Spring. I tasted the best dim sum in the world and soaked up the atmosphere of this vibrant Asian city, where the British past and Chinese present crash against each other in chaotic fashion. Little did I know then of the political chaos that would unfold in Hong Kong in 2019.

The Hong Kong Consulate became a centre of expertise and the first regional rapid deployment team after the 2004 tsunami. This happened because large numbers of Hong Kong staff deployed to Bangkok to support the back end of the crisis operation, i.e., handling calls, casualties and relatives after the initial evacuation from the disaster zone. Having crisis-capable staff a short flight away gives an Embassy the potential to scale up its operation quickly. Hence, the doctrine of "scaling up and paring back" emerged, in which the Foreign Office would commit maximum resources to a crisis immediately, even if it scaled back later.

In any crisis, the first forty-eight hours are critical. If you get off to a slow start in making key decisions about the response, the press and British public will be on your back and you won't recover. You also need every member of staff to have the training and preparation to know what to do when the worst happens.

Bangkok, Thailand, January 2005
On 8 January 2005, I flew to Bangkok for some time off, having been in the tsunami disaster zone from the beginning, working more than two hundred hours. I was the last person to leave from those who deployed on day zero. In the intervening thirteen days, the press and grieving relatives went on the warpath against the Foreign Office. Teflon-shouldered Mandarins deflected criticism towards the Embassy. People like David Fall and myself were royally rogered, with the only support from London being "Just bend over,

old boy, here's the Vaseline." A day or so after my departure, a full rapid (*sic*) deployment team rushed to Phuket to our aid. A year later, Sir Michael Jay, the Permanent Under Secretary at the Foreign Office, was criticised personally in the press. Having been lost for words for a year, he wrote an impassioned letter, in which he mounted a staunch public defence of the work of the British Embassy with its scant resources. I emailed him and said, "At last. Well said." He didn't reply.

In the aftermath of the tsunami, the National Audit Office conducted a review of the experiences of British Nationals affected by the tsunami and their report was published in November 2006. Manifestly, the key failing in the UK response was a lack of strategic focus, with neither grip nor urgency in recognising the magnitude of the challenge at hand.

At a more personal level, the NAO commissioned the Zito Trust to interview tsunami survivors, and a summary of those findings is included in the report. Among the wide-ranging conclusions, a consistent theme emerged of Foreign Office staff not having the right skills to act with empathy and care in a disaster zone. The training offer today is much better than it was in 2004, with an excellent Consular and Crisis Faculty. However, I still fear that too few staff receive training to deal with the unexpected. And there is a growing deficit of staff with the skills and experience to think on their feet and respond in a pragmatic and caring way when the worst happens.

Almost twenty years on from the tsunami, it feels as if the Foreign Office has gone full circle. The doctrine of deploying maximum resource at the start of any crisis appears to have been chucked out the window. Through COVID, the Afghan and Sudan crises, the modern Foreign Office stumbles from one flat-footed crisis response to the next. COVID was unprecedented in scale. The latter two crises, while serious and extensive, were small when compared with the 2004 tsunami and the concurrent crises of 2011 around the Arab Spring, New Zealand earthquake and Japanese tsunami.

In the modern FCDO, crisis response has been reduced to establishing towering structures of bureaucracy in London, far removed from expertise or delivery, to meet an increasingly impatient and dissatisfied minister's unrealistic expectations. Armies of senior officers jockey with each other with no obvious role except to reassure the big boss that everything at the front is going exactly to plan, whatever the realities on the ground. The most harrowing crisis many have faced has been whether to choose quinoa or chia seeds with their fairtrade salads from Waitrose. The vast majority of junior colleagues I've led in a crisis have been outstanding in their energy and commitment. But there has been no sustained effort to ensure all staff in the organisation have the basic skills they need to operate when the worst happens. Meanwhile, in the case of Afghanistan, the Permanent Secretary is nowhere to be seen, away on an unexplained holiday, in a weird parody of Russia's military high command. We have stopped learning and keep making the same mistakes.

This also talks to a fundamental lack of partnership between Ministers and Officials. For all their earnest desire to see the civil service improve, bullying by Ministers in the current government seems more often to solidify a leaden bureaucratic inertia in Whitehall. While Jack Straw's apology to British victims of the tsunami was half-hearted, we did learn and make improvements. We made mistakes during the rolling crises in the spring of 2011, but I felt that junior ministers like Alistair Birt were on our side, and we were working together in real time to support British nationals better. James Cleverly does appear more highly regarded than his two immediate predecessors. But that amounts to damning with the faintest praise. The system appears broken.

Sometime before my first stint in the disaster area finished, I bumped into a couple at the Embassy Office in Phuket who needed assistance. I invited them in and sat down in an area we had set aside for talking to relatives. Their daughter was in a group of six young women on holiday and had drowned when the tsunami struck Phi Phi Island. Though it had been a few days, I remembered their daughter's name immediately, and said that I had met her friend in Krabi. They'd flown out from the UK and wanted to take a bunch of flowers to the place she had died and a letter, to help them say goodbye.

What do you tell a parent whose heart has been torn into shreds by the sudden and unexpected loss of a beloved child? Even today, I struggle to process the scale of that grief. I sat next to Mum while she showed me photos of her daughter from an album she had brought. I said how beautiful her daughter was, and how she must have made them proud. In the back of my mind, I wasn't sure there was anything practical I could do to help, as Phi Phi was a disaster zone. But a Thai colleague discovered that the Thai Prime Minister was flying in to visit the island the following day; we were able to get both parents on a boat to the island with Thai government officials, so they could leave their letter and flowers for their girl.

I was glad to help and saw it as my duty, aware that no small act or kindness can make a grieving relative feel better at the worst moment of their life. However, jobsworth incompetence and a lack of empathy can make things a hell of a lot worse. As the Foreign Office continues to stumble haphazardly from one crisis to another, it must renew its focus on equipping staff with the skills they need when things go badly wrong.

As I left Paris in the spring of 2016, I didn't necessarily expect that there would be a crisis during FIFA 2018 in Russia. But I was determined that the British Embassy would be ready for anything.

18. PAPER TIGER, HIDDEN DRAGON

Tajikistan, March 2016

"We're definitely going to die now," I remarked coolly. Our car thundered at unseemly speed through a darkness made more obscure by billowing clouds of dust. High in the Zarafshan Mountains, the Anzob Tunnel wasn't paved with tarmac and appeared lit by candles. It has variously been called the tunnel of death and the tunnel of fear. I pondered briefly which of the two was worse.

Vinny Sollers, my new energy expert, sat stone still and silent beside me. Had I been able to see his face, I assume it would have been pale.

In the distance, two faint orbs of light grew larger. A heavy truck hurtled towards us, and I hoped it wasn't loaded with untethered metal spikes, in case of a sudden braking incident.

After five kilometres of arse-clenching on the back seat, the car emerged into blinding daylight.[87] Aside from the occasional burned-out car at the side of the road, the rocky scenery was stunning, a mix of juniper forests and glaciers. We stopped briefly

---

87 The Anzob Tunnel was built by Iranian contractors in the early noughties to open the route to Uzbekistan. Particularly during the winter, the Anzob Pass was practically unnavigable. An avalanche in 1997 killed forty-six people on the pass, prompting the need for a tunnel. However, the initial construction of the tunnel was so poor that traversing it became only slightly safer than taking your chances with the high-altitude pass. Locals talk of people dying of carbon monoxide poisoning in the unventilated tunnel during traffic jams.

at a roadside toilet. It consisted of an unventilated concrete cube atop a ditch, with a gash hacked out of the floor for people to crap through. When Vinny emerged, his face had turned a shade of green; the bogs were clearly better at Balliol. Tajikistan looked and felt like central Asia's poorest country.

We'd been on a two-day fact-finding visit to Tajikistan's capital, Dushanbe. It was a surprisingly neat, yet unremarkable city. The British Embassy was small and sleepy. With the Ambassador away, his Deputy acted as our personal tour guide and organised a programme of meetings. The four key themes were poverty, migration, corruption and energy. Since the collapse of the Soviet Union, this small mountain state had been growing at a respectable clip of over 7% per year. However, around one third of Tajikistan's people remained below the poverty line. Shepherds grazing their flocks on high mountain meadows suggested a subsistence farming far removed from the relative glamour of the capital.

Over a million Tajiks[88] had moved to work in Russia, sending their surplus income home. Prior to 2014, remittance payments were estimated to make up almost half of Tajikistan's GDP.[89] After the oil price collapse precipitated the 2014 Russian financial crisis, the value of the rouble in the average Tajik worker's pocket more than halved, causing a fall in the value of the somoni, Tajikistan's national currency. The sectors of Russia's economy most hit by the related economic recession were those with significant groups of migrant workers, including construction, trade and hospitality; there was less work available for Tajiks and Uzbeks, stemming the monetary flow of remittance payments.

As is so often the case in poor countries, endemic corruption in Tajikistan also stole valuable capital away to offshore accounts or white elephant projects. My visit happened after the world's

88 Unofficial figures suggest as much as 40% of Tajikistan's population lives and works abroad. Significant numbers of Uzbeks also live and work in Russia.

89 Between 2011 and 2015, Tajik workers sent approximately $17.7 billion in remittances from Russia.

largest flagpole in Dushanbe had been overtaken by a taller more tumescent rod in Saudi Arabia.[90] I also, regrettably, missed the chance to visit the world's biggest teahouse. But the fourth issue – energy – offered scope for real economic development. Despite being a small country geographically, its high mountains and rivers offer Tajikistan huge potential in the hydro-electricity sector. But therein lay a source of tension with neighbouring Uzbekistan.

When the Soviet Union collapsed, it left a convoluted set of borders between the central Asian states,[91] many of which remain contested to this day. In 2008, Uzbekistan closed all but two border crossings into Tajikistan and insisted that Tajiks needed visas to travel. As our car approached the border, the volume of traffic reduced to a trickle and the kilometres of razor-wire ticked up. A checkpoint was deserted except for Kalashnikov-wielding Tajik soldiers.

Uzbekistan, March 2016

Vinny and I said farewell to our driver and went through passport control on both sides of the border. On Uzbek tarmac, a small huddle of men waited hopefully for an occasional traveller wanting a taxi ride to Tashkent.

"We had better make sure our taxi has seatbelts," Vinny offered. "Our FCO travel insurance won't cover us if it doesn't."

I looked sceptically at the beaten-up GM saloon at the front of the line.

"Yes, I have seat belts. Very modern car, I take you." The first driver grabbed our bags and ushered us excitedly into his car.

The plastic, patent yellow seats didn't look standard issue. Seatbelts there were, though nothing to clip them into.

"What do you think we should do?" Vinny asked anxiously.

---

90 An even bigger pole has since been erected in Egypt, at 201 metres, pushing the Dushanbe erection down to third place.

91 The borders between Tajikistan, Uzbekistan and Kyrgyzstan are very convoluted, and fighting between villages remains a common occurrence.

I found the fixation on Foreign Office travel insurance amusing, so leaned forward and said to the driver in Russian, "I'm afraid we can't travel in your taxi, old chap, because you don't have appropriate regulation seatbelts."

We got out of the car, the driver angered and shamed by our sudden change of plan. The second taxi driver stepped in helpfully, offering to take us in his very good car with seatbelts, at which point the first driver started yelling at him in Uzbek. Whereupon the third driver attempted to mediate – and wonder whether, given the upset, he might be the right driver for us. Soon all the drivers were in a melee arguing with each other about this unsatisfactory situation, while my bag and Vinny's were still in the boot of the first car.

I walked up to the first driver and in a polite, yet firm voice said, "Look, I'm sorry, but can you give us our bags back, please?"

This enraged him further. He retrieved our bags and hurled them to the floor before uttering a curse and biting his thumb in my direction. In a cloud of wheel-spun tyre smoke, he roared off, almost hitting the other taxi drivers on the way.

"Well, that went well," I said, as we clipped our seatbelts in place in the second taxi.

Christopher Allan was new in town as Britain's Ambassador to Tashkent. Young and ambitious, he laid on a terrific programme of meetings for us, including dinner at his Residence with a range of Embassy and NGO contacts. For canapés, I recall individual salted Pringles, with a small squeeze of cream cheese topped with a brown micro-herb. This Ambassador knew how to captivate his guests. Once I popped those suckers, I couldn't stop.

Much larger than Tajikistan, Uzbekistan gave the impression of a country living in a state of self-imposed economic isolation. More so even than Belarus, Uzbekistan clung to a Soviet-style economic model, led by an elderly and out-of-touch apparatchik in Islam Karimov.[92] Wealth was channelled towards elites and ever-more inefficient state-owned monopolies. There was hardly any foreign investment and the main crop in this arid place was cotton, a decision seemingly taken by Soviet diktat. Tajik plans to build dams for hydropower would restrict water supplies to parched Uzbek cotton fields.

The Uzbek som currency wasn't readily convertible, fostering a black-market rate, more favourable than the official. At dinner, I counted out a three-inch-thick wad of banknotes to pay for my steak, chips and beer. It reminded me of my first visit to communist Laos in the mid-noughties, and similarly huge wads of kip. Much as Ukraine had fallen far behind neighbouring Poland, Uzbekistan was now dwarfed by neighbouring Kazakhstan.[93] Its economy wasn't as stone-age as, say, North Korea's or Turkmenistan's, but it didn't seem far off.

However, the main purpose of my trip to central Asia wasn't to study the economies of these two states. Of more interest was that neither had chosen to join the newly established Eurasian Economic Union.[94] The research establishment at the Foreign Office saw the Union as Russia's attempt to bind former Soviet states into a geo-political project. "We shouldn't give it the time of day," they'd say, foaming at the mouth. I'd always regarded that as naïve and short-sighted: the European Union has taken seventy years to reach its current fragile state; ASEAN,[95] which the UK invested significant political capital to become a dialogue partner of, is fast approaching sixty years. The EEU was less than a year old.

---

92 Islam Karimov died suddenly on 2 September 2016. His replacement, Shavkat Mirziyoyev, has since pressed ahead with economic reforms to open the country and sought to improve relations with neighbouring Tajikistan.

93 In 2015, GDP per capita in Kazakhstan was $11,390 compared to $2,160 in Uzbekistan.

94 Initially launched by Russia, Kazakhstan and Belarus, Armenia and Kyrgyzstan soon joined.

95 Within the ranks of the Association of Southeast Asian Nations are included those well-known paragons of liberal economics: Myanmar, Laos and Cambodia.

Far bigger forces were at play than a nascent economic union of five former Soviet countries. In 2013, Chinese Premier Xi Jinping had announced a new Silk Road project: China would use its enormous economic might to invest in road, rail and sea infrastructure to strengthen trade routes, including through central Asia, to Europe. Uzbekistan, with its historic Silk Road cities of Samarkand, Bukhara and Khiva, and Tajikistan, were in the crosshairs of China's grand aims.

On the back of three decades of high-octane investment and export-fuelled economic growth, China had almost limitless wells of surplus capital. It could bestow largesse on poorer neighbouring states with not many questions asked in return for political influence.

This was undoubtedly coming into conflict with the old economic model in which former Soviet states maintained close political allegiance with Russia through the inducement of soft loans and sweetened deals on cheap energy. Put simply, the Kremlin couldn't match Chinese cash. Russia was burning through its capital following the double-tap collapse of global commodity prices in 2014 and again in early 2016. A rainy-day reserve fund set up in 2008 to manage external economic shocks was being eaten away to plug Russia's fiscal deficit.[96]

While Russia's economy continues to dwarf that of its former Soviet neighbours, it was nonetheless ten times smaller than China's. China was still clipping along at 7% growth, while Russia was emerging from a recession that cut GDP by almost 4% in 2015. Belt and Road investments in roads, rail and power and all points in between have allowed China to unseat Russia as the largest foreign investor in central Asia. Much of this investment, which came with Chinese labour to complete the works, was of dubious economic benefit. And poor countries like Tajikistan were bartering assets to

96 The Reserve Fund was established in 2008 with $125 billion in capital; by late 2016, that figure had dropped to $16 billion. It was set up for the very purpose of meeting gaps in the federal budget that may emerge, e.g., from a sudden drop in the oil price, so in that regard, it was performing the function for which it was established.

fund Chinese infrastructure projects, giving away land and lucrative concessions to gold and other mineral resources.

But there was a deeper significance too. The economic glue that had helped to keep the Soviet Union together was Russia's status as the lender of last resort. That model has crumbled with China now the largest creditor to central Asian states. In 2023, with Russia suffering economically because of the war in Ukraine, China also became the largest trading partner. From the perspective of modern central Asian leaders, the Eurasian Economic Union project looked increasingly like a paper tiger, against the not-so-hidden Chinese dragon.[97]

If you step back to look at the map of central Asia, it's easy to see why the imperial powers of Britain, from its redoubt in India, and Russia played a Great Game for influence over the lucrative Silk Road during the eighteenth and nineteenth centuries. It's in Central Asia where the argument that Russia is bent on recreating the Soviet Union disintegrates. China today is the dominant power. And Russia's paranoia about NATO to its west is in part fuelled by a sense of being overmatched on its eastern flank.

• • •

"I'm not even going to tell you what Craig used to get up to in here," Chris Allan said, as I sat in his office waiting to go to another meeting.

I already knew about the allegations that former Ambassador Craig Murray had had sex with Uzbek women in return for assistance to receive UK visas. My legs felt sticky, so I got up from the plastic sofa, preferring to stand.

Unashamed of his reputation for drinking and womanising, Murray's biggest crime in the eyes of the Foreign Office was his penchant for criticising the dissident-boiling antics of Uzbekistan's

---

97 To this day, neither Tajikistan nor Uzbekistan has joined the EEU.

then leader, Islam Karimov.[98]

Until the shambolic withdrawal of NATO from Afghanistan, Uzbekistan had been an important ally of the US and UK, as a key transit route for military supplies into Afghanistan. Mentioning human rights abuses to London distracted attention unhelpfully from the war on a bigger enemy – terror. It was a classic example of the Brits cherry-picking on values to suit the exigencies of the operation at hand, and to stay close to the Americans.

The Great Game mentality was still very much alive and kicking in King Charles Street on Russia policy. 'Joined-up government' has been bandied around the British Civil Service ever since Tony Blair first coined the phrase in 1997. Of course, bureaucratic organisations are necessarily self-serving. In my experience, relations between Whitehall departments are often characterised by turf warfare and competition rather than genuine collaboration. But within the budget statement of July 2015 was a call for a more integrated approach to dealing with security and defence threats. A new UK joint security fund of £1.5 billion per year was set up, with the UK intelligence agencies set to benefit from increased funding. In the spirit of "joining up," therefore, a joint Russia team would be established at the Foreign Office. It would have two heads, a Foreign Office diplomat and a representative from the intelligence agencies. For the first time, all the major departments and agencies of the British government that worked on Russia could work together in King Charles Street.

On one hand, this made complete sense. It was right that the UK government strove to be unified in its policy and operational approach towards Russia. But on the other hand, it occurred to me that the policy of the UK towards Russia was already pretty sewn up. Under Philip Hammond, direct dialogue with Russia was seen

---

98 Among many alleged breaches of human rights, hard-line Karimov was said to have approved the boiling alive of political opponents. Craig Murray pointed out the duplicity of US and UK policy by turning a blind eye to alleged human rights violations in Uzbekistan in return for support in the post-9/11 war on terror.

as a weakness, even though the Americans,[99] Germans and French were actively engaged. Maintenance of sanctions was paramount, despite the moribund state of the Minsk accords. The UK would communicate about Russia (in Ukraine) to other states, rather than communicating directly with Russia. Unquestioning solidarity with Ukraine was prized above seeking peace.

I have considerable respect for the work of the UK intelligence community and would never compromise that. However, agencies, like armies, are also, like bureaucracies, self-serving. They need an enemy to justify increases in resources. This is a universal truth and not restricted to the corridors of Whitehall; the same is undoubtedly true in Moscow. It would never be right to allow generals to choose when to go to war, nor with whom. Likewise, spooks should be the covert tools of foreign policy, not its author.

It worried me that putting the hawks in King Charles Street would weaken efforts at diplomacy even further, from a very low base. As part of this drive towards 'joined-up government,' pleas to London for deeper engagement with Russia were increasingly unwelcome. I'm not a pacifist and believe that aggression should be overcome with aggression. But the available evidence shows that the hard-line UK policy of poking the Russian bear has undermined the cause of peace in Ukraine since 2014.

---

99 Despite the poor state of US–Russia relations, Secretary of State John Kerry had a virtual hotline to Sergei Lavrov to seek diplomatic solutions.

19. ENGAGE, ENGAGE, ENGAGE, EXIT!!!

Moscow, Russia, May 2016

"Brexit, Brexit, Brexit!" Daniel Kawczynski, Conservative MP for Shrewsbury, thumped his hand on the coffee table and looked at me with a creepy, demented smile. I wasn't sure if he was flirting or grandstanding.

As a career diplomat, I kept my personal political opinions to myself; my life revolved around making sense of what others thought. As it happened, I'd grown up a conservative. I'd idolised Margaret Thatcher as she took on the corporatism that had brought the UK economy to its knees in the seventies. And I'd inherited her latent Euroscepticism, persuaded that the European institutions were self-serving, sclerotic and democratically unaccountable.

Age and experience working in the UK public sector had moderated my views; Brussels appeared no worse than Whitehall. Seen from Moscow, where my daily movements were scrutinised by the FSB, the European project was about more than pointless regulation and the bend of a banana. There was a greater set of economic, social and cultural benefits that no one in the UK talked about enough. I'd become a "reluctant remainer."

Ahead of the referendum, the UK parliamentary Foreign Affairs Committee was visiting Moscow and St Petersburg to study the

UK's relations with Russia. On the surface, there didn't seem that much to study. Some good stuff was happening; a Cosmonauts exhibition was about to open at the London Science Museum that would prove popular. Princess Anne would visit Archangelsk in August to commemorate the World War II Arctic Convoys. But under Philip Hammond, the government-to-government relationship was in the cooler.

The assembled members relaxed with a coffee in the Ambassador's Residence waiting for the next guests. We'd walked part of the way back from the State Duma, as the traffic was jammed, across the Bolshoi Moskvoretsky Bridge, where Boris Nemtsov had been shot in the back.

On the economic side, I'd lined up Alexander Medvedev, deputy chair of Gazprom. Since our first drunken argument over Korean food, I'd kept in touch with Ivan Zolotov; we'd meet for dinner each month to share snippets and he'd helped me arrange the meeting. Not surprisingly, the parliamentarians asked lots of questions about the Nordstream II pipeline. Periodically, No. 10 had asked for advice on the UK position on Russian gas, but every time the answer from the Department of Energy and Climate Change was the same; the UK imported so little gas from Russia that we had insufficient skin in the game to influence EU policy.

With the Brexit referendum on the horizon, the UK had even less leverage; taking a strong stance on Nordstream II would cause a bust-up with either the Germans – who were in favour – or the Poles – who were against – and we needed both countries' support on EU reforms. Our approach therefore was to lobby for transit conditionality, that is, assurances that gas transit via Ukraine (and the associated revenue) would be protected even if Nordstream II was built. It was all, frankly, a bit bonkers, insisting that Russia export gas via a country that no longer purchased its gas. Medvedev pitched Nordstream II to the UK, a country that imported very little gas, precisely because the Brits were set against the project behind the scenes. The MPs listened politely and asked about

Ukraine transit.

The Resident Representatives of the International Monetary Fund, World Bank and European Bank for Reconstruction and Development discussed Russia's economy. The view was the same: Russia was looking to liberalise and deepen economic relationships with partners, despite the constraints of sanctions, a declining workforce and an over-dependence on low-value-chain exports. The EBRD representative was opposed to sanctions, which had seen lending to small grassroots companies, with no links to the Russian state, cut.

The FAC was a mixed bag of characters. The then chair, Crispin Blunt, was earnest and serious, and the Scottish Nationalist MP Stephen Gethins was impressively well-briefed and engaged.[100] Kawczynski was a curious mix: hard-line Brexiteer of Polish descent; openly gay and pro-Russian. Nadhim Zahawi spent much of his time on a sofa scrollaxing (no doubt checking his tax returns).

The FAC report was issued nine months later, in February 2017. It argued that "refusal to engage with the Russian Government is… not a viable long-term foreign policy option for the UK." While clear on the areas where significant disagreements existed between the UK and Russia, it pointed to weaknesses in UK policy including on sanctions.[101] The recommendation to set out clear conditions for sanctions removal was palmed off by the Foreign Office in its official response, listing a set of Russian responsibilities that were

---

100 I'm a committed Unionist, but nonetheless, credit where it's due.

101 *FAC report* "The FCO should be open to considering any proposals that the Russian Government may advance to resolve the situation in Ukraine outside the Minsk II process that are in line with international law. Russian actions demonstrating compliance with the rule of international law in Ukraine could be linked to the gradual removal of sanctions and would provide Russia with a route map to restoring positive relations with the West. We invite the FCO in its response to this report to detail the exact responsibilities of Russia with regard to the Minsk II agreement. The measure of success in relation to sanctions is their no longer being needed. It is therefore imperative that the international community recognises the need for an achievable route to rapprochement."

not included in the Minsk Agreements.[102] This was a reminder of how toothless the FAC is as a check and balance on the executive.

The report also suggested people-to-people engagement, including through universities. It pressed the FCO to invest in its internal expertise to understand Russia better, including through analytical and Russian-language skills.

• • •

At around the same time the FAC was in Russia, Tom Fletcher, author of *The Naked Diplomat*, produced a "Future FCO Report." The nub of it was about making the Foreign Office more agile, expert (including in diplomatic skills and foreign languages), diverse and digitally savvy: an organisation fit for diplomacy in the twenty-first century. Sir Simon McDonald, the Permanent Under Secretary who had commissioned the report, quickly announced that it was too radical; rather than drive forward ambitious change, he repackaged pre-existing low-energy initiatives under the banner Diplomacy 2020. A bit like the character CJ in the seventies comedy *The Fall and Rise of Reginald Perrin*, he clearly didn't get where he was today through radical reform.[103] Most of Tom's recommendations continue to gather dust.

• • •

102 *Government response* "The Minsk Agreements provide the framework for resolution of the ongoing conflict in eastern Ukraine and the restoration of Ukrainian sovereignty over all of the Donbas. Implementation of these Agreements should remain the focus of international efforts. Russian responsibilities under the Minsk Agreements are clear: Russia must stop equipping the separatists; it must use its influence over the separatists to ensure they also meet their Minsk commitments; and it must withdraw all foreign armed formations, military equipment and mercenaries from the territory of Ukraine." [Note these responsibilities are not set out in either the original Minsk Protocol or the Minsk II agreement, even if they were implied.]

103 Predictably, the very issues of workforce agility and expertise continue to bedevil the newly created Foreign, Commonwealth and Development Office seven years after the Fletcher report was issued.

Saint Petersburg, May 2016

"Will he mind if we drink alcohol?" Alexei Kudrin asked me in Russian. I turned to Vince Cable MP, who had no objections. The leader of the Liberal Democrats was visiting to promote *After the Storm*, his book on UK economic policy after the global financial crisis. His visit had been supported by Nonna Materkova, a London-based Russian philanthropist who'd set up an NGO focused on promoting dialogue about arts and the creative industries in the former Soviet Union. Her partner when setting up the venture was Kudrin, whose path I'd crossed the year before. Like many well-placed Russians, Kudrin was involved in several business, charitable and academic ventures. Another was his support for the privately funded European University of St Petersburg.

My friend Max Bouev, the head of the economics department at the university, had moderated a discussion with Vince about the book the previous evening. In the morning, Vince visited the university to meet faculty in the grand surrounds of their palace campus close to the centre of the city. The academics appeared mostly disengaged and the conversation would have been dreary but for some good questions from a younger economics professor, Yulia Vymyatnina. Kudrin showed up, formally thanked the faculty for the event and invited Vince for lunch. I grabbed Yulia's card on the way out, as she seemed a good person to stay connected with.

On this mid-April trip, St Petersburg had already laid on four seasons' worth of weather, from snow when I arrived, rain in the evening, a chilly dawn and warm daytime sun. Nonna had booked a table at a restaurant at the Greek market. Over lunch, Kudrin was interested in the upcoming Brexit referendum. As the Lib Dems were the only decisively pro-European mainstream political party in the UK (in England at least), Vince's views on the Brexit debate were predictable; the often toxic debate about migrant labour, he argued, was tinged by a creeping rejection of "otherness." I agreed with this: as we have seen in the huge labour crunch that has followed Brexit, large parts of the UK economy from agriculture, hospitality and social care through to financial services depend on migrant labour to thrive.[104] And there is something fundamentally odd about the Tory policy picture of 'let's train British fruit pickers' while importing highly skilled labour from non-EU countries. The considerable benefits to the UK of EU membership were sadly lost in white noise about the relatively small (though still significant) number of illegal migrants and the failure of the Home Office to prevent them from entering the country.[105]

Vince asked about economic reform in Russia, and I explored how the Embassy might best engage in this space. Kudrin was clear that Russia needed a more open and less confrontational political and economic relationship with Europe. The Embassy could add value through engagement outside Moscow and St Petersburg. Lots of economic and civil initiatives were happening across the country and it would be an easier operating environment than Moscow in particular. At this point, the conductor Valery Gergiev and composer Rodion Shchedrin showed up and joined our party, whereupon conversation shifted towards the arts.

It was a pleasant lunch that left me with a few helpful nuggets of insight to dwell upon. I'd been struck by the absence of students at the meeting with the European University; if I wanted discussion about the future of Russia's economy, I'd be better off talking to the next generation.

Vince Cable was lower maintenance than most politicians or seniors I looked after during my career. Relaxed, easy-going, urbane yet interested. Lacking in airs and graces. His visit made me think about working with other senior non-governmental British figures

---

104 The catastrophic collapse of the UK labour market post-Brexit has illustrated the benefits of the free movement of labour and the consequences of erecting artificial barriers to limit it.

105 Even before the referendum, I considered both the Tories and the Labour Party to have made an error in fighting the rising influence of the UK Independence Party by starting from the broad-brush acceptance that migration was bad in principle.

as entry points into dialogue with Russia.[106] I wrote to him shortly
after his visit to suggest he might return to St Petersburg to talk at
the International Economic Forum in June. He seemed keen, but it
was never going to work. The Conservative general election victory
of 2015 had dealt a crippling political blow to the Lib Dems and
ended their period in coalition government; despite his economic
credentials, it would have been odd for the UK government to push
Vince forward as a speaker.

I therefore thought about Jim O'Neill, the British economist
who first coined the term BRICs.[107] I'd met Jim shortly before my
posting to Moscow, when he gave a lunchtime talk on economics
at King Charles Street. He was a junior minister at the Treasury,
but I thought that might send a positive signal on engagement. Jim
seemed very keen to participate and it appeared the Chancellor,
George Osborne, wasn't opposed. But the idea was killed at birth
when it hit the Russia team.

• • •

Moscow, June 2016

Laurie Bristow wasn't happy. The Russian government was blanking
him by refusing to grant senior-level meetings in the Ministries.
His counterpart in London, Alexander Yakovenko, was similarly
unhappy. He too was being blanked by the FCO and other government departments in Whitehall. In the diplomatic episode of the
gameshow *Blankety Blank*, no official in either Foreign Ministry
was prepared to write "Ambassadorial meeting" on their cards.
Diplomatic meetings had emerged as a new way to cancel direct

---

106 We would talk about Track 2 dialogue a lot with London, but very little of
substance got off the ground. And I still wondered why we couldn't just get our
ministers to talk directly to their Russian counterparts.

107 The original term referred to Brazil, Russia, India and China. South Africa
was included when the group of emerging economic powerhouses formed as the
BRICS forum of political and economic dialogue.

bilateral engagement.

Fortunately, Laurie was due to cross paths with Yakovenko in St Petersburg. The Russo-British Chamber of Commerce was celebrating its 100th anniversary. As part of the celebrations, Laurie would join a round-table discussion at the economic forum.

The prospect of England playing Russia in the European Football Championships in France also seemed like too good a public diplomacy opportunity to miss. Christophe, the Consul with whom I'd visited Paris, thought we might invite a wide range of senior Russian contacts to a screening at the Residence. This might include Governors from the various host cities for FIFA 2018 in Russia. I thought it was a great idea: make contacts and show our commitment to seeing a safe and successful World Cup in Russia for travelling British fans. Unfortunately, the match was to be played on a Saturday and it was obvious that the manager of the Ambassador's Residence didn't want the faff of a weekend gig. The dour Welshman dug his heels in. I wrote to Laurie, who made a habit of saying how much he disliked football, and he refused point blank. I followed up in a professional way, challenging this and reinforcing the arguments for the event, and he didn't respond. From that point on, I enjoyed a professional, though rather strained, relationship with Laurie.

· · ·

Two months after our first meeting, I was pleased to see Yulia Vymyatnina again at the Ambassador's Residence in Moscow. I'd designed and set up[108] a half-day economic policy development event – a bit like *Dragons' Den* but less intimidating. Fifty economics students worked in mixed teams to develop ideas to drive growth, presenting their ideas to an expert panel who asked questions.

---

108 I invited students from the three economics universities in Moscow I worked with most closely: Plekhanov, the Higher School of Economics ICEF and RANEPA.

Together with Yulia, the panel was made up of the World Bank Resident Representative, a colleague from the Finnish Embassy and Oleg Zamkov, an academic from the Higher School of Economics.

I'd observed that much of the Russian tertiary education system was didactic in approach: students soaked up knowledge from learned professors and regurgitated it through essays and exams; the pedagogy was more Asian than European in some ways. The format I designed asked for their unfiltered opinions. Despite the novelty of this concept, the students settled into it well and seemed to thrive under the spotlight of questioning. Every presentation was different. But the ideas were overwhelmingly liberal, focused on creating a more open economic relationship between Russia and other countries, and bearing down on government corruption and wasteful spending.

Laurie signed certificates for all the students, and everyone enjoyed photographs on the balcony before the event closed. It was a bright early June day, so I decided to walk home and caught up with Yulia along the embankment. We agreed to team up again, in St Petersburg. It occurred to me that I could run these sessions all over Russia and neighbouring countries with very little effort. Indeed, fifty students felt like an easy number, and I wondered how I could run this type of event on a larger scale.

• • •

Saint Petersburg

The Europeans were in St Petersburg in larger numbers for Putin's yearly economic forum. Commission President Jean-Claude Juncker attended, justifying his visit on the need to maintain dialogue with Russia, despite the challenges with Ukraine. Italy's Prime Minister, Matteo Renzi, joined Putin's plenary session, where he loved up St Petersburg, bigged up Russian–Italian trade and tried to avoid all mention of Ukraine and sanctions. By mid-2016, half the EU member states had re-established bilateral economic commissions with Russia. Just a week before the Brexit referendum, the UK was looking increasingly isolated in Europe on Russia policy and closer to the US.

Putin's plenary session followed the same script as the year before; Charlie Rose once more posed questions and Putin again ran rings round him, sniping about Western foreign policy.

More entertaining exchanges happened at the Russo-British Chamber of Commerce roundtable. Laurie made a decent speech about ongoing collaboration, Alexander Yakovenko made some barbed remarks from the side-lines and the whole affair got petty. The two Ambassadors were clearly not banya buddies. But in circumstances where neither Ambassador was getting any significant government access in the respective capitals, the event might have been an opportunity for them to talk like grown-ups and forge a deal to unlock barriers. That assumed, of course, that both Ambassadors had the clout in their Ministries to secure agreement to a deal. In the end, they bickered like schoolkids.

· · ·

Moscow

"Yeahhhhh!" I leapt out of my seat and punched the air, knocking over the beer of the guy on the next table.

In the seventy-third minute, Eric Dier had stepped up and thumped a beautiful free kick into the top corner of the Russian net. Dressed in a brilliant white England replica shirt, I was the only Englishman in the crowded Moscow bar where the game was being screened live. Vinny, clinging on to his Welsh identify, leaned away and covered his face, hoping no one would notice we were together.

I apologised profusely in Russian and bought the guy another beer. We shook hands on it, but he still looked a bit pissed off. And then the inevitable happened. Russia equalised.

The whole bar erupted, men and women jumping up and down,

celebrating like lunatics as I had before. And I couldn't help but think that the majority were cheering, pointing at and sledging the dickhead in the white shirt! It was brilliant. I didn't get even a bit of trouble and I suppose in some ways, I was glad to leave the bar with honours even.

But as I looked at the screen, I saw scenes of violence in the stands in Marseilles. The Orel Butchers, a group of nationalist football hooligans from Russia, were attacking England fans. The Russian government distanced themselves from the thuggery, but they could have done more to prevent this had they wanted to. The dire nature of the bilateral relationship meant they simply didn't.

England has a bad track record when it comes to hooligans letting down their country abroad. However, the British police make it much harder for known yobs to travel to football tournaments; I was determined that they do so for the 2018 World Cup in Russia.

• • •

Having assumed England would beat Russia in the Euros, I also predicted that the UK would vote to remain in the European Union. While it would be incorrect to say that everyone in the FCO was a staunch remainer, it's fair to say that most were. British staff in Moscow chancery were overwhelmingly deflated when Britons voted in favour of Brexit. For me, this wasn't only about the UK leaving a vital economic, social and cultural community. It was also a harbinger of a hardening of UK policy towards Russia, as we drifted inexorably towards even closer alliance with the US. It seemed ironic that the fate of UK policy towards Russia seemed to hang on who won the upcoming US presidential election.

20. CITIZENS OF NOWHERE

Moscow, Russia, July 2016

I n my peripheral vision, I spotted the police officer approaching through the queue of traffic. Ahead, the traffic lights were stuck on red. I gripped the steering wheel and stared at the Ministry of Foreign Affairs building, aware of his looming presence. As he raised his baton, the lights turned green. *You can shove that stick up your arse.*[109] I slammed my foot on the accelerator and shot off like Lewis Hamilton at the British Grand Prix.

Moscow had been tense since the end of June, when CCTV captured a police officer wrestling an American diplomat to the ground outside the US Embassy. The diplomat can be seen squirming until he is able to enter the opening door of the building. He succeeded in getting his body onto diplomatic territory and became as untouchable as Anne Sacoolas. The Russian authorities claimed he was a spy and immediately expelled him and another diplomat. Had he not broken free, he might have ended up sitting in front of Russian news cameras the following day in cuffs. Either way, word had got out that the police should stop US and British diplomatic vehicles on sight.

My escape at the traffic lights was the third time I'd evaded the baton-pointing police. Once they tried to stop me as I left the

---

109 In the Embassy, we nicknamed the black and white police batons "pozhalyista sticks," after the Russian word that can signify "you're welcome," "if you please" and "please."

Embassy. Another time, as I drove out of a shopping mall following a visit with Katharine and the kids. W-T-F!

Diplomats are not immune from being stopped by the police if they are committing an offence under local law. But as far as I was concerned, this was blatant harassment, and I wasn't going to play along.

Then one Saturday morning as we went to the kids' school for swimming, a police car waited patiently on the garden ring waiting for me to emerge. They stopped me, briefly and courteously, before letting me go on my way. They'd made their point, I'd made mine, and after that the harassment seemed to melt away a little.

• • •

Kazan, Russia

I stepped off the train into bright sunshine at seven in the morning, fresh and revived after a shower in my overnight cabin. The overnight service from Moscow to Kazan was extremely comfortable; plenty of time to watch old Soviet movies, have a few drinks and still get eight hours of sleep. Two students waited patiently on the platform by my carriage, holding a plate with a golden mound of stuck-together breakfast cereal. Or that's what it looked like. They invited me to eat a piece of chak-chak, the national sweet of Tatarstan. The morsel was pleasant, crumbly and sweet like Frosties.

We drove a good way out of Kazan to a resort hotel decked out with coloured banners. Fresh-faced students bustled here and there. RANEPA, the Russian Presidential Academy of National Economy and Public Administration, had invited me to participate in their yearly international summer campus. Two hundred or so students from across the world gathered for a week of educational, social and cultural learning. A solitary English girl, Brioney, had made the trip out from Bath, which was nice to see. Across a couple of days, I delivered a talk on economics and another economic policy-development seminar. The students seemed engaged but exhausted: each day they'd be woken up early, exercised till they were red in the face and lectured at ad nauseum before enduring (in my view) slightly cringeworthy entertainment until past midnight. It was alcohol-free, which Brioney joked was to prevent them all shagging during the brief hours they were meant to be asleep.

It had a slight air of Soviet Youth Pioneer Camp, and I wasn't entirely convinced of its educational benefit. But the scale and organisation of it was impressive. And the social media reverberations rippled on for many months afterwards; participants from across the globe posted and reposted photos and memories of their international chums. World peace, comrades! It strengthened my desire to run my economic events not over half a day but over a week. And not with fifty but with a hundred or more.

I also spent time with Gabriel di Bella, the affable Argentinian IMF Resident Representative. Gabriel was making the most of his time in Russia and told me he had excellent access in the Moscow Ministries and regionally. He was perennially optimistic, including on Russia's economy; the Central Bank and Finance Ministry continued to do a good job of managing macro-stability despite the ongoing slump in oil prices and sanctions. Whenever I took a harder-line view, he'd be more moderate. People view things in different ways. But Gabriel was undoubtedly an accomplished economist, and I valued his judgement.

The Republic of Tatarstan has benefited from considerable oil and gas wealth and appeared to have invested it wisely. During my free time, I took a trip into Kazan to visit the local government to discuss preparations for the 2018 World Cup. The city was bright and modern, and the sleek football stadium looked fit to host World Cup games. I presented the minister with a British Embassy-branded football shirt as a memento, with hopes that a British team might get a chance to play in his city.

And then another train ride for a chilled-out thirteen-hour daytime run to Ekaterinburg. You get a different view of Russia when you watch the vast open plains roll by and make an occasional stop at a sleepy village or town. As it was summer, lots of the little houses had vegetable patches in the garden. Life for ordinary Russians seemed simpler and far removed from the high politics of Moscow.

Sidney, our man in Ekaterinburg, was absent, and I was covering his job for a week. Poor old Sid always looked like a rabbit on Red Bull in the headlights; despite the easy-going pace of life in the Urals, he struggled to cope with the isolation from the Moscow mother ship. And the situation in Ekaterinburg was only going to get more stressful.

Volgograd, Russia, August 2016

I visited Volgograd around the time of my economist Oksana's birthday. She'd be there with her family and would accompany me for a meeting with the local government. I'd spent months remembering her birthday and kept telling her, just to help me remember.

Birthdays for Russians are a big deal and I'd been doing my cultural homework at parties in the Embassy. Flowers – never given in even numbers, and definitely not yellow – would be presented. Don't celebrate the day before! Effusive speeches were made, praising the birthday boy or girl to the high rafters. In England we just take in a cake and hope no one makes a fuss; indeed, at my advanced age, I'd sooner forget it. But miss a Russian birthday and you might not forget it. Ever.

It was baking hot and cloudless, and I was met by a young man from the local government. Driving to the centre of communist-controlled Volgograd, the city looked run down. I remembered that Oksana's birthday was on one day and her brother's two days later, something like that. How sweet. That made it doubly difficult to forget.

The official sat opposite me in the minibus, shifting uncomfortably in his seat. "Your colleague Oksana will meet you at the government building," he said.

"Great, looking forward to seeing her," I beamed, bursting with excitement.

His eyes darted nervously, and he avoided eye contact. "It was her birthday yesterday."

The colour drained from my hot face. "Oh, yes, of course." *Holy shit!* Oksana was the kindest, humblest person: she never made a fuss, and tolerated the weird working arrangements at the British Embassy without complaint. As we drew up, she waited outside the government building in a plain blue dress and enormous mirrored shades. What little I could see of her face was set like stone. I offered birthday wishes in the most exaggerated manner; she barely spoke. I leaned in to kiss her cheek and she ducked away like a bantam-weight boxer dodging a punch.

My meeting with the deputy chair of the Volgograd government was formal but constructive. It had taken ages for them to agree to this single meeting. The head of the local World Cup Organising Committee was more pleased to see me. I also presented them with a British Embassy football shirt. That meeting paved the way for good collaboration during the tournament itself.

Meeting over, the young official escorted me on a walk around Mamayev Kurgan, a hill overlooking Volgograd, formerly known as Stalingrad. Here, over five months, the most ferocious battle took place between the Nazi and Soviet forces in World War II. Several times Mamayev Kurgan changed hands. Marshal Vasily Chuikov, who oversaw the defence of Stalingrad, is buried here, his granite statue built into the hillside, immovable. Vasily Zaitsev is also buried here, his sniper skills immortalised in the Hollywood movie *Enemy at the Gates*. At the top, "The Motherland Calls" stands majestic, a realist statue of a fecund Soviet woman defiantly holding aloft a mighty sword. From the hilltop, the partially built football stadium was visible in the distance and I wondered whether it would be complete in time.[110]

Oksana's mood had lightened slightly when we said farewell at Volgograd Station. Outside the station stood a replica of the

---

110 As it turned out, England would play Tunisia in Volgograd during the World Cup and the connections I built proved handy closer to the tournament.

Barmaley, a fountain depicting six children dancing in a circle, which survived the unimaginable destruction of the battle. The Soviets turned Stalingrad into a merciless killing zone, feeding in enough troops and weapons to prevent its capture while building up massive armies in the flanks. The encirclement of 265,000 Axis troops at the end of November 1942 and their eventual surrender on 2 February 1943 was the key turning point on the Eastern Front in World War II. Volgograd is a fascinating, sombre and moving place to visit. I boarded another overnight train to Moscow and reflected once more on the immense sacrifices Russia will endure to defend their motherland.

· · ·

Edinburgh, Scotland, August 2016

"You look like a British diplomat," Elizabeth Smith[111] said.

"I'm not sure whether that was meant as a compliment," I replied with a smile.

We settled down for afternoon tea in the genteel surrounds of an Edinburgh hotel. Already seventy-six years of age, the baroness was relaxed and happy to discuss the machinations of Labour Party politics under Jeremy Corbyn. Behind the gentle exterior was a sharp mind, and she was soon asking about my work in Russia. Very much Old Labour, she told me of her fascination with Russia from student days, as well as her disdain for American exceptionalism.

After her late husband the former Labour Party leader John Smith passed away, she had set up the John Smith Fellowship Trust. It organised twice-yearly fellowship programmes for emerging leaders from the countries of the former Soviet Union, with the aim of promoting shared values of tolerance, respect and openness, together with good governance. She has loads of

---

111 Baroness Smith of Gilmorehill is a Labour peer and the widow of the late John Smith, who led the Labour Party from 1992 until his death in 1994.

experience working across the region, so we discussed my plans for engagement with future generations – and the reason for my visit to Scotland.

I'd got wind that a delegation from Glasgow was visiting Rostov-on-Don in September. The cities had established a twinning relationship in 1986 which was alive and well. It was one of several partnerships between British and Russian cities that emerged in the decades after the Second World War. I wanted to see for myself what it was all about. Baroness Smith kindly joined me for a visit to Glasgow City Council, where we heard about cooperation across a range of fields from jewellery design and music to art and gymnastics. It all looked positive, so I decided to join the visit to Rostov. And stay in close touch with the baroness.

• • •

Rostov-on-Don, Russia, September 2016

My mouth was dry as a lime digger's clog as I sat, massively hungover, in a VIP section filled with dignitaries from cities around the world. Legions of kids in bright red and blue sang the Rostov-on-Don anthem enthusiastically. Students waved large flags from the balconies. A brief performance recounted the proud history of the city, dating back to Catherine the Great. When the show was over, I shuffled out with the Glasgow team, and we wandered around the nearby display of art by local schoolkids. A baillie[112] led the delegation, civic chains around his neck, studiously looking at every painting.

Before long we boarded a minibus to the Olympic Reserve Gymnastics School.

"You are a murderer!" Vladimir Fudimov, the director of the school, beamed and wrapped me in a hug.

Vladimir and I had got on like a house on fire the night before,

---

112 Effectively, a deputy mayor.

at a city day reception with lots of food, music, dancing and even more hooch. His schtick was to ply his guests with as much booze as possible in a show of exaggerated hospitality. I vaguely recall Lev from the Royal Conservatoire of Scotland getting his violin out at around 4 a.m. and performing on the street.

Led by his wife Lia, a gymnastics coach, students of various ages laid on a performance for our group. It's one thing to watch gymnastics on TV but quite another to see young kids effortlessly doing all sorts of somersaults and tumbles. Collaboration on gymnastics had helped Scotland rise in the rankings, through yearly two-way study trips. A small group of Scottish girls would come to Rostov each year and a group of Russian girls would make the return trip to Scotland.

This was just one form of cooperation between ordinary people from both cities. Wider collaboration happened in other areas, including puppet theatre, music and art. Glasgow Kelvin College also ran a yearly exchange programme.[113] All small-scale stuff but important to everyone involved. I considered twinning activity like this to be thoroughly positive. Far from the glare of media headlines about our appalling two-way relationship, it brought ordinary people from the UK and Russia together.

After a jug of water and an afternoon nap, I joined the Glasgow delegation for dinner in Theatre Square, followed by fireworks and a free concert for city residents by a popular Russian girl band.

Vladimir couldn't join us, but the following day he collected me from Rostov Airport. My flight to Moscow had been delayed by several hours and he offered to take me back to his place to relax for a while. On the drive out of town, we passed Zmievskaya Balka. Here, 27,000 Jews and Soviet citizens were murdered by the Nazis between 1942 and 1943. Women, children and the elderly were often gassed in trucks while the men were simply shot. It was

---

113 I hosted a group of students from Glasgow Kelvin for tea at the Residence on their way home from their summer study visit shortly before visiting Rostov myself.

another chilling reminder of the hatred that warfare can unleash.

Vladimir and Lia live in a humble flat in a *khrushchevka*, a low-cost, low-rise, concrete-panelled block built during Nikita Khrushchev's time. It was a hot day, so Vladimir lent me some baggy shorts and a T-shirt to relax in while Lia prepared manti dumplings and salads. Just the loveliest people, with whom I remain good friends, despite everything.

• • •

Riga, Latvia, September 2016

The immigration queue for non-EU citizens at Riga Airport was long. I sailed up to the EU desk and quickly stepped onto European Union soil. The contrast couldn't have been more marked. After I left Rostov, I'd transited Moscow and was now passing through Latvia for the first time. An overnight stay awaited, ahead of another visit to Kyiv. Riga was a pretty, efficient and welcoming city. It wasn't that I disliked Moscow; my family was perfectly happy there and we had a good and rather privileged life. But as a British diplomat, I lived in a goldfish bowl, my every move watched over and questioned by the Chekist big brother. In Latvia, I was conscious of entering a wider community of people. The EU is not perfect by any means but was trying hard to build a life of democracy, prosperity, harmony and peace. While I had been a reluctant remainer before the Brexit referendum, my short visit to Riga made me acutely aware of how life in Russia had made me less reluctant.

• • •

I'd admired David Cameron's gambler instinct in running a G8 summit in Northern Ireland. But he was a fool to call a Brexit referendum when he was under no significant pressure to do so. And he was a coward to jack in his job when the result went the wrong way. When Theresa May gave her first speech as Prime

Minister on the steps of Downing Street, I felt briefly inspired. She was talking about creating real opportunities for working-class people who were 'just about managing.' It was like she'd turned the Tories into the Labour Party.

The joyless Hammond was gone as Foreign Secretary – hooray! Boris Johnson took his place, and the early signals were that we would take a completely different tack on Russia. I was optimistic for the first time in a while.

International Trade and Exiting the EU were established as separate Cabinet-level ministries. Boris was too popular in the Tory Party to ignore. But May wanted to limit his influence over foreign policy as much as possible. Hammond was in Treasury, David Davis in DExEU and Liam Fox in Trade. So, Bo Jo would be hemmed in on all sides by Russia-hawkish head-bangers.

When May stood up for her first Tory Party conference speech as leader, my initial optimism faded. In a bizarre turn, she called for a reimagining of citizenship, saying, "If you believe you are a citizen of the world, you are a citizen of nowhere." While she couched this in the context of global multinational firms tripping around the globe and evading taxes, what I heard was: "Love the United Kingdom, not Johnny foreigner." It was the ultimate repudiation of multiculturalism that Vince Cable had hinted at earlier in the year. As Prime Minister, Theresa appeared more Maggie Blackamoor[114] than Maggie Thatcher.

I didn't consider global citizenship a pinko left-wing fantasy but rather a point of view in which people were curious about their fellow men and women from different countries, cultures and faiths. As a diplomat, I travelled around constantly, curious to understand Russia and her people, and keen to search for common ground at a time of enormous bilateral tension. Was I a 'citizen of nowhere'? Theresa May's speech marked the moment my lifelong

---

114 Maggie Blackamoor is a fictional character played by David Walliams in the satirical comedy series *Little Britain*. She vomits on gay people and people of colour.

conservatism, rooted in self-reliance and personal responsibility, and ironically prompted by Margaret Thatcher, died. Politics was no longer about mixed market economies versus socialist command and control but rather nationalism against internationalism. Or Little Britain versus Global Britain.

. . .

Moscow, Russia, September 2016

An S-class Mercedes limousine pulled up outside the Embassy and I ushered Oksana into the rear seat. We drove in comfort along the embankment to Moscow's financial district and a fancy restaurant on the sixtieth floor of one of the skyscrapers. It was my belated birthday treat and she seemed genuinely moved at the gesture.

I'd travelled so much over the summer of 2016 that I had become a citizen of everywhere. But then at the end of September I broke my leg and for a few months became a citizen of going nowhere.

. . .

The expat director of the Russo-British Chamber of Commerce was asked to resign his position over the summer. We wanted this British citizen nowhere near the Embassy in future.

21. MEDDLING

Moscow, Russia, September 2016

Someone commented at the morning meeting that Theresa May "doesn't 'do' personal warmth."

Like the worst Tinder date imaginable, Theresa May met Putin at the G20 summit in Hangzhou, China. There was nothing substantive to discuss on Ukraine, as the UK remained decisively outside the Normandy peace tent. The core foreign policy priority for the UK with Russia was on Syria, but there too, Russia saw the UK as a bit-part player. The government had lost a 2013 Westminster parliamentary vote on military intervention following a rebellion by thirty Conservative MPs; this had left Her Majesty's government chipping in from the rough, with Turkey, Russia, France and the US playing the most active roles. Putin came to the 2016 bilateral with a completely different plan for the evening: specifically, an amorous desire to re-establish some form of sanctions-compliant economic collaboration.

Russia's Economic Minister, Alexei Ulyukaev, had joined the May–Putin bilateral and was keen to move forward. Officials from Russia's Finance Ministry met me and the Embassy head of trade and prosperity issues, to explore practical follow-up. Alexei Kudrin was also asking us about economic engagement; he'd been appointed to head up a presidential export panel on the Russian economy.

But Theresa was most definitely not swayed by Vladimir's charms. So, UK–Russia relations remained cold and decidedly limp. However, agreement was reached to make 2017 the UK–Russia Year of Science and Education.

• • •

Moscow, Russia, November 2016

Alexei Ulyukaev was arrested by the FSB on 12 November near the Rosneft headquarters, yards from the British Ambassador's Residence.

Ulyukaev had been one of several critics of state-owned oil giant Rosneft's purchase of Bashneft, the oil company expropriated from oligarch Vladimir Yevtushenkov two years previously. In October 2015, Rosneft paid the regal sum of $5.3 billion for Bashneft, straight into Russia's federal budget. This helped to plug the still-yawning gap in state finances caused by low oil prices.

Rosneft CEO Igor Sechin invited Ulyukaev to his office and presented him with the gift of a basket of wine and sausages. It just so happened to include $2 million in cash stashed at the bottom. You can imagine the scene in Sechin's office.

"Alexei Valentinovich, I know we haven't always agreed, but please accept this gift of wine and sausage, and let's move on to mutually beneficial cooperation."

"Ah, thank you, Igor Ivanovich, you really are too kind. It's certainly a large basket." Pausing with a nervous smile. "But wait a minute, you haven't stashed $2 million in dodgy bank notes in the basket, like some B-grade seventies crime drama, have you?"

Laughing heartily. "Fuck your mother! This is the best sausage you ever tasted."

Lurking nearby and almost falling over themselves like Keystone Cops, FSB officers pounced on Ulyukaev to arrest him as he was about to depart the scene in his Maybach.

There is no reason to believe Ulyukaev was free from corruption, like any other senior state official in Russia. Indeed, the Panama

Papers leak of April 2016 revealed his beneficial interest in a company called Ronnieville registered in the British Virgin Islands.

But why would an apparently intelligent man, accomplished economist and government minister take *only* $2 million, and paid in banknotes? And in Igor Sechin's office? It didn't completely add up. I sent a stream of reporting to London on the unfolding drama.

What did seem clear was that the old guard of the former KGB *siloviki* was reclaiming the higher ground on the future of Russian economic policy from the so-called economic liberals. This was happening for two reasons.

Firstly, the Russian energy sector had been struggling since the oil price collapse of 2014 and the decision to free-float the Russian rouble. Western sanctions hadn't dented oil production, which continued to rise. With energy prices still relatively low, the types of oil exploration sanctioned – shale, deep water and Arctic – weren't a good bet in the short term, so new investment was frozen, literally. Russia continued to exploit mature fields. However, in a bid to bear down on inflation, a free-floating rouble had brought with it higher interest rates, which strengthened the rouble. As a result, whenever the oil price fell, the rouble wouldn't fall by a commensurate amount, depressing the rouble value of each barrel of oil exploited. From consistently bringing in 3,800+ roubles per barrel of oil before the oil price decline, the rouble price of oil fell gradually throughout 2015 to an average of around 3,000 roubles and seldom crept above 3,200.

Over the much longer term, a less profitable energy sector might have prompted a rebalancing of Russia's economy and a movement into new industrial sectors as the state searched for new ways to drive economic growth. But it was clearly not in the interests of people like Sechin or other oil and gas fat cats to let that happen. It wasn't just that their profits were down: a lower rouble price of oil meant lower tax receipts from the energy sector, which meant reduced influence for their companies. The second phase of Russian monetary policy – the economically liberal, free-floating rouble, for which Ulyukaev was an advocate – ran counter to deep-rooted vested interests.

Second, where other state-owned enterprises had benefited from the economic nationalism that emerged from the imposition of Western sanctions, the energy companies wanted a piece of the pie. Buying Bashneft was another step on the road to transforming Rosneft into a state-owned monopoly, along the lines of Saudi Aramco. I joked that Rosneft might soon change its name to Gosneft.[115] Laurie hated me referring to the re-Sovietisation of Russia's economy even though that appeared, self-evidently, to be happening.

A Rosneft with a greater share of oil exploration in Russia would enable Sechin to cement his value as an indispensable member of Putin's inner circle. The $5.3 billion Bashneft purchase was a down payment to the state. A cooked-up pseudo-privatisation of Rosneft's shell company in November 2016 provided a further $10.8 billion to the exchequer. Sechin had been viewed as on the back foot after the Black Tuesday collapse of December 2014. He was now back with a vengeance.

In the ensuing court proceedings against Ulyukaev, Sechin refused four court requests to give evidence. He was suddenly bullet-proof. Making a scapegoat of the Economy Minister sent a powerful message to other liberals who wanted to take him on. "If you think you're in charge of economic policy, you can eat my sausage."

The machinery of Russian economic policy therefore shifted. One year after Ulyukaev's arrest, the rouble price of oil had risen again to 3,800. Two years later, it was 5,400. Russian foreign exchange reserves also started to creep up again; the war chest was being filled.

If the West had wanted to weaken Russia's oil and gas sector, the best approach would have been to buy roubles. Some people thought I had gone stark raving mad when I suggested it, as if I

---

115 Many Soviet industrial entities had names that began with Gos, which is a contraction of the word *gosudarstvennoy* or state.

were proposing some sort of sanctions-busting support. After the war in Ukraine started, I suggested we fix a rouble cost per barrel of oil based on a pre-war exchange rate. Rather, officials and journalists crowed about the collapse of the rouble. In March 2022, the rouble price of oil was over four times higher than its level in late 2013 when the oil price was at its highest pre-war level. Not only did Russia earn $590bn in export revenue in 2022, but it did so at an extremely high exchange rate, with western customers increasingly forced to pay in roubles.

• • •

"The Democrats picked the only candidate who couldn't beat Trump" was the stinging assessment of a member of my team.

I couldn't have agreed more. In 2016, I predicted the UK wouldn't vote in favour of Brexit and that Donald Trump would win the US presidency. My first prediction proved wrong, sadly, but I remained confident about my second.

Trump was tapping into a "great unheard" of ordinary rust-belt Americans in Intercourse, Pennsylvania and Arsecrack, Arkansas. Hillary Clinton embodied the self-obsessed entitlement of "dynasty" candidates on both sides of the American political divide.

Allegations swirled about Russian interference in the US elections following an embarrassing hack and leak operation over the summer; the revelations caused embarrassment to Clinton's campaign. Meanwhile, Trump was facing all manner of (I'd argue, equally damaging) allegations about his sexual misdemeanours, including a taped conversation of him bragging about grabbing women's pussies.

Russian intelligence agencies were undoubtedly playing in the US elections, even if they used proxies they could (try to) disavow. Offensive intelligence operations had become the *ordre du jour* of the Russia, US and UK relationship in particular; we were all at it! The big question remained whether, during a presidential and

congressional election season which saw total campaign funding
of $6.5 billion, it really swung the outcome. If the Russians spent
even 5% of that sum on the US election, pumping out social media
bots and hacking Democrat servers, I'd be surprised. But as a Brit,
I wouldn't say I really cared that much.

I did notice that polling for the US presidential elections revolved
more deliberately around what the pollsters wanted to believe was
true. This seemed part of a general decline in the credibility of
polling organisations in the US and elsewhere. Economic pollsters
were increasingly more likely to get forecasts wrong than right,
especially in the run-up to the Brexit referendum.[116] The sudden
rise in popularity of Podemos in Spain and Syriza in Greece had
taken polling organisations by surprise. Somehow, constituencies
of disenfranchised people who wanted a say on political change
(for better or worse) in their countries were being missed. The
Trump factor sat outside a metrosexual middle-class median that
pollsters felt comfortable with. Pollsters were simply unable, or
unwilling, to measure the Trump effect. When Clinton lost, it was
clear the sour grapes and bad feeling on Capitol Hill about Russian
interference would be heard like a scratched record well beyond
the election itself. I'd argue that it has tinged US policy towards
Russia since Joe Biden came to power, with the disastrous results
we see today in Ukraine.

· · ·

2016 was a great year for Embassy social events. In midsummer,
British and Russian colleagues performed an evening of Shake-
speare sonnets and scenes at the Residence. I reprised the role
of Orsino from *Twelfth Night*, with the beautiful Sveta as Viola,

---

116 David Davis, the Brexit Minister, and some parts of the right-wing Tory press
accused government officials of a pessimism bias in economic forecasts about the
potential impact of Brexit.

secretly in love with me and disguised as my male page. Vinny did a hilarious turn as Malvolio in cross-gartered yellow stockings.

We held a five-a-side football tournament and a popular charity concert in the garden of the Residence. Music fanatic Steve from Visa Section had formed a friendship with Russian blues artists in Moscow who agreed to perform for beer and bratwurst.

But over this loomed the spectre of the free Christmas party. It had become a toxic issue with a cabal of British colleagues, led by Fred; I was seen as a tyrant who inflated prices in the Hammer and Pickle to impose undemocratic festive joy. The vicar, Ivor, a retired army officer who had previously worked at the Prince's Trust, dipped his jolly hockey stick in unhelpfully. He saw the social committee as a potential cash cow to raise funds for restoration at St Andrew's Church; his wife, the bar manager, quietly stirred the revolutionary pot in the background. Many would describe Ivor as a colourful character,.[117] I found him a pain in the arse.

While I was on my family holiday, a plan was hatched to unseat me from the social committee at the annual general meeting. A bit like the US elections, a major campaign was in full swing – with equal bile but without the billions. Weekend lunch gatherings on the compound whipped the British staff into a foam-speckled frenzy at the injustice of free parties. And then one day, Fred got in the lift with me and casually told me to step aside or be pushed. I didn't see it coming.

I sat alone in my office when Martin's personal assistant – the designated election official – popped his head around my door with a smile. He passed me the folded yellow post-it note and left to allow me a moment's privacy. On it were the words:

---

117 The following year, Reverend Ivor was recalled early from the parish of St Andrew's in Moscow by the Anglican Church. His bull-in-a-china-shop approach had rubbed too many people in the Church community up, and in the wrong way. They weren't entirely convinced their blessed vicar was pure in heart, nor that he would see God. For my part, I wasn't sad to see the back of him. Malcolm, a decidedly meeker vicar, arrived in September 2017 and the parishioners rejoiced that he should inherit the parsonage.

Ian – 77
Fred – 75

I punched the air silently. Then I laughed, as the tension evaporated. I couldn't believe it. A hundred and fifty-two people voting in an Embassy social committee election was nuts; practically everyone who worked at the Embassy had turned out. Just as they did for Donald Trump, *The Huffington Post* might well have given me a 1.7% chance[118] of winning the election. As most of the diplomats were accompanied by a spouse or partner, Fred's campaign banked two votes for every diplomat.

But the stubbornness I inherited from my mother had kicked in. Screw you, I thought, as I wrote personally to every Russian member of staff in the Embassy. My campaign was simple: "I know you wouldn't normally vote, but if Fred becomes chair, your Christmas party will be cancelled. So please vote for me and let's rock on in the Residence!" Having never previously voted, they answered my call.

Despite the challenges and suspicions swirling around the building on Smolenskaya Embankment, staff worked hard for a moderate wage and deserved a Christmas party. It didn't cross Fred's mind that the Russian staff, who made up the majority at the Embassy, would have an opinion on the matter. He didn't think he needed their votes.

I didn't see Fred for a few days after, but his sidekick, Barney, popped his head around the door. "Congratulations," he said. "But how come staff from the Visa Processing Centre[119] were allowed to vote?" For a moment of unbelievable pettiness, he was looking

---

118 As soon as I saw *The Huffington Post* prediction on US election day that Hillary Clinton had a 98% likelihood of success, I knew instinctively that Trump would win.

119 The Visa Processing Centre was run by an outsourced private company and while its offices were elsewhere in Moscow, a small number of their staff were embedded in the Embassy Visa team to ensure smooth cooperation.

to unpick the result by rendering some votes invalid. A handful of
Russian staff who worked for an Embassy contractor had become
the equivalents of the hanging chads in Florida that killed Al Gore's
bid to become US President in 2000. For my part, I didn't mind that
the contractors weren't fully detached from the Embassy. Fred lost,
a bitter taste of Russian election meddling in his throat.

22. THE KREMLIN CHRISTMAS TREE!

Moscow, December 2016

The Americans were being played. The Anglo-American School of Moscow (AAS), had been "closed" by the Russian government. Or had it?

My son started at the AAS in August 2016. It opened in 1949 to provide a western-style education for the children of (initially) US, British and Canadian diplomats in the Soviet Union. Organised along the lines of a US private school, it had amazing facilities, a fantastic community and events all year round. We loved our visits there with our son and, later, our daughter.

On 29 December 2016, Barack Obama announced the expulsion of thirty-five Russian diplomats in response to alleged election meddling. Shortly before making way for Donald Trump at the White House, it was his final foreign policy pea-flick as President.

Speculation swirled around how Russia would respond. Sergey Lavrov proposed publicly that Putin evict thirty-five American diplomats; that was odd.[120] Several western news outlets ran a story, quoting a US source, that Russia had ordered the AAS closed as well. Wikipedia was immediately updated to refer to the school in the past tense.

---

120 Lavrov wouldn't have spoken out of turn from the Kremlin. He was teeing up Putin to look magnanimous.

I was suspicious. Russia likes to overmatch in a diplomatic dispute, to hit their adversary harder in response. But targeting 1,200 kids, most of whom weren't American or British? Pissing off seniors in the presidential administration with kids or grandkids at the school? Not to mention the Chinese, Indians, Vietnamese and other friendly embassies? They were never going to do it.

The Foreign Ministry had clearly hinted the school might be in the crosshairs to start the ball rolling. Someone had leaked the closure as a given[121], and the story exploded from there. The Wikipedia page added to the story. As the school was closed for the holidays, its website was unchanged, and the Americans controlled that. It was fishier than Billingsgate Market.

Panic erupted among parents. "Oh, my son has been up crying all night, as he's due to finish his International Baccalaureate in the summer," my neighbour wailed. The American Embassy approached us to see if we might provide practical support. [122]

And then the coup de grâce.

Putin invited the children of US Embassy families to a New Year's party at the Kremlin to see his Christmas tree. It was an offer the Americans didn't accept. Rather than expel any US diplomats, Putin paused, waiting to see how the land would lie with Trump as President.

It was a case study in Russian tradecraft. A major line of attack in Kremlin propaganda is that the Americans (and to a lesser extent, the Brits) are hysterical about Russia and overreact constantly. The Americans played the part impeccably. Russian officials condemned the Yanks as "angry and shallow-brained losers."

You don't have to appreciate the tactics. But if you want to engage with Russia, you should at least try to understand them. I took a screenshot of the Wikipedia page and sent it to London, which piqued their interest.

---

121 Russian Foreign Ministry spokesperson, Maria Zakharova, alleged the Americans leaked it.

122 The school was co-sponsored by the American, British and Canadian Embassies.

Diplomatic schools are not explicitly provided for in the Vienna Convention on Diplomatic Relations. The UK government moved away from the formal recognition of diplomatic schools a few years ago and several, mostly in eastern Europe, had been closed. However, several countries ran diplomatic schools in Moscow, so the Russians picking on our school was well out of order. Most importantly, Russia has a diplomatic school attached to its Embassy in Kensington, that has operated since 1954.[123] My position was simple and easy for the reciprocity-obsessed Russians to understand: "if you close our school, we'll close yours".

· · ·

"Did you organise this shit then? Did ya?" Fred's wife Wilma got right up in my face, waving her hands for emphasis.

With the festive spirit in full flow, Fred and Wilma missed the free minibus transport to the Residence for the Embassy Christmas party and arrived late. When I'd tracked Fred down after his post-election sulk, I offered him the role of deputy chair of the social committee. He brought some good ideas, sourcing local suppliers for beer that we could pay for in roubles, and putting in place a voluntary rota to man the bar, to reduce costs. But the free party still grated with him and, clearly, with Wilma.

I chipped in £100 towards the cost, as I did every year, but the party was nonetheless a shoestring affair. Fred, and his sidekick Barney, cast their eyes over every kopek.

"You should have project managed this better," a colleague Jimmy leaned in and shouted, while jigging along to "Dancing Queen" in the garden room.

The Wi-Fi wasn't working, so the disco descended into five ABBA songs on repeat. It didn't deter most people, who drank and danced

---

123 There is also a Russian Mission School attached to the Russian Mission to the UN in New York.

happily or escorted friends and family for tours of the Residence. "Kremlin selfies, anyone?"

I gave Jimmy a wide berth on many issues, as he wasn't sighted on the intelligence, but we collaborated just fine. He also spent a lot of time socialising with British expat and Russian contacts. As I watched Jimmy's attractive Russian colleagues shuffling around him on the dancefloor, I worried that his inner lounge lizard might one day get the better of him.

· · ·

Like Bilbo Baggins, I hobbled to the door after each knock to meet another guest. They'd remove their shoes and coat and present me with a small gift. I broke my leg on the eve of (not) running the Moscow 10k in September and, until that point, had been training with a local running club. They were all so supportive after my injury that I decided to organise a Christmas get-together at our apartment. My Russian chums gathered chairs around a coffee table, and we sat, drank, ate and chatted for the evening. Some broke off from time to time to dance in the lounge.

My friends not only trained together; they went out for meals and evenings at the theatre, to concert halls or art galleries, and in the summer they travelled all over the country to different running events. Whenever I introduced Russian friends at an Embassy event, I was often surprised to see them on Instagram days later socialising together.

Not long before, I'd hosted British colleagues for an evening of homemade pizza; they had a nice time, stood chatting in small vertical clumps, and I vowed to organise a similar event the following year. It was an interesting insight into sociological differences between the (generally speaking) individualistic Brits on the one hand and the Russians on the other, for whom the group is a powerful connecting force.

Ivan Zolotov, my Gazprom friend, joined us for Christmas lunch with his wife Olga. Having served in London at the Soviet Embassy in the nineties, he took great pride in carving the turkey. Our friends were great with the kids, who enjoyed spending time with the visitors like they were family guests.

We gave Ivan Ivanovich, the building supervisor, a case of English beer for Christmas. The kids called him Mr Poleteli; whenever he saw them in the yard, summer or winter, he'd grab their wrists and swing them round in the air, crying, "*Poleteli, poleteli*" ("Let's fly").

· · ·

As 2017 started, no one thought the relationship between the US and Russia could be worse under Trump than it had been under Obama. But the jury was out.

Having been grounded for three months by a broken leg at the end of 2016, I looked forward to a new burst of travel in the New Year.

I started in a frosty St Petersburg with another economic policy event. Yulia Vymyatnina had joined me in putting another group of fifty students through their paces. As in Moscow, the ideas presented by each group were economically liberal and outward facing.

Minsk, Belarus, February 2017

Shortly afterwards, I ran a similar event in a snowy Minsk. Arriving in Belarus had become slightly more complicated since my first visit in 2015. In February 2017, Belarus allowed five-day visa-free access for eighty countries, in a bid to open its doors a crack. Russia retaliated by imposing controls on its border for foreign visitors trying to enter via Belarus. Prior to that, flights and rail journeys had been unimpeded by border controls, much like in the EU. The action was clearly a minor warning shot from the Kremlin across the bows of Alexander Lukashenko as he contemplated closer integration with the wider world. But in fact, the ramifications of the visa-free travel arrangement would be felt by the EU much later, and in very different ways, when refugees massed on the border with Poland.

Krasnodar, Russia, April 2017

Then it was on to the agricultural city of Krasnodar in the south of Russia, another host city for FIFA 2018. It was the first and only time I travelled out of Russia to join a programme with Laurie Bristow. The trade team had organised a UK roadshow with all kinds of events. I joined a "reading out loud" competition, with Russian school kids reciting a passage of their favourite book in front of a panel of judges, including me. It was all very jolly.

I delivered another economic policy event at the crumbling campus of Kuban State University. A couple of students objected to their peers talking down military spending and talking up corruption in front of a British diplomat. It was a fascinating illustration that outside of Moscow and St Petersburg, in the less affluent universities, with the less high-performing students, the Kremlin narrative resonated more. Laurie came to the university to deliver a speech, albeit in English, and was good; he could be very engaging and likeable when he allowed himself to get over his introversion and intellectual superiority.

I also visited Sveta's mum and sister for dinner, bringing gifts of giant macarons from Moscow. My Russian colleague is from the south and ethnically Adygean.[124] She had also recently become the first Foreign Office member of staff to pass the flagship Foundation Qualification. The residential school project that had started in 2015 with my first visit to Kyiv had run into the sand, with very few people going on to take the tests to receive the qualification; I was gradually being drawn into sorting that out.

Kyiv, Ukraine, May 2017

With the weather warming up in spring, I was back in Kyiv for my third visit, for another economic policy event at the prestigious

---

124 Adygea is one of the North Caucasus republics, home of the Circassian people who battled against the Russian empire over the centuries. The Circassian Princess was romanticised by Mikhail Lermontov in his book *A Hero of Our Time*.

Kyiv-Mohyla Academy. It was much like the events I had organised in Russia and Belarus. However, there was a more specific focus on economic reform as part of Ukraine's drive towards greater EU integration. Corruption and maladministration re-emerged as major barriers to real reform. I presented Embassy certificates, signed by Judith Gough, the Ambassador to Ukraine.

I had been in Kyiv the preceding September, with the weather glorious and sunny, for a regional economics conference at the Embassy. Understandably keen to show commitment, staffers in London wanted to make a UK–Ukraine free-trade agreement a top post-Brexit priority. This seemed bonkers. I didn't have a problem with the principle, as the EU had its Deep and Comprehensive Free Trade Area with Ukraine. But I suggested, given the long list of higher-priority countries to do deals with – the US, the EU, China, India, pretty much every G20 country – that Ukraine shouldn't be at the top of any list, on volumes of trade alone, not to mention deeper governance challenges. FTAs aren't meant to be political gifts. I also suggested that, given its much greater relative size, the UK should at least enter talks with the Eurasian Economic Union in parallel with any Ukraine trade talks. It prompted a tumbleweed moment.

Novosibirsk, Russia, May 2017

"If you visit Siberia, you must drink vodka like Siberian man," Professor Sergei Sverchkov said across the lunch table in his outer office.

RANEPA's largest campus outside of Moscow is in Novosibirsk, and I decided to pay my first visit. Laurie had been due to join a trade roadshow to the city in April but had cried off, claiming to be sick, although not so sick that he couldn't be in his office at the Embassy every day.

Four hours by plane from Moscow, Novosibirsk is less than halfway across Russia's vast landmass. With summer approaching, it was gloriously sunny, warm and humid. My hotel looked out over the grand Novosibirsk State Opera and Ballet Theatre, which is larger than Moscow's Bolshoi. Building of the theatre was completed during World War II and it would initially have housed significant numbers of dancers and musicians who were evacuated to Siberia in the face of a rapid Nazi advance. That evening, I wandered the streets, curious to find an "English bar." With a black London cab parked out front and a life-sized colour cut-out of HM the Queen in the entrance, the "Twiggy Bar" wasn't hard to find.

The following day, I delivered a speech at the university about economic policy to a large lecture hall packed with students.[125] Afterwards, Sergei the director invited me for formal discussion then lunch in his office. Among his staff was Viktor Markin, double gold medallist for the Soviet Union at the 1980 Moscow Olympics. The modest, trim former athlete told me about his work on sports development at the university.[126] After seven vodka toasts, Sergei was satisfied that I'd passed the test, and we could be brothers. I warmed to both men immediately. Having discovered that I needed to fly to Ekaterinburg that evening, I headed to the hotel for a litre of water and a pre-flight sleep. I had planned to go to the ballet that evening, so I gave my front-row ticket to Sergei's personal assistant. Sergei's driver took me to the airport, and we chatted in the car about our respective fathers' lives as soldiers during the Cold War. I felt sad to be leaving Novosibirsk so soon. I'd enjoyed my first visit to Siberia, and I had made a good contact to work with in building academic cooperation.

Before we'd arrived at the airport, I received a call to tell me my event the following day in Ekaterinburg had been cancelled. Sod it. Such a shame to depart.

That evening, Sergei strode into the hotel lobby with two female colleagues. "Ah, Ian, my brother, I'm so glad you decided to stay!"

---

125 Sergei had also invited other universities in Novosibirsk to send representatives to listen in.

126 I recall he abstained from the vodka sprint that was inflicted on me over lunch.

23. THE CAATSA WAY

Moscow, Russia, April 2017

B o Jo was a no-go. Again.

On 8 April 2017, the Foreign Office issued a statement that Boris's planned visit to Moscow on 10 April had been called off and that US Secretary of State Rex Tillerson would go instead on the 12th. It was deeply humiliating. No. 10 had called the visit off at the last minute, the second time they'd blocked a proposed visit by Boris since he took up office. Tillerson's visit had been telegraphed since 21 March.

The context was Syria. On 6 April, Trump had ordered a major Cruise missile attack on Shayrat Airbase, Syria, following a chemical weapons attack that had killed eighty people in the village of Khan Sheikhoun. Where Obama's red lines had been marked out faintly in soft chalk, Trump's were laid out in permanent marker. Russia reacted angrily, but that was not necessarily a bad thing. Tillerson's visit to Moscow went ahead, and although the headlines were frosty, it paved the way for Lavrov to visit Washington in June.

However, Boris's visit to Moscow would have been the first by a Foreign Secretary for five years. The Americans clearly didn't want Boris fouling their lines. Theresa didn't want him shitting the bed by shifting UK policy more explicitly towards dialogue after a period of leaden, joyless silence under Hammond. She'd placed him in a weakened Foreign Office in the hopes he would do no harm.

So, the Prime Minister sold out her Promethean Foreign Secretary in the interests of maintaining her control. Having "taken back control" of the keys to British foreign policy from the European Union, Theresa was handing them to the Americans.

My early optimism about any improvement in Russia–US relations under Trump was short-lived. Summoning up the ghoulish spectre of Cold War zeitgeist, there was bipartisan support on Capitol Hill to pen in the new President on Russia. A new Countering America's Adversaries Through Sanctions Act (CAATSA) was under construction which would not only lock existing sanctions into law but lay down a huge list of additional measures to sanction Iran, Russia and North Korea.

Key EU member states, including Germany and France, together with the European Commission, were furious; some of the proposed CAATSA sanctions would give the US powers to sanction at will those EU firms operating in Russia. Some of my European colleagues talked icily about introducing updated EU legislation to block the extra-territorial application of American law.[127]

I organised a lunch at the Residence for some US and EU colleagues, as I had good relationships with both groups. But it was painful. The jovial Wolf had returned to Berlin and my new, not jovial, German counterpart was spiky with the Americans, which I found in poor taste. He was in a doubly foul mood after German company Siemens had been caught with its pants down, supplying gas turbines to a Russian company that promptly shipped them to Crimea.

In King Charles Street, colleagues downplayed tensions, reassuring us the UK could influence US legislation to limit the impact on British firms. But once again, they were missing the point. Russia saw sanctions that had been in place since 2014 as fundamentally unjust because of their attachment to a Minsk Agreement that Ukraine wasn't honouring. They hadn't affected

---

127 An earlier EU blocking statute had been agreed in 1996, limiting the application of US sanctions against Cuba on European firms.

Russia's policy towards Ukraine, but rather strengthened resentment and resistance. The toughest sanctions, on finance and oil production, had not damaged Russia's economy enough to change Putin's calculus. The Kremlin saw CAATSA as further proof of US law makers punishing Russia unfairly. Further trouble seemed inevitable.

* * *

Saint Petersburg, Russia, June 2017

2017 saw my final visit to the St Petersburg International Economic Forum. I met Ivan Zolotov and Max Bouev for dinner at a jazz restaurant.

Having lobbied us and other European countries on non-attendance at the event in the preceding three years, the American business community turned up in force; around a hundred companies and a face-to-face meeting with President Putin. Typical.

For the main event – President Putin's plenary discussion – I took my seat in the cavernous hall for the third and final time. Megyn Kelly of NBC News moderated the session, which ran for two and a half hours. Following the yawn-fest of Charlie Rose for the preceding two years, this was a more combative affair. On alleged Russian election meddling, on Ukraine and Syria, Megyn slugged it out toe-to-toe with President Putin, not pulling any punches in her questions, not letting Putin off the hook when he tried to evade or patronise.

Many of the themes were constants. Kelly hammered Putin on US election interference, and he wouldn't back down. At one point, he snapped, accusing the US of interfering constantly in Russia's domestic affairs. In a separate, one-to-one interview the same day, Putin said, "Every action has an equal and opposite reaction," reinforcing the core principle of reciprocity in Russian tradecraft:

if you hit us, we'll hit you at least as hard in response.[128] On Syria, Putin was defiant: 4,000 Russians [i.e. Muslims from the restive north Caucasus] were illegally in Syria and instability there posed a real threat to his country; if the US wanted to resolve the crisis, they should work in partnership.

There was an element of Groundhog Day; some of the lines were near identical to those I'd heard him use two years before. He once again pointed to the alleged coup d'état in Kyiv on 21 February 2014 and the failure of Ukraine to comply with its obligations under the Minsk agreements. He accused the US of clinging onto a unipolar world in which they set all the rules. Strikingly, he brought up again the four-decade negotiation between Russia and China to resolve a disputed border area. His point, not for the first time, was that negotiation was better than accusation.

Many of Putin's lines can be cut and pasted into the present day. If you want to solve conflict, work with Russia; we don't like sanctions, but we'll live with them; if you ignore the interests of Russian-speaking people then Russia, as a sovereign country, will take decisive action [whether you like it or not]. On the latter point in particular, Putin has shown time and again that this line is blood red.

Putin seemed to enjoy the cut and thrust of questioning, despite being called out several times on key points of detail. He had home-field advantage, playing to the largely Russian audience, who laughed loud and often at his ripostes. And the choice of Megyn Kelly was interesting. Donald Trump famously refused to attend a pre-election debate that she moderated in late 2016; despite his towering ego, Donald didn't have the donuts to face up to Megyn. She was magnificent.

Also on stage were three heads of state or government. Indian Prime Minister Narendra Modi's pitch was almost exclusively "Please come to India." The Austrian Chancellor, Christian Kern, stuck to platitudes and generalisations, with a ruthless determination not

---

128 Putin also alleged that the US interferes in the elections of countries around the globe.

to express a clear view on either Minsk or sanctions. President Dodon of Moldova, like a Putin Mini-Me, followed Kremlin lines on breaking down a unipolar (i.e., US-dominated) world and not forcing Moldova to choose between Russia or Europe.

I'd started to pay closer interest to Moldova over the preceding year, and as luck would have it, I was covering for the Ambassador for a week in July.

. . .

Chisinau, Moldova, July 2017

"And here is Vladimir Putin's wine collection," the tour guide announced.

I looked at the alcove, piled with dusty wine bottles, with a Russian desk flag and a brass plaque engraved with Putin's name.

We boarded the buggy and sped off through cool limestone tunnels lined floor to ceiling with racks of wine. Each tunnel had its own street sign, like an underground town. Cricova Winery has a labyrinth of 120 km of tunnels which maintain a cool temperature year-round and are perfect for wine storage. Foreign dignitaries often visit and hence the President of Russia's collection, together with many more, including Angela Merkel and Alexander Lukashenko. Putin is rumoured to have celebrated his 50th birthday there.

With its warm summers and rolling hills, the Republic of Moldova – a small jigsaw piece of land wedged between Romania and Ukraine – produced much of the wine for the Soviet Union, and Russia was for many years a significant export market. However, Russia imposed a ban on Moldovan wine in September 2013. It was a move to apply pressure as Moldova – together with Ukraine – prepared to sign an EU association agreement in Vilnius.[129] The impoverished country on the western edge of the former Soviet

---

129 At the Eastern Partnership summit, where President Yanukovych of Ukraine had also been expected to sign an agreement before he cut a deal with President Putin on debt and gas pricing.

space is the least well-known rubbing point of European and Russian interests.

Under glorious sunshine, I spent a week in the capital, Chisinau, working out of the small Embassy in a side street with a friendly and committed team of mostly country-based staff. They set up a good range of calls with governmental, non-governmental and international contacts.

It was clear that Russia's levers in Moldova are in some ways longer than in Belarus or Ukraine. The population, mostly Romanian speaking, is considerably smaller. And a long slither of land to the east of the Dniester River remains frozen in unresolved conflict dating back to the downfall of the Soviet Union. Starting in 1990, Transnistria fought to secede from Moldova as the Soviet Union fell apart; 1,500 Russian "peacekeepers" remain stationed in Transnistria to maintain a status quo that has held since a 1992 ceasefire.

In a curious arrangement, much of the electric power generated in Moldova comes from the breakaway region; it receives gas from Gazprom, but customarily doesn't pay for it, with little risk of supply disruption.[130] Transnistria nonetheless charges Moldova for the electricity it uses. All the while, Russia presses Moldova to repay its accumulated debt for gas supplied to Moldova as a whole, including Transnistria. The total gas debt to Russia, at around $8 billion, equates to two thirds of Moldovan GDP. Despite more recent efforts to import gas via Romania for the remainder of Moldova, Transnistria's gasometer keeps piling up further debt. And there is no obviously available plan to resolve the mounting debt, as Russia wants to be paid. So, the debt hangover locks in the status quo in Transnistria, and slows the pace of Moldovan integration with Europe, to Russia's benefit.

A wider challenge facing Moldova is of brain drain. With around a quarter of the population holding dual Moldovan and Romanian

---

130 As Moldova is such a small country, Gazprom can live with the risk of carrying the modest (by its standards) debt burden.

citizenship, young and talented Moldovans have a free ticket to work anywhere in the European Union. Many still work in Russia. As a result, Moldova is heavily dependent on remittances from the diaspora, which make up around 16% of GDP. The appeal of migration is strong in a country with an undeveloped economy and deep-rooted corruption. A massive banking fraud in 2014/15 stole $1 billion, equivalent to an eighth of Moldovan GDP. An oligarch and the prime mover in Moldovan politics at that time fled the country in 2019 in the face of an international arrest warrant. Moldova was also at the centre of the "Russia laundromat" scandal.

After a non-stop merry-go-round of corruption scandals, in 2020 Moldova voted overwhelmingly for a pro-European President in Maia Sandu, of whom most people (in the West, at least) speak highly. Most Moldovans would like to see further political and economic integration with Europe, and they should be supported in this. This effort is more likely to succeed if Moldova can stay on good terms with Russia while strengthening relations with the EU.

When President Dodon said in St Petersburg in 2017 that forcing Moldova to choose between Europe and Russia would lead to a loss of statehood for his country, he was saying, "Don't mess with Transnistria". In 2022, when Ukraine stopped Russia's advance before Odessa the risk of a Russian move on Moldova subsided. However, it is also clear that destabilising activity in Moldova has increased since the war in Ukraine commenced.

It is ironic that the war in Transnistria emerged out of a rise in Moldovan nationalism, which, among other things, sought to ban minority languages, including Russian. Policymakers, in London and Washington, should avoid the mistakes made in Ukraine and encourage Moldova's government to take account of the needs of all ethnic and religious groups as this small, optimistic country looks to reform and open up further.

• • •

Moscow, Russia, July 2017

With almost no naysayers, in July 2017 the US Congress and the US Senate passed the Countering America's Adversaries Through Sanctions Act. Exactly three years after I arrived in Moscow, on 31 July 2017, Russia responded, ordering the reduction of the US diplomatic presence in by 755 personnel. This was enormous, representing an almost two-thirds cut in US staffing.

Putin had paused after the US presidential election to see how the dynamics of the relationship changed under Donald Trump. The Trump-Putin bromance had initially appeared promising. But the idea of Trump negotiating with Putin so inflamed lawmakers on Capitol Hill that the Russia-US relationship lurched sharply to the right.

Laurie Bristow was on leave, so I was left in charge in Moscow. At the request of the Cabinet Office, I have agreed to remove 231 words here about the Anglo-American School of Moscow. Suffice it to say, the Americans were panicking that the AAS might be caught in the massive staff cut. In Laurie's absence, I advised the Americans not to take the Russian bait, but rather get the school to announce it was still open for business, which is what happened. I became vice-chairman of the Anglo-American School governing board, to support my US Embassy colleague in keeping the ship steady. The State Department appointed an Ambassador to explore a possible change in status for the school which might remove its diplomatic accreditation. While packaged as an attempt to kick the can down the road, I worried that the can was headed for an own-goal.

One hundred American diplomats left Russia and over six hundred Russian staff lost their jobs in the biggest down-shift in the US diplomatic presence in Russia in a generation. I went to a farewell party for the diplomats and felt genuinely bad for those people going, particularly the American colleagues I'd come to know well and like.

. . .

That autumn, a Chancery colleague left the British Embassy at the end of his three-year posting. He had been appointed to one of the senior positions in the Russia team in London. He had never done anything to compromise himself or cast doubts on his reliability. However, when he got back to London, he was denied the appropriate security clearances to work on Russia, effectively leaving him out of a job in the short term. I took this as a further sign that the diplomats had lost control of Russia policy in London.

24. THE FUTURE IS YOU!
(BUT NOT YOU...)

London and Cheltenham, September 2017

Cossack wrestlers going to the Highland Games? Yarn bombers of Tring planning a UK–Russia crochet federation? Three years after sanctions were introduced, most government departments got the chills from anything with the word Russia on or near it. So, everything *outside the scope* of sanctions, however minor, would float upwards for a decision. With the risk appetite of an agoraphobic sky diver, the Russia team blocked most initiatives, citing an impenetrably neurotic array of reasons why not. Anything big got sent to No. 10 for final refusal.

It was late September and I'd travelled back to the UK for two weeks to prepare a paper for a cross-Whitehall meeting on economic engagement with Russia. My aim: to unblock the system so low-level decisions could be made without so much sweat and hand wringing. The Cabinet Office asked me not to detail here the specifics of my work in London during this period, and I agreed to redact 234 words.

During his time, Tim Barrow had the confidence and cojones to cut and thrust through Whitehall; despite the overwhelmingly hawkish stance of the British government under Theresa May, he could nudge the system towards small steps of engagement. But since his departure there had been a huge growth in Russia-related staffing in the UK, at a time when the Embassy was increasingly under-staffed. I crossed paths with Laurie during my time in London and, by comparison with Tim, he looked outgunned in this gathering.

Time back in the UK allowed me to meet Dr Sangeeta Ahuja, who was waiting for her diplomatic visa ahead of a posting to St Petersburg as HM Consul General. She was part of a long queue of diplomats waiting for Russian visas after an almost one-year blockage in the system. Russia has more diplomats in the UK than the Britain has in Russia,[131] because they employ fewer local staff; it's a simple equation. For the bulk of my time in Russia, we got by on the bare bones of our arses.

• • •

"Is it going to be some sort of communist love fest?" the Right Honourable Charles Hendry asked, through the crackle of a poor phone connection.

"Well, the origins are rooted in the left-wing youth movement, but I'll have complete control over our event," I explained to the former Conservative MP and Energy Minister, who was active on the Russo-British Chamber of Commerce. I reassured Charles that I'd never been one for promoting Marxism-Leninism. He was due to be in Russia for another event in St Petersburg, so a side visit to Sochi was easy enough to organise.

Since my first student economic policy event the previous June, I'd organised similar events across Russia,[132] as well as in Ukraine and Belarus. Students liked the intellectual freedom to put forward their own ideas, and most academics seemed to appreciate it once

---

131 This asymmetry would become amplified by events of March 2018.

132 When Charles called, I was with Vladimir Fudimov and his family in Rostov-on-Don; I'd just delivered a seminar at the Don State Technical University and we were having lunch on the banks of the Don River, looking across at the near-complete Rostov Arena.

they'd tamed the urge to pour out their considerable wisdom for students to record verbatim. Now I wanted to organise something bigger, with students from across Russia, maybe two hundred in total. So, the idea of a Russia–UK Student Economic Forum (RUKSEF) was born.

Russia would host the World Festival of Youth and Students in Sochi in October 2017. It would be the largest festival since a 1989 extravaganza in the totalitarian glory hole of Pyongyang. I'd been down several dead ends with potential Russian partners and through a blizzard of bureaucracy with London. Tagging onto an event rooted in the post-war anti-imperialist student movement wasn't my first choice. However, organising my forum at a festival hosted by Russia would minimise disruption and show willing during the UK–Russia Year of Science and Education. The cost of accommodating and feeding the students would be met by the festival, minimising my costs; this allowed me to set aside funds for a study tour to the UK.

A major snag was that Russian universities can't receive funding directly from the British government; for understandable reasons, Igor Chirikov at the Higher School of Economics didn't want his butt cheeks branded with the words "Foreign Agent." In the end, we arrived at a fix whereby the Embassy would channel funding through Roman Chukov, Russia's Y20 representative. He had sufficient cover in the presidential administration to be able to justify the activity as supporting youth engagement. And as 2017 was the Russia–UK Year of Science and Education, it looked above board.

"SOMEONE OUTSIDE SPOKE to me. They know who I am!" Trevor from the Home Office was jumpier than a cat on a hot tin roof.

I looked out of the small telephone shop at the top of Old Arbat and couldn't see anything dodgy. My colleagues had travelled out from London with burner phones and needed SIM cards so they could make phone calls and access the internet.

"Yeah, possibly," I replied, in no hurry to allay his anxiety. Colleagues visiting Russia for the first time often landed in a state of anxiety, as if they expected to happen upon scenes reminiscent of *Doctor Zhivago*.

Milly from the Russia team, however, was more chilled and seemed to be enjoying the experience of visiting a new city for the first time.[133] Both were in Moscow to participate in a young diplomats' forum that had been organised as part of the wider festival programme. RUKSEF was on the horizon, but it still felt like I had a mountain of work.

• • •

Sochi Olympic Park, October 2017

"It is Russia's past and Russia's future," the academic from Higher School of Economics remarked, with a thin smile.

I admired the space shuttle built during the Soviet period and a large white police control truck parked beside it.

With the weather in the Sochi Olympic Park pleasantly warm and sunny, RUKSEF ran from 16 to 20 October. In the end, I secured around 130 students from across Russia. It wasn't the number I'd hoped for, but after all manner of mucking around, I was content.

At the end of the first day, I hosted a reception at a hotel outside the main festival area.[134] It was an informal affair and because for many students it was their first time meeting a British diplomat, I channelled my inner Austin Powers for a whole host of increasingly silly group photographs. Possibly taking the fun a bit far, I picked up Nastia, a student from the Higher School of Economics. Someone took our photograph which I posted on Facebook and

---

133 If you can't rock up to a new city alone and just crack on and make the most of it while you are there without wanting to phone home or find McDonald's, then diplomacy isn't for you.

134 The logistics of getting agreement to bus students out of the festival to the hotel posed yet another bureaucratic headache, to add to a long list.

Instagram. All perfectly harmless.

The Olympic media centre in Sochi was a riot of activity, from Syrian man-dancing Assad supporters to groups of Russian student communists in logoed-up chintz jackets to African students playing music on traditional instruments, singing and joking loudly. The spirit of left-wing youth solidarity was invoked in every vast corridor.

I had expanded my half-day format to cover four days, with more layers to the exercise, and added in experts to discuss specific topics with the students. Roger Munnings, the chair of the Russo-British Chamber of Commerce, joined for a significant period and was generous in the time he spent with the students. Gabriel di Bella from the IMF got involved throughout and joined one of the teams.

Trevor and Milly came down to witness the end of the event. "It's like watching diplomacy in real-time," Milly gushed. Trevor spent most of his time wide-eyed and looking scared half shitless. I wasn't sure from this whether we should let officials from the Home Office visit foreign countries more, or less. The goons were around but largely blended into the background and didn't give us any trouble.

For the students, it was a high-pressure, highly competitive four days, with a lot of fun in between. Their final presentations were fantastic, with a clear focus on liberalising Russia's economy; tackling corruption; diversifying into new high-growth sectors, including the knowledge and green economies; building up expertise in the workforce away from a heavy reliance on STEM, where Russia has historical strengths; and building a more open and less antagonistic relationship with the West. They crafted a declaration from RUKSEF with the goal of making it a yearly event. I selected the best twenty-six students for a study trip to the UK the following February.

Charles Hendry travelled down from St Petersburg, accompanied by Vinny, and invested a lot of his time supporting the event. He was the godfather of the group, bringing gravitas and good humour throughout and closing the forum with a thoughtful speech.[135]

The World Festival closed with a concert in the football stadium that would soon host Ronaldo and others during FIFA 2018. Putin attended and declared to the thousands of students, "The future is you."

"You need to take that photograph of you and a student down from Facebook," lounge lizard Jimmy from the Embassy said anxiously down the phone, as I was about to board my flight.

"Err, yes, OK, although it was all pretty harmless," I replied. *What's all the fuss about?*

"I know, and I understand. Someone will want to discuss it with you when you are back."

I returned to Moscow unsure whether the future was me. At the Embassy, I made it clear I'd done nothing untoward, and that was the end of the matter.

· · ·

My two weeks of bureaucratic toing and froing in Whitehall didn't prompt significant change. The blockage in day-to-day decision-making on Russia across Whitehall remained as immovable as a toilet filled with an excess of bog roll by a man with catastrophic diarrhoea. However, by the low standards of UK–Russia political engagement, something was starting to shift.

Theresa May's authority had been dented by her decision to take the UK to a general election on 8 June 2017. This left the Tories with no overall majority, and reliant on support from the Democratic Unionist Party. It also left the Foreign Secretary unzipping his overly restrictive policy trousers, ready to thrust himself into the moist and mesmerizing diplomatic depths of Russia.

135 By chance, Charles bumped into liberally minded Deputy Prime Minister Arkady Dvorkovich and bigged up the work we were doing. It was a rare moment when the UK and Russia connected in a positive spirit of cooperation.

. . .

Within weeks, Jimmy's diplomatic posting to Russia was terminated by the Foreign Office with immediate effect, and he was put on the first plane back to the UK. The future wasn't him.

25. FLYING HIGH

Moscow, Russia, December 2017

"Ah, it's you again," Boris Johnson said as he got out of his car at the entrance to Plekhanov University in Moscow. At the third attempt, the Foreign Secretary had made the trip to Russia. His was the third visit in the space of a month. In November, Justin Welby visited Moscow for ecumenical and pastoral meetings, including with Patriarch Kirill of the Russian Orthodox Church. Junior Foreign Office minister Sir Alan Duncan visited in early December to meet his counterpart, First Deputy Foreign Minister Vladimir Titov. Among other things, they put pen to paper on a deal to exchange visas, to clear a backlog of British and Russian diplomats waiting to travel to the respective capitals on postings.

Boris's visit had two main parts. He would hold talks and have lunch with Sergei Lavrov. The symbolism of a face-to-face meeting was important. As a Foreign Secretary hadn't visited Moscow for over five years, the list of challenging issues was long. The banter and body language between the two was, I thought, a good sign. The idea of Philip Hammond in Moscow on a dark winter's day conjures up images of the dementors from *Harry Potter*, feeding on human happiness and generating feelings of deep despair in any person close by. It seemed like the foundations were laid for Boris and Sergei to create a long-overdue grown-up channel of dialogue and deconfliction.

The media focused on the light-hearted clash between the two in their press conference on alleged Russian meddling in the Brexit referendum. Lavrov stuck to the standard Russian playbook of plausible deniability.[136] He would also have been conscious that his visitor was Britain's third Foreign Secretary since the start of the Ukraine crisis[137] and that Boris, whose ultimate goal wasn't to be Foreign Secretary, was already on manoeuvres within the Tory Party.[138]

Back at the Embassy, a small window of time had been allotted for Boris to meet staff.

"What happens if he wants to read our material?" one colleague asked in a preparatory meeting.[139]

"Just chat to him about your work," someone replied.

The second major piece of Boris's schedule was a speech to Russian students.

Despite the efforts I'd made to build relationships with Russian universities, no one wanted to touch the British Foreign Secretary with a rubbered-up pole. The Higher School of Economics said a big "hell no" and stopped answering my calls for a while. RANEPA wasn't letting the mop-haired lothario anywhere near their students. In the end, my old friend Ruslan Abramov, whom I'd first met at Plekhanov in 2014, made it happen. I'd visited his faculty often, he brought several groups of students to the Embassy, and we met for dinner from time to time. That investment helped him persuade the rector that hosting a major speech by a visiting

---

136 The scores of Russian think tanks and internet agencies that received funding from Russian intelligence agencies were playing in the social media sphere in the UK; their activity spawned all manner of toxic memes, including around the wave of migrants finding their way to Albion.

137 There would be three more before war in Ukraine started.

138 A week before travelling to Moscow, Boris Johnson broke Tory ranks by expressing concern about the direction of Theresa May's negotiations over a Brexit deal. It was the first shot in his battle to oust May and, in his words, "get Brexit done."

139 In 2019, the BBC alleged that Theresa May tried to restrict Boris Johnson's access to sensitive intelligence material while he was Foreign Secretary.

Foreign Minister was a good opportunity for the university.

Waiting for Boris's car to arrive, the Embassy WhatsApp group set up for the visit was alive with chat from breathless, over-excited colleagues in the convoy.

"Ooh, look we are coming up to a traffic junction now. Do you know what it's called?"

"No. Do you?"

"No. But look, when the traffic lights change from red, they turn green."

"OMG, that's totes amaze!"

With the rector, I escorted Boris through the historic building to a lecture room where several hundred students waited with bated breath. A summary would be: I like Russia, but events in Ukraine and Syria have shown that we are drifting closer to full-blown conflict, and time is running out to find a solution. That's why I came to Moscow, to have a dialogue. There was a lively question-and-answer session that Boris seemed to handle quite well. Russian state news showed video footage of his speech but none of the speech itself.[140]

I gathered a group of students, including a selection of the best students from RUKSEF, to meet Boris at the university. And then he was whisked off to the airport.

Boris's visit to Moscow was unremarkable, but fine; it's rare to achieve big things at first meetings. The measure of any diplomatic engagement is in its impact over a longer time span and UK foreign policy towards Russia had been rooted in short-termism for several years.

Afterwards, as I enjoyed a celebratory dinner with the rector, Ruslan and other staffers, washed down with great quantities of vodka, I wondered how long Boris would stay in King Charles Street.

---

140 The reporter explained the facts of the speech without highlighting any of the points that hinted Russia needed to change course. State-run media highlighted only the Kremlin's core script.

• • •

Bangkok, Thailand, December 2017

Katharine and the kids clapped and cheered at the end of my duet with retired Police General Israphan Snitwongse, in which we'd sang the Thai pop song, *Khon Mai Samkhan*[141]. Though my posting to Thailand had finished eleven years previously, I'd stayed in touch with the former Deputy Commissioner of the Royal Thai Police, who I respect greatly, and with whom I'd worked closely. He was considerably more senior than me, but I had built a relationship of trust through my understanding of Thai culture. I visited him often at Police Headquarters or we'd meet up for meals and karaoke, and I spent as little time as possible talking about those things I most needed to discuss. But when I had a particularly difficult or sensitive case, he always ensured I received the cooperation from the Police that I needed, and he knew I would do anything I could to help him and his officers. So I looked on him as much as a mentor and a friend. And I've stayed in touch because good relationships don't end at the completion of a diplomatic posting. The General borrowed a guitar from the band on the stage and promptly performed *Love Potion Number Nine* without any accompaniment, as I'd told him my son enjoyed the song.

Despite the challenges I'd faced, Thailand is a country that I love dearly, and I can still speak the language better, I suspect, that most British members of the Embassy today. We visited the Embassy and had lunch with my former Thai colleagues, including my beloved political analyst, Khun Nuttanee ('Pe Mai'), who is now retired. We enjoyed a week by the sea in Hua Hin. Our son was unwell one day, so our daughter spent the day with my friends Mouse and Ton, senior officers in the Royal Thai Police and Royal Thai Air Force; she was the safest British tourist in Thailand that day. On our final night, we stayed on the banks of the Chao Praya

---

141 Literal translation: unimportant person.

river, and I made pizza for my dear friends Chet, Nee, Eddie and Lek. It was a special way to end the year 2017.

And as we entered 2018, fresh-faced new diplomatic staff started to arrive in Moscow. Perfect timing, as we put the finishing touches on ensuring the Embassy was match-ready for the 2018 World Cup.

. . .

St Petersburg, Russia, January 2018

I grabbed the drink from the Russian soldier and, not dwelling on the oddity of the encounter, ran on. My legs felt like lead, my chest hurt, and I was hot despite the sub-zero temperatures. Having recovered from my broken leg of 2016, I'd started running again and in early 2018 was fitter than I'd been for a long time, by the relative standards of a middle-aged man with asthma; at weekends I could run Moscow's undulating, ten-mile garden ring road with relative ease, even with temperatures down at minus-ten. Pasha, a friend from my running club had secured for me an entry to the Road of Life half-marathon; I had missed the entry deadline but was desperate to participate as part of a bucket-list of things to do before my posting to Russia finished in the summer. The course follows a road from the shore of Lake Ladoga to the outskirts of St Petersburg, along which Soviet forces kept Leningrad resupplied during World War II until the siege was broken on 27 January 1944.

Problem was, I had picked up a chest infection and had started a course of anti-biotics the previous day. On the eve of the race, Pasha and his wife collected me from St Petersburg airport and took me for a pasta-heavy dinner. They also insisted on taking me to look around the Erarta museum, which I tried to enjoy despite a splitting headache and body sweats. I was glad to finish the half-marathon alive and passed up the offer of buckwheat porridge from the soldiers manning the Russian army field kitchen at the finish.

I was also in St Petersburg to participate in a seminar at the European University on the role of central banks in responding to financial crises. Yulia Vymyatnina invited me to join Professor Charles Goodhart – a former member of the Bank of England's Monetary Policy Committee – in a panel discussion. I presented my research on the three phases of Russian monetary policy since the outset of the Ukraine crisis. Sangeeta had recently arrived as Consul General and sat in the audience to listen.

In Moscow, between my various travels, I'd spent hundreds of hours studying the movement of the rouble against the dollar and other currencies, using constantly moving oil prices as a triangulation point. It was clear that the combination of a competent Central Bank Governor and Finance Minister had steered Russia through the economic twists and pressures of volatile oil prices and sanctions. In the third phase of Russian monetary policy, a weak rouble was prized. It still amazes me, even today, how often western media has a wet dream every time the rouble takes a tumble.

The economic nationalism prompted by the Ukraine crisis and the imposition of sanctions meant companies like Rosneft and Gazprom played an even greater role as guarantors of federal finances, even when energy prices fluctuated.

It's clear to me that by February 2018, Russia had digested and largely defeated the sanctions effect. By the Foreign Office's own economic analysis, any state that is subject to sanctions will find ways either to evade them or lessen their impact over time. Russia's economy didn't look the way it might have, had the events of 2014 not taken place. But the country had emerged after four years of sanctions in a better position to manage them than at the start of the Ukraine crisis. Wittingly or not, Russia was better prepared to deal with the shock of 2022.

Kyiv, January 2018

"You can't make me take the exam," the colleague from our Embassy in Astana, Kazakhstan, said spitefully.

"Well, I guess not," I replied. "But I can terminate your participation if you aren't going to take part."

She harrumphed and agreed to go along with the tests. Ever since the Foreign Office had set up its City and Guilds certificated qualification in 2015, only a handful of staff around the world had passed. Sveta in Moscow was the first, but very few followed her example. Even after we'd paid for staff to fly to Kyiv and Moscow for expensive residential schools, they'd go away and still not take the tests.

Although my job was busy enough as it was, I had decided to take on the additional role of Director of the Diplomatic Academy for Eastern Europe and Central Asia.

"So, you want to turn it into a sort of boot camp?" Andrew Lepoidevin had said on our video call when I set out a new approach.

"Well, yes. They study all the materials beforehand. And we fly them to Kyiv, where we talk about what they learned before they sit the required tests under exam conditions." I wanted to 'flip' the classroom.

"I think it's a brilliant idea." As always, Andrew, our Learning Adviser for Eastern Europe and Central Asia,[142] was completely supportive.

Staff who wanted to attend my school would get an enjoyable trip to the gorgeous city of Kyiv. However, they'd need to study hard in the process. James Sharp, shortly to become Britain's Ambassador to Azerbaijan, agreed to help me facilitate the school, with Andrew.

"Oh Ian, I was up until midnight revising," said a colleague from our Embassy in Armenia with a proud smile.

It was a tough week of study in Kyiv. But it was also fun, especially the camaraderie of colleagues from ten countries across the region. We enjoyed an evening meal at a Caucasian restaurant in the Podil district. Snow fell as we ate, and the pedestrianised street resembled a Christmas card as we walked back to the hotel.

The colleagues from Kazakhstan failed their exams. However, the majority of the twenty participants passed with flying colours,

---

142 Andrew was based in the Academy team in Bucharest at the time, supporting embassies across the former Soviet Union.

including Elkhan and Tengiz, two security guards from Baku. The FCDO Foundation Qualification enjoyed a pass rate of 3% before my residential boot camp; in Kyiv, we turned in a pass rate of over 80%. Staff at my school were buzzing from the experience, and it was further proof that colleagues show an amazing ability to respond well and out-perform under pressure.

A limp human resources consensus has descended on the Foreign Office in recent years that setting high expectations on staff isn't inclusive. As with the Foundation Qualification, the Foreign Office still isn't good at holding staff to account when they duck out of taking foreign-language exams.[143] For an organisation that attracts the brightest graduates in the UK, this inability to ask staff to sit an exam they've been paid full-time to study towards is quite remarkable. If we want to have more diplomatic umph in Moscow, we need to become stricter in insisting all staff, starting with the Ambassador, arrive at post with the right mix of training, skills and experience, including in the Russian language and basic diplomatic tradecraft. The Foreign Office has seen a huge increase in Russia-related resources; they now need an imposition of love tougher than that doled out daily by the FSB to the ill-equipped kids they send out to the Embassy in Moscow.

Glasgow, February 2018

All in all, I thought I looked pretty decent in a kilt.

My students from RUKSEF had enjoyed a lightning one-week study tour to London and Glasgow. In England, they had a tour of the City of London, including a visit to the London Stock Exchange, they spent a day at the Foreign Office, and I took a small group into the House of Lords for tea with Baroness Smith and another peer. In Scotland, they were hosted by the city council and the Adam Smith

---

143 A significant number of the 27% of foreign-language students at the FCDO who do not hit their C1 attainment target fail simply because they don't take the exams, customarily offering excuses about not being ready.

Business School at Glasgow University. I also took them for a day trip to Edinburgh, where I gave a speech on UK–Russia relations at Edinburgh Business School. While in Edinburgh, I caught up with an old friend, Mike, who runs a deli[144] that was recommended as one of the best in Scotland by *The Times*. I invested in a box of the finest Scotch eggs, which I offered the students. Sasha from Sakhalin told me it was weird, to my great distress.[145] As weird to him as frozen raw elk meet had been to me in Moscow.

The highlight of the week was a RUKSEF dinner hosted by Charles Hendry at his "castle" thirty minutes outside of Glasgow. I rented a kilt and all the accoutrements for the evening. The Lord Provost of Glasgow joined, as did the vice-chancellor of Glasgow University, together with members of the Glasgow–Rostov-on-Don twinning association. The students were greeted by a piper on arrival and Burns's ode to a haggis at dinner; they loved it. It was the perfect way to end a fabulous week for the students, some of whom later returned to the UK for work or study. I was absolutely determined to keep the RUKSEF programme alive in future years.

· · ·

Moscow, February 2018

"Ian, large crowds of angry Russian protesters are marching on the British Embassy," a colleague said, anxiously.

I looked around at my teams and calmly issued directions, synthesising everything I knew.[146]

Many of our staff were deployed outside the Embassy responding to the bomb attacks in St Petersburg and Moscow; it remained unclear whether any British people had been killed in the blasts.

---

144 181 Delicatessen in Bruntsfield.

145 Having shelled out a princely sum for these fine eggs, I didn't even get to eat one myself!

146 When you manage a crisis, a key skill is to process a vast amount of information quickly, to make sense of what needs to be done and then delegate tasks out for action.

British tourists were gathering at airports trying to get out of Russia as quickly as they could, although all flights had been grounded. We needed teams out at the airports as soon as possible before the mood started to get ugly.[147]

The pressure was immense. And it almost felt like the real thing.

Afterwards, Christophe came up to me, breathless, and said, "You were absolutely bloody amazing."

I always perform at my best when the shit is hitting the fan, staying calm when others are flapping and focusing my energy on the task at hand. Pressure offers me respite from my inner chaos and I get a lot of energy from helping others, knowing that life hasn't always been plain sailing for me..[148] However, the main reason we aced the pre-World Cup 2018 semi-live crisis exercise[149] was the considerable work Christophe, as the British Consul, and Vinny, as my secretary to the Crisis Committee, had put into our preparations. Since my visit to Paris in early 2016, I had set the Embassy on a path to ensure all members of office staff were trained and equipped to move into a crisis role should anything bad happen during the World Cup. Several Champions League and Europa League fixtures in Russia involving British football teams had given us ample opportunity to test our readiness in a real-world way.

We weren't expecting anything bad to happen, but if it did, our working assumption was that we'd have to cope on our own in Moscow for at least a week, until (and if) reinforcements arrived from London. The Head of the Crisis Management Department remarked that he'd never seen so many Embassy staff attend a

---

147 I remember a video call with the Embassy in Cairo at the height of the Arab Spring, and the Ambassador saying he was too busy to go to the airport, where hundreds of anxious and increasingly angry Brits were gathered.

148 I've never been sure calmness is career-enhancing in the Foreign Office: people get more attention by flailing around telling everyone how busy they are and how stressful it is (but how they are just about coping).

149 A semi-live crisis exercise is organised by the Foreign Office's Crisis Management Department and seeks to replicate a real-life crisis scenario, to test an Embassy's ability to respond.

pre-exercise briefing; the large conference room was packed as absolutely everyone wanted to get involved.

A new Deputy Head of Mission, Linette, had arrived at the Embassy and "observed." Laurie was meant to step aside after the first shift and let someone take over as the Crisis Lead, to simulate a change of shifts.[150] However, he suffered an attack of the Klingons and couldn't break away from the simulated casualty situation in one of the Embassy flats.

But overall, the Embassy received glowing praise for its performance. The next few months were likely to be high-pressure. But I knew the Embassy was prepared for any situation fate might throw at us.

The preceding three months had verged on 'as good as it gets' for me in career terms, and personally. Everything I touched turned to gold, I was high on life and sprinting my final five months in Moscow.

Within a few days, the Salisbury nerve agent attack took place.

---

150 When running a crisis over an extended period, you need a shift system in place, principally to ensure that operations can continue to function over a period of weeks or months. If everyone is working for twenty-four hours a day from the start, you won't last a week before the system collapses.

26. PERSONA NON GRATA

Moscow, Russia, 17 March 2018

"What's happening?" Katharine asked over the phone. She'd called seconds after I sent her a text message from the lift lobby outside Chancery.

"We're staying."

"Oh, OK," she replied, characteristically calm. "It's just that I got two text messages from you simultaneously. The first said, "Heading home" and the second, "We're staying.""

"Ah," I replied.

I got into the habit of sending my wife a short text message most days after work to say I was heading home.[151] My text message from the evening before had been held and delivered at the same time as my message to confirm that I had not been expelled from Russia. Clever bastards.

• • •

After Laurie read the list of twenty-three names, it took a couple of seconds for me to process the fact that I hadn't been expelled. I

---

151 I varied my routes and transport; sometimes I'd walk and sometimes drive. But as the Russians would see me as soon as I left the Embassy compound, I figured letting my family know I was coming home was a risk I could take.

immediately told the members of my team who'd been expelled that they'd been brilliant and offered to help them in any way I could.

One thing was clear: the Russians had cleaned us out. Most of the new British diplomats who had arrived in Moscow in January would be going home in six days.[152]

The political and economic teams were left with four people. Of those, I was due to leave Moscow immediately after the World Cup ended in July. One political colleague was due to go in October. Vinny was due to leave in November. By not expelling the three of us, Russia was claiming a two for the price of one deal, as they knew we would shortly leave Russia anyway. It was blindingly obvious that neither country would be issuing diplomatic visas for new officers anytime soon.[153] So, we were the designated survivors. Come Christmas, the mighty Chancery operation would be reduced to the one officer who managed diplomatic visa negotiations with Russia's Ministry of Foreign Affairs.[154]

I wandered into the East Wing, past Christophe's office. He sat staring into space, stunned. The man who had done more than most people to get the Embassy ready for the 2018 World Cup was going home. I was gutted for him. His door was closed, and I thought it best not to disturb him.

Zainab, the Embassy communications chief, was chuntering around the top floor, crying, wailing and tearing at her robes as if she'd been kicked out twice, when in fact she was staying. Most people were quiet; many had drifted off to see family and process the bad news.

Before I'd decided whether to be happy or sad about staying, I clicked into crisis mode and turned my mind to repairing the Embassy ship.

---

152 Russia gave the UK seven days to evacuate the expelled British diplomats, but we achieved the feat in six.

153 New British diplomats would start to arrive in Moscow only in early 2019, almost a year after the mass expulsion had taken place.

154 Defence was down to one officer, a Royal Navy captain: Technical and Comms down to one officer, good old Fred.

On first sight, we were holed below the water. I discounted the loss of Chancery colleagues on the basis that UK foreign policy towards Russia was in a deeper coma than the Skripals following the Salisbury attack. The World Cup and keeping the Embassy afloat were our biggest short-term priorities. From my perspective, losing Christophe was the biggest operational hit. A new, short-term Football Liaison Officer had arrived in Moscow in January to work with Christophe, but he was one of the twenty-three people expelled.

But there was life in us yet. Our Head of Facilities Management, Hamish, was an effective and experienced Foreign Office colleague. He'd had a succession of overseas jobs, including in consular; he was the perfect person to replace the almost irreplaceable Christophe. I wandered into this office and asked him, in principle, whether he'd like to take on running the consular and World Cup coordination operation. He didn't think twice. I also spoke to his wife, employed as a local member of staff as Head of the Accommodation Team, and she was prepared to step up and run the whole facilities management operation.

I asked a British colleague from the East Wing if he'd like to come into the West Wing to help in Chancery, and he agreed. The capable Deputy in Ekaterinburg was keen to come back to Moscow and have an opportunity to work in Chancery. Two staff had been due to leave Moscow, and I asked them both to extend for a few months until after the World Cup; one agreed to provide extra cover in Ekaterinburg. The wife of one colleague was a fluent Russian speaker and she was keen to work in Chancery too.

With the announcement to expel twenty-three British diplomats, Russia also signalled its decision to close the British Council operation in Russia immediately and the British Consulate General in St Petersburg in the summer. Recently arrived Sangeeta and her deputy would be available to relocate to Moscow and work in Chancery at some point. The bilateral arrangement for temporary, one-month working diplomatic visas had survived the Salisbury attack, so I spoke to the Directorate about setting up a rolling programme of working visits by colleagues from London. I patched up the Chancery ship as well as I could, and Laurie agreed with the changes I proposed.

We had wider pressures elsewhere across the network too. In Ekaterinburg, the Consul General had left post early for personal reasons. Yelena had continued to suffer harassment. The Ministry of Foreign Affairs tried to push her out of her job. Their line of attack that was local staff shouldn't be representing the Consulate at official meetings and, by inference, passing themselves off as British diplomats.

This was crazy. Yelena was the most hard-working colleague in Ekaterinburg, working non-stop to set up meetings all across the region for the diplomatic staff. Sometimes she might go to meetings herself. In the end, we managed to find a way for her to stay in her job.

This whole affair illustrated the difference between the British and Russian approach to staffing their diplomatic missions. Most of the staff at British Embassies and Consulates overseas are locally employed; it's less expensive and they have better local knowledge and connections than any diplomat deployed from London. Russia has a larger number of diplomats in London and Edinburgh than the UK has in Russia, because they don't rely on local staff as much. That gives us power that we never capitalise on, either when local staff are being picked on unfairly or on the back of events that would soon unfold.

· · ·

"Hey, you crashed into the back of my car!" the man yelled, as I got my daughter out the back of our car to go into the Usachovskiy Market near home.

"Sod off," I replied in Russian, before heading in to stock up on fruit and veg.

I had not long returned home from the Embassy after learning my fate. Being accused of a road traffic accident when I'd parked a good couple of metres behind the car concerned was the latest act in a festival of weirdness that had unfolded in the preceding week.

A few days before, I'd wandered home along Denezhniy Pereulok and spotted an attractive young Russian woman smiling at me outside the apartment block. As I opened the heavy outer door, she followed me in. Ivan Ivanovich towered at the top of the stone stairs and tersely asked who she was before kicking her out. I wondered whether someone had taken a photograph of the moment for my undoubtedly large file in Lubyanka.

My walks to work were accompanied as never before by couples of twenty- and thirty-somethings in poncy clothes with man bags. Being followed to the Anglo-American School by a tail car that morning was just a small scene in a much more elaborate show.

• • •

"Who the bloody hell posted a photo on Instagram?" Fred whinged, as he wandered past the small clump of Chancery colleagues.

"The photo has been taken down now, Fred, so give it a rest, eh? Everyone is under pressure," I replied.

The night before, we'd held a farewell party for the officers and their families who had been expelled from Russia and would depart the following day. Ever the professional, Christophe took on the role of compère for the evening, his humour and light-heartedness preventing the occasion descending into a wake. Laurie made a speech, told everyone they were the best colleagues he'd worked with, and briefly broke down. It was touching. A photograph of the expelled colleagues was taken on the Residence balcony, with the Kremlin in the background.

One of my RUKSEF students, Marina, messaged me later that evening from St Petersburg to express her sadness that a member of my team was leaving Russia. An expelled member of my team had posted the balcony photograph on Instagram, and Marina had seen it. I contacted the colleague immediately and told them to take the photograph off Insta, so it was only visible for a fairly short period of time.

It was irritating but frankly not the end of the world, as the officer concerned didn't have a big social media following.

• • •

"God save the Queen!" I shouted defiantly, my fist in the air. I was stood at the main vehicle gate to keep an eye on the assembled press photographers for anything suspicious. With Laurie's flag car out front, the minibuses carrying the expelled British diplomats, their families and pets turned out of the British Embassy compound and set off for the airport.

I wandered back into the Embassy reception, which was now eerily quiet. Vinny was red-eyed. We wandered back up to Chancery, which felt like the *Mary Celeste.*

"I always find the best way to water down alcohol is with more alcohol," a colleague said, as we drank Belarusian Aperol watered down with Russian prosecco.

The new acting Defence Attaché was there, a Royal Navy captain who'd just lost all five of his military colleagues. The mood in the room was remarkably upbeat, considering there were hardly any of us left. Perhaps because there was more alcohol to go around than before.

• • •

Linette promptly disappeared to London to "be there" to meet the expelled diplomats when they arrived in the UK. In the process, she would "be there" getting plenty of visibility for her valiant efforts in front of ministers and Sir Simon McDonald, the Permanent Under Secretary. She was taking it all for the team. What a brick!

My biggest priority now was to ensure the Embassy was ready to support the tens of thousands of England fans[155] turning up for the World Cup in three months' time; after events at the 2016 Euros in France, their safety was paramount. The British press would bay for Russia to be stripped of the World Cup or for England not to play, but I never thought this would happen. In the cold light of day, Novichok was another blot on a scruffy inked-up pad of bilateral grievances between Russia and the UK. Other countries wouldn't see it as in their interests to take a stand on soccer because of Salisbury. But I had to make sure my heavily depleted squad was ready.

---

155 The final total was around 32,000.

27. ROGERED BY THE RUSSIANS

Singapore, 2006

Shehzad Tanweer appeared on the grainy video image taken at the Woodall service station on the M1. It was around 5 a.m. and he was quibbling with the cashier about payment for petrol and snacks. I found it remarkable; within four hours, he'd detonate a homemade bomb in a rucksack on a London Underground train between Liverpool Street and Aldgate Stations, killing seven people.

Peter Clark, head of the Metropolitan Police Anti-Terrorist Branch, clicked onto the next slide. Following the 7 July bombings in London, the Met was showing off the forensic detail of its investigation into the bombers' journeys that fateful morning. I had accompanied a small group of Royal Thai Police Special Branch and Thai National Intelligence Agency officers to Singapore for this briefing. The whole thing was organised by the British High Commission and Singapore Police Force, with British Embassies across south-east Asia inviting small groups of interested guests. The night before, the Singapore police had hosted me and my Thai colleagues for delicious chilli crab at a lovely spot by the sea along the East Coast Road.[156]

---

156 My glasses needed repair, so one of the Singaporean officers took them from me; in the morning, one of his officers appeared at my hotel to return my newly repaired specs. That's a level of service that the Met might not match.

Peter Clark was impressive and the level of detail of his team's work represented the shock-and-awe equivalent of forensic policing investigations. The UK has the most surveillance activity of any country in Europe by number of CCTV cameras and ranks as one of the highest in the world, behind the US and China. But I was nevertheless fascinated that, for example, an ATM camera caught the back end of the blast from the number 30 bus on Tavistock Square. And the theory that Hasib Hussain may have purchased batteries at Boots[157] after his bomb hadn't exploded as planned at the first attempt on a Tube train. But it was the way the Met had traced the full route of the attackers all the way back to their bomb-making factory at a council flat in Leeds that impressed me most. SO13 had a motto, "Short on sleep, long on memory", which seemed apt; they would be relentless in hunting down clues until they either indicted terrorists or pieced together the fragments of atrocities to prevent future attacks.

$$\bullet \ \ \bullet \ \ \bullet$$

Moscow, Russia, April 2018

Russia overmatched the UK in the first phase of the tit-for-tat response to Salisbury, just as they overmatched the Americans with the massive cut of 755 in the cap on US Embassy staffing in Russia imposed in the summer of 2017.

The UK expelled twenty-three diplomats; Russia expelled twenty-three British diplomats. But they also shut us down in St Petersburg[158] and closed the British Council operation. This is important. They matched our twenty-three and raised us two offices and, de facto, a further thirty or so country-based staff.

I believed we should strike back hard, at the very least, to

---

157 Hussain was caught on camera coming out of a Boots store in King's Cross Station after the first three bombs had detonated on Tube trains.

158 Cleverly, they shut St Petersburg without expelling Sangeeta or her deputy, which allowed them to focus their energy on clearing out the Chancery operation in Moscow.

improve our bargaining position. Not doing so made the UK look weak and accentuated Russia's advantage in numbers of diplomats and facilities in the UK. I pushed several ideas at the time which were not adopted. The Cabinet Office has asked me not to detail my specific proposals, and I have redacted 260 words from the text.

The handwringing in London about how to respond in the post-Salisbury tit-for-tat soon started to make more sense. At the end of March 2018, the US, Ukraine and a host of other countries announced the expulsion of over one hundred undeclared Russian intelligence officers.

On the surface, this was a stunning act of collective solidarity with the UK by twenty-eight EU, NATO and other countries. However, the UK, US and Ukraine collectively expelled the biggest number of Russian spooks, ninety-six in total. The most any other country kicked out was four, in what looked like reluctant, semi-embarrassed tokenism. And in most cases, Russia matched up the expulsions with reciprocal expulsions. It was, I fear, another example of the UK talking about Russia rather than to Russia, like a skinny schoolkid calling on their friends in the playground to tackle a bully rather than working things out for themself.

On top of the huge cut from 2017, the US lost a further sixty diplomats and were forced to close their Consulate General in St Petersburg.[159] Russia's window to the West was now officially closed to Albion and the Americas.

· · ·

I folded my post-it and pushed it across the table with the names of those Country-Based staff who I thought were possibly 'dodgy'. The other designated survivors handed in their notes too. We were gathered in the meeting room to consider the latest Russian escalation.

---

159 Russia would also later close the Anglo-American School's small campus in St Petersburg.

After the mass expulsions by allied countries, Russia had hit back at the UK by imposing a cap on the British diplomatic presence of around 160. They used this figure, as, they argued, it matched the number of Russian diplomats in the UK. This was the identical play that they made against the United States the year before; we aren't expelling any named diplomats; we're simply ensuring that you have no more diplomatic staff in Russia than we have in your countries. So, on top of the twenty-three diplomats expelled in March, and the closure of St Petersburg, and the British Council, we had to lose another fifty or so staff to live within the 160 cap. The difference was, we got to choose which staff to cut; this was both heart-wrenching, to decide the fate of loyal staff, but also an opportunity to lose those people we had suspicions about.

But herein lay another missed opportunity. London had tied itself in knots about the legality of closing further Russian offices in the UK in the tit-for-tat. They could still have hit back at the cap by placing a supplementary cap on the number of diplomatically accredited Russian officials in the UK.

Putting it another way, from April 2018 there were approximately 320 staff spread across the British and Russian Diplomatic missions in our respective countries: how many would you think were Russian citizens? 180, 200, or 220 maybe? The figure was around 280. The UK had less than 40 diplomats in Russia, within its cap of 160; I argued we should reduce the number of accredited Russian diplomats in the UK to a comparable number, within their overall cap of 160. By doing so, we would have taken out well over one hundred Russian diplomats from the UK in a single hit.

This would have had an immediate and crippling impact on Russia's presence in the UK. It would have critically undermined their business model and forced them to hire more expat Russians, creating more opportunities for UK influence in the long term. It might also have brought them back to the table to cut a deal, including on the UK office in Saint Petersburg, and/or on the treatment of Country-Based Staff working at British Diplomatic Missions.

Such elegant ideas prompted much teeth-sucking in London. Boris Johnson trumpeted the mass expulsion of Russian undeclared spies as a huge success. Defence Secretary Gavin Williamson famously said that "Russia should go away and should shut up." It seemed to me the only thing being shut up was the British Embassy. Despite all the mincing and chest-thumping we made ourselves look weak, and Russia despised us more.

· · ·

Hampshire, England, May 2018

The Russia team held a strategy get-together in an 18th-century fort by the beach. I decided to travel back to the UK for a week, principally to hunt for a house for my family, with the end of our posting to Russia looming large. It was nice to see many of the twenty-three expelled officers, but the mood was vengeful. After we'd shot the bolt on the mass expulsion of Russian spies from allied countries, there was a thirst for new ideas to punish Russia, as the UK had come off second best in the initial diplomatic tit-for-tat. No one seemed to grasp the idea of closing down more Russian diplomatic premises or putting a huge dent in the number of Russian diplomats in the UK, for reasons that escaped me.

Everyone wanted to "internationalise" our policy in some way, by which they meant working more in concert with other countries in a united front against Russia. This seemed ironic for a United Kingdom that had chosen to step away from membership of a grouping of twenty-eight countries in Europe. A number of ideas emerged from this seaside gathering including a self-congratu-latory roadshow where we told other countries how we'd come out better after Salisbury. Boris's move to engage with Russia had been briefer than most of his relationships, a low bar that even he couldn't jump[160]. I couldn't help but wonder whether we might give actual diplomacy a more sustained effort, for the first time in over five years.

• • •

In early September, Alexander Petrov and Ruslan Boshirov, prime suspects in the Salisbury case, appeared on television for a cringe-inducing interview with Margarita Simonyan, editor in chief of Russia Today. After a painstaking six-month investigation, the Metropolitan Police had pieced together the details of their attack on Sergei and Yulia Skripal. The two officers – real names Alexander Mishkin and Anatoliy Chepiga – were clearly being shamed publicly for their appallingly lax tradecraft in mounting an attack in broad daylight under the full gaze of Salisbury's surveillance apparatus. The GRU, Russian Military Intelligence, suffered a fall from grace following the Salisbury attack. Shortly after the attack, four GRU officers were apprehended in the Netherlands attempting to hack the Organisation for the Prohibition of Chemical Weapons. The head of the GRU died in November 2018, his predecessor having died suddenly in January 2016.

I always believed the Met would trace the identities of the Salisbury attackers. In London, colleagues were foaming at the mouth to seize on this big reveal to "go again" with another round of sanctions and internationally coordinated expulsions of Russians. But this was never going to work.

Driven on by a baying press pack and Parliament, Theresa May decided to go early in March, prior to the identity of the attackers being known. The UK had come out worse in the tit-for-tat exchange that followed, unable to game the tactics to our advantage. Our breathlessness played into the Russian narrative of making

---

160 In fairness to Boris, Theresa had blocked him for a full year before his brief visit to Moscow.

accusations without evidence and assuming guilt absent proof of innocence. Allied countries expelled small numbers of diplomats[161] in solidarity, but they weren't going to go again. President Macron would join Putin at the yearly St Petersburg economic forum in June. Donald Trump and Vladimir Putin would hold their summit in Helsinki in July. There was a heavy sense of other countries wanting the UK to move on. Had we waited until we had clear evidence of the attackers' identities, we could have devised a better-thought-through, and stronger, response.

Anyone who believes that the UK came out better from the post-Salisbury tit-for-tat is, I fear, either deluded or misinformed. The Brits were royally rogered in a manner that would have made even Prince Andrew blush. In response, we barely left a punch unpulled.

---

161 Apart from the US and Ukraine, who together expelled seventy-three Russian diplomats.

28. FOOTBALL AND COMING HOME

Moscow, Russia, July 2018

"Dami i gospoda!" I boomed at the top of my voice like a town crier on Nuneaton high street. "Ladies and gentlemen!" The white and gold room was packed with guests. But I had their full attention, offered a broad smile, and launched into my speech which I delivered in Russian and English. I hosted a lot of events at the Residence, and this was my signature intro. I'd seen too many colleagues mumble half-apologetically into a microphone while the Russian crowd continued chatting; with a loudmouth like mine, I never needed a mic.

It was the World Cup round of sixteen play-off game between England and Colombia, and I hosted a live screening for Embassy contacts. My counterpart at the European Union delegation in Moscow – a Spaniard – showed up in a Colombia baseball cap, which I promptly threw out the window.

At the behest of London, my speech had been loaded with content about promoting LGBT rights in sport. Afterwards, my friends Alya and Katya, in a moment of fun, kissed each other on the lips while someone snapped their photo. They both wore England flags on their cheeks as they had come along to support the Three Lions. Katya's husband Max had a mini-meltdown and insisted that no one post the photograph on social media. The last thing Max wanted was the damned Brits using his wife for gay propaganda.

Our World Cup operation ran as smooth as silk. Having lost almost eighty staff in the post-Salisbury tit-for-tat, the Embassy still had over eighty staff who had been trained in crisis operations over the preceding two and a half years. Despite many of our crisis team and deputy team leaders having left the Embassy, we promoted other staff into more senior roles. Sveta became our Head of Welfare and Rostering. The loveable Irina Chesnokova, our administrative oracle and the grand matriarch of the country-based staff, became our Head of Logistics. And as had always been planned by Christophe, consular staff from across the region, with visa-free travel rights to Moscow, set up a large consular operation; this was headed by the excellent Rufus Drabble, Consular Regional Director from the Hague, and Neale Jones, Consular Regional Ops Manager based in Baku.

London secured visas for a five-person 'Rapid Deployment Team' to help us, although in truth we would have been fine without. Throughout the World Cup, the Embassy stopped normal business operations and moved fully into World Cup mode, operating seven days a week, eighteen hours per day. Using his excellent skills in Excel, Vinny produced a marvellous spreadsheet that anyone could use to look up their precise shift pattern. The top floor of the East Wing became our permanent operations centre.

A West Midlands Chief Superintendent and a Met Counter-Terrorism Detective Chief Inspector co-located with us in the ops centre; they were a good laugh to be around, reminding me of my old days with Hampshire Police. Whenever any policing issue with England fans cropped up, they were in touch with the British police contingent out in the field. Peter Tatchell was arrested in Red Square protesting LGBT rights, and I was told his arrest and swift release were handled professionally. When two scrotes were caught on camera using Nazi salutes in Volgograd, the British police actively supported Russian efforts to run them out of town and ensured they were up in front of the magistrate back in the UK.

• • •

I spotted the two men at a bar near Red Square and introduced myself before ordering a beer. My cousin Lexi had mentioned her two acquaintances from the London metals exchange were travelling to Russia for a World Cup match, so I decided to say hello.

"There's been a lot of news in the UK about how bad it's going to be here, but it's actually really good," the more talkative one said.

After a pleasant chat and hearing about the eye-watering cost of some of the UK charter packages, I looked around. The centre of Moscow was rocking, with a kaleidoscope of Russian and international fans drinking and meeting new people.

There had been a lot of press coverage of potential violence against England fans, in particular members of the LGBT community. The Foreign Affairs Committee had criticised the government for not doing enough to protect England supporters. As a result, my sister-in-law didn't want to send her footie-mad son to stay with us in Moscow to watch a match; I thought, we're here with our five- and eight-year-old kids, and it's perfectly fine.

Most ordinary Russians I met were thrilled to be hosting a global football tournament and excited to meet fans from the thirty-one countries that sent teams. In truth, Russia showed the world how warm its welcome could be.

Of course, the World Cup followed on the heels of Putin's re-election and signs of a toughening of the environment for free speech; Russia seemed on the precipice of choosing between greater repression or closer engagement with the West. The negative British media coverage before the tournament simply proved to me the need to build even stronger people-to-people links. Linette, who led the deployed field team at the England matches, lavished praise on Volgograd for its outstanding welcome. It's perhaps ironic that Volgograd has the oldest twinning arrangement in the world, with Coventry; the only example of sending Russians to Coventry that made sense in British foreign policy.

We ran a textbook operation for the 2018 World Cup. Indeed, I'd argue that I wrote the textbook. My new police chums described the Embassy as the most prepared they had encountered for a major sporting event, and I took that as a massive compliment. It was the certainly the easiest five weeks of work that I could recall.

However, much of the credit is owed to the UK police; they ensured that most England fans could enjoy themselves free from aggro, having seized the passports of well over 1,000 known yobbos to prevent them from travelling to Russia. Despite Salisbury, cooperation with the Russian police and security establishment was first-rate.

That autumn, Linette launched a roadshow to showcase her, sorry, the Embassy's tremendous and almost-impossible-to-believe-if-you-hadn't-been-there preparations for the World Cup. I wasn't invited.

• • •

St Petersburg was glorious in the early evening midsummer sun, and I headed directly to the Consulate General. After less than six months as HM Consul General, Sangeeta was relocating to Moscow.[162] Running her own post had been a dream opportunity for her, and she had got off to a decent start; now, she was understandably deflated. I thought we should have put up a better fight to keep the St Petersburg operation open, or at least take a bite out of Russia for its closure. I decided to travel up and have a last supper with her and her husband Jan before travelling back to Moscow in style by the overnight Grand Express train. We enjoyed sumptuous Georgian food washed down with much prosecco at a restaurant under the walls of the Peter and Paul Fortress, looking across the Neva River towards the Hermitage. With the white night

---

162 The Consulate General continued to operate in a more limited capacity until the start of August 2018, with Sangeeta's deputy holding the fort.

sky refusing to fall into darkness, the Consulate driver[163] arrived to collect us and deliver us to the Moskovsky railway terminal. It was emotional, to put it mildly. But we were soon aboard and rolling out of the station, enjoying a final farewell tipple before retiring to our respective cabins.

We agreed that Sangeeta should run the political side of the house to allow me to focus my attention on preparations for the World Cup. However, it was clear she wasn't happy with feeding the sausage machine of breathless policymaking in London, and by August she decided to leave Russia and return to the UK. I was sad to see her go but respected her decision.

Sangeeta wasn't the only post-Salisbury casualty; the gentleman I'd enticed into the West Wing decided that the pressure cooker wasn't for him. Having arrived in Moscow in January, he voluntarily withdrew and left the country before the World Cup. When applying the cap, another British colleague voluntarily stepped forward to withdraw with his wife. Linette muttered darkly that he'd "done his own legs," which I interpreted as meaning he disagreed with the direction of the UK's foreign policy line towards Russia.

Even after the tit-for-tat, we continued to hemorrhage Diplomatic and Country-Based staff. I decided to extend my time in Moscow for five months until December.[164]

· · ·

Philip Barton's [165]private secretary got in touch to ask me how Laurie was bearing up. From my perspective, the Ambassador seemed fine. Whenever his wife Fiona was away, he'd hole up in

---

163 The driver and all the Consulate staff would be out of a job by the start of August.

164 When you have kids, there are only three breakpoints in any year when it's advisable to leave post for schooling reasons. On balance, I didn't want to stay until the summer of 2019.

165 Philip Barton was at that time the FCO Director General responsible *inter alia* for Russia and Ukraine.

one of the Embassy transit flats and appear at the morning meeting looking as if he hadn't washed his hair. However, he was a long way removed from the British Ambassador who left his Embassy dressed only in pyjamas to negotiate with protesters massed in the nearby shopping district. I never felt I'd have to dive into the cupboard for the comedy giant sedative syringe and straitjacket for Laurie.

• • •

In the teeth of Tory Party resistance to her Brexit negotiation strategy, Theresa May looked increasingly like a lame duck Prime Minister with every passing day. Having been on manoeuvres for several months, Boris Johnson resigned on 9 July. Jeremy Hunt became the UK's fourth Foreign Secretary in the four years since the start of the Ukraine crisis. I saw him as a journeyman who'd maintain the policy status quo on Russia. Having made his fortune in the online training industry, Hunt did arrive at the Foreign Office with at least one idea of his own: he wanted to double the number of foreign-language speakers. Great idea! Having over 1,000 foreign-language speakers would in fact have represented a quadrupling of talent, as just over half of Foreign Office language students didn't reach their targets. I joked that if we just got existing students to sit their exams and pass, we could tell Hunt that we had indeed doubled foreign-language use. In the end, we haven't even achieved that.[166]

• • •

Ivan Ivanovich grabbed our bags and loaded them up in the back of the car, giving the driver stern instructions along the way. He chatted constantly to the kids and gave them each a gift bag with

---

166 The system assumed that Hunt wouldn't be around for long, as it seemed a matter of if, more than when, Theresa May's time in office would come to a grinding halt. This proved a good bet, and the Foreign Office quietly forgot the doubling target after Hunt moved on in July 2019.

chocolates and little treasure chests, filled with Russian sweets.

It had been a grim few months since the World Cup. I'd kept Chancery on life support with the help of the former deputies from Ekaterinburg and St Petersburg, a couple of officers on monthly rotation from London, and the dude who managed diplomatic visa negotiations.

I visited Warsaw in July, for a conference organised by Foreign Office researchers with a Polish Research Institute; the conclusion was that the UK should engage with Russia via other, Central Asian States, who had more influence! I visited Novosibirsk again, where I finally enjoyed front-row seats to the ballet with Sergei Sverchkov and his wife Galina; it wasn't quite at the level of Svetlana Zakharova in Swan Lake at the Bolshoi, but it was pretty darn good. I paid my third visit to Rostov-on-Don to join the Glasgow delegation at the boozy annual city day celebrations and see my good friend Vladimir Fudimov and his family. The second and final RUKSEF student competition ran successfully, hosted this time by Vladimir Mau's RANEPA. I spent a couple of weeks in Ekaterinburg with Yelena and the small band of country-based staff, including a side trip to Perm, which is twinned with Oxford. Laurie, Linette and I passed occasionally like ships in the night, our relationship strained for reasons I never understood; by that time, I'd lost the ability to give a damn.

But it was now time for me and my family to leave Russia. Before I left the shuttered and stuffy confines of Chancery for the final time, I wrote to Philip Barton and Laurie and, among other things, observed that we pulled our punches in the Salisbury tit-for-tat.

In Money Lane, before we got into the taxi, Ivan Ivanovich gave the kids a big hug and Katharine took a selfie with him. He'd been like an uncle to our kids, and we'd always got on well. I shook his hand, hugged him and saw the tears pooling in his eyes. With the old Red Army soldier watching us from the frozen pavement, we drove away from our Moscow home for the final time.

Our farewell rail journey took us via St Petersburg. We met Ivan Zolotov and his wife for dinner. After Katharine had settled the kids in bed at the hotel, Ivan had a wander and found a bookshop, where he bought me a souvenir book about the English Embankment. Before saying farewell, my friend remarked, "You know, if you Brits go looking for a fight, you want to be careful that you don't end up getting one."

• • •

I sat in the German-themed restaurant in the nondescript agricultural city of Bryansk, where my colleague had been hauled off the train from Kyiv in 2015 and enjoyed a few beers with my food. Young people and families danced to Russian pop songs, and no one paid me much notice. It was a pleasant evening among Russian people just getting on with their daily lives, close to the Ukrainian border that Russian troops would smash through three years later. I'd returned to Russia for a month from mid-January 2019 to provide cover in Ekaterinburg, the highlight of which was taking a dip in a frozen river with my German and French counterparts to mark Orthodox Epiphany.

After a deeper chill in the diplomatic relationship, a new batch of visas had been exchanged between Russia and the UK; fresh-faced and wet behind the ears, new British diplomats started to arrive in Moscow from London. It really was, now, time for me to leave Russia, and I had decided to drive home, via Ukraine and the EU.

In the morning, I stood at the frozen roadside, ten kilometres from the Ukrainian border looking up and down the road; absolutely nothing. I was soon blasting down the final stretch of empty highway before rolling past the four-kilometre queue of commercial vehicles backed up at the border, going nowhere fast. Immigration formalities for me were swift and within minutes I was in Ukraine. I was aware of a great pressure being lifted from my shoulders. And feelings of relief, regret and despair at the utter futility of my efforts over the preceding five years.

EPILOGUE

I n my rear-view mirror, I watched the police car catch up to mine and its blue lights flash. Sod it. I pulled over to the side of the road.

The officer appeared at my window, saluted and said something to me in Ukrainian.

I replied in Russian, and he clearly understood, but he wasn't having any of that. He whipped out a handheld device and tapped in his message, which appeared on the screen in English.

"You have been stopped for overtaking on a bridge, which is illegal in the Republic of Ukraine."

"Ah, I'm very sorry, I wasn't aware of that," I replied.

He tapped at his screen again. "Why do you have Russian number plates on your car?"

My mobile sat on the centre console, the Union Flag phone cover facing up. I pointed at it, looked him in the eye, tapped my chest and said in Russian, "I'm a British diplomat. I've been working in Moscow for four years to support Ukraine and am finally travelling home to see my family in England. *Slava Ukraini!*"

In Russian, he replied, "Well, as you are diplomat, I'm unable to charge you with any offence in my country." He saluted and disappeared. Moments later he reappeared, reached through my car window and shook my hand.

As I drove the seventy kilometres from the charming city of Lviv in western Ukraine to the border with Poland, the road was tree-lined, sun-dappled and potholed. Along this road three years later, pitifully long queues of women, children and the elderly waited to flee their country after it had been invaded. But on this day, commercial trucks were lined up at customs and, unlike at the Russian border, there was a heavy volume of passenger traffic and holiday coaches. Ukrainians were taking advantage of visa-free travel to visit the European Union for work, leisure and trade.

I shamelessly used the diplomatic lane to shave an hour off my wait and found myself in Poland. Soon, I raced along modern motorways in a high-speed, friction-free current of people, goods, services and investment which is the adrenaline coursing through the economic arteries of Europe. Driving, with the stereo turned up to the max, I could see and feel why Ukrainians wanted to build a more integrated economic and political relationship with Europe. Ukraine is a country with wonderful people and so much promise; it deserves our support on this journey.

Before an overnight stop in western Poland, I visited Auschwitz. It was surprisingly busy with visitors for a grey day in mid-February. Student groups, including from Israel, posed for photographs by the remains of gas chambers the Nazis destroyed to cover their traces. Many visitors wandered lost in thought through the rows of buildings, laid out with cold Teutonic precision and neatness; the place where humanity and kindness went to die with the degradation and murder of every innocent victim. It was a vivid and harrowing reminder that, beyond the purely economic benefits, the greatest achievement of the European project has been an era of peace. That era of peace has now come to a juddering halt.

It took me two nights and three days of good driving from the border with Ukraine to be reunited with my family at our new home in the rolling north downs of Hampshire.

After a month of much-needed annual leave, I reported to King Charles Street, my headquarters for the previous twenty years. In the rush to transfer EU legislation into UK law under "Operation

Yellowhammer," I authorised a significant proportion[167] of the individual sanctions against Russians. In the grand scheme, sanctioning individuals who have no assets in the UK and are unlikely ever to visit seemed slightly pointless, although it kept me busy. I then spent a while preparing advice for Dominic Raab on a complex disclosure case, the subject of which I am unable to discuss.

After a few months, my dream job came up, and I was appointed Vice-Principal of the International Academy, responsible for, among other things, driving up the Foreign Office's still appalling record on foreign-language usage. It was undoubtedly one of my most enjoyable and rewarding roles as a British diplomat, and a nice way to end. I was fortunate to work with some incredible colleagues and learning professionals including, among many others, Julia Powell and Marie-Louise Childs, with whom I've stayed in touch.

This travelogue skims lightly over a complex period of my career, namely my four and a half years in Russia. It does not, and never could, seek to justify Russia's mindless and needless invasion of Ukraine; this unconscionable and, in my view, avoidable war has displaced seven million people from their homes, killed well over one-hundred-thousand service personnel from Ukraine and Russia, plus countless innocent children and civilians. Rather, I ask three questions: was the Tory foreign policy non-engagement with Russia the right approach; is the Foreign Office equipped with the right skills to engage with and understand Russia, and therefore advise ministers well; have Western sanctions materially altered Russia's posture towards Ukraine and made conflict less likely?

The UK policy, introduced under Philip Hammond, of talking about Russia rather than to Russia has failed. In the almost-ten years since the start of the Ukraine crisis the Europeans and, until the arrival of Biden as President, the Americans sought actively

---

167 Probably 35–40% of all the individual sanctions against Russians and separatist Ukrainians, including entities, going back to the original designations made in 2014, at the start of the Ukraine crisis.

to engage with Russia despite the considerable challenges. And there had been a troubled but stable status quo before the sudden deterioration in relations at the end of 2021. The self-imposed exile from negotiations towards a peaceful resolution in Ukraine in 2014 reduced Britain's role to flag-bearer for Ukrainian liberation and potential NATO membership, and drumbeater for sanctions; in my view, this undoubtedly inflamed hostility in the Kremlin and suspicions about so-called NATO encirclement. Today, the UK has no political influence in Moscow and no scope to effect their actions in Ukraine. The Russians view us as fawning puppets of the Americans, and I worry that the cluster of British behaviours post-Brexit has burnished that reputation in Europe.

Of course, this has happened at a time when the UK retreated from internationalism through the painful process of withdrawal from the European Union. The deep-rooted lack of intellectual clarity in the UK's position towards its European identity, its role as a military power and its relationship with both Ukraine and Russia seems at least in part linked to the constantly revolving door at the top of government. Since 2014, we have seen five Prime Ministers, six Defence Secretaries and seven Foreign Secretaries, each with different and often conflicting approaches. When Europe is on the brink of full-blown conflict and we send in Liz Truss, we should all start dusting off plans for an Anderson shelter in the garden. Determined to help Zelenskiy fight to the last Ukrainian, the Little Britain Tories are making the world less safe. I find it staggering that, despite the Conservatives making a complete hash of most contemporary domestic policy challenges, they can garner cross-party support on foreign policy.

The Foreign Office has been woeful in its approach to Russia capability. Despite a huge increase in Russia-related resource in London, the Embassy in Moscow is a Potemkin house, mocked by the Russians and largely ignored by a massive Whitehall machine. Russian-language attainment still lags behind the Foreign Office average, which remains short of the Foreign Affairs Committee target of 80%. I never saw a serious plan to ensure all officers in speaking roles arrive in Moscow with their C1 standard in the back pocket, like P plates on a newly passed driver. And following a twenty-year disinvestment in basic diplomatic tradecraft, too many young officers arrive in Moscow keener to be locked-in policy wonks than out-there diplomats, meeting regular Russian people and "getting under the skin" of the country. We just aren't (to use that hackneyed phrase) levelling up with Russia on the open field of play.

Of course, efforts to improve diplomatic capability have been further delayed by the decision to merge the Foreign and Commonwealth Office with the Department for International Development, in September 2020, six months into a global pandemic. Three years on, the new organisation remains paralysed and directionless at an executive level. The challenge of unifying two culturally opposite departments through COVID, Afghanistan withdrawal and war in Ukraine has been beyond the undoubtedly intelligent Sir Philip Barton. He was given the comms cover legend of 'Mr Kind' shortly after taking on the role. The Foreign Office still awaits 'Ms or Mr Visionary and Decisive Leader'. It is also grimly ironic that the cut in overseas development assistance funding that accompanied the merger, broadly correlates with UK spending on weapons to Ukraine following the outbreak of war in February 2022. I wonder how different Ukraine might be today had western allies spent tens of billions on governance reform in 2014, rather than on weapons since 2022. Guns not butter is the new Tory shibboleth.

Sanctions haven't worked and seem unlikely to work any time soon, if at all. From the point at which Minsk conditionality was applied, sanctions merely elevated Russian resentment toward the West and stoked an economic nationalism that ensures state-owned enterprises are protected at all costs. This resentment was heightened by a perception that Ukraine wasn't being held to its responsibilities under Minsk, specifically a process of political engagement with the Russian-speaking Donbass. Sanctions haven't been painless, but Russia's Central Bank and Finance Ministry have been effective in insulating Russia's economy and reserves and minimising the damage since the end of 2014. War in Ukraine hasn't had sufficient impact to alter Putin's calculus. And by the Foreign Office's own economic analysis, sanctions are likely to reduce in impact over time as countries take steps to evade them and/or to reorient their economic model to cope.[168] Russia is simply shifting its trade east with, for example, huge increases in energy exports to India and China.

I say this having studied Russian sanctions closely for nine years. Like a rusty old cannon, I was wheeled out of retirement in early 2022 to authorise a significant chunk of the sanctions against Russia after the invasion of Ukraine. The truth is, we hit diminishing marginal returns on sanctions within the first couple of weeks after war started. Every sanction since then has been a sticking plaster on feelings of inadequacy that we can never give Ukraine quite enough weapons to beat Russia, and that we would sooner not send our own troops. As a result, Russia and Ukraine have fought each other to a bloody standstill, like the Somme. Neither the UK nor the US are promoting the idea of a ceasefire, to allow a (frankly) decades-long peace process to recommence. Nine years on from the onset of conflict, we remain convinced our strategy is working!

As for me? I requalified in Russian language in 2021, without any additional tuition, studying through the medium of reading papers, watching Russian telly and talking to people. In 2023 I became a Fellow of the Chartered Institute of Personnel Development, and hence my particular focus in this book on the skills and capabilities of the grand old 'Office'. I took early retirement the day before my birthday in July 2023, with my security clearance intact and a strong performance record. One of my aims in writing this book is to inject a greater sense of urgency into efforts to improve

---

168 I'm sure this advice falls into the category of information ministers don't want to hear.

the Foreign Office for the benefit of the thousands of committed individuals who work there in support of UK interests. However, I suspect that many of my former colleagues are now pricing in the possibility that the FCDO won't survive contact with the next general election.

In terms of some of the characters mentioned in this book, Vinny and Christophe continue to go well in their FCDO careers, and Sveta is still working at the British Embassy in Moscow, doing great work. Yelena in Ekaterinburg was eventually made redundant after many years of exemplary service. Oksana now works in the UK; she forgot my birthday last year, so we are now even. Nastia, the former student, also lives in the UK; whenever I meet her and her husband, I never pick her up!

The Foreign Office's performance in Russian language is still way below average.

Having stayed open for seventy-four years, through the countless crises of the Cold War, the Anglo-American School of Moscow closed for the final time in May 2023. It had been subject to all manner of obstruction after its diplomatic status was given away.

The Russian Embassy School in London and the Russian Mission School in New York both remain open.

Despite the huge weight of sanctions, Russia is expected to return to economic growth again in 2024.

Russia still has more diplomats in the UK than the UK has in Russia.

Leaving the Foreign Office after a career of stratospheric highs and slough-like lows, I know that diplomacy is a rum and much misunderstood career. It imposes two requirements on the officer: that they reliably keep the secrets they hold, thanks to the work of the UK and allied intelligence community; and that they refrain from offering an opinion on government policy in public while in Crown service. I left the FCDO in large part because I wanted, publicly and for the first time, to offer an opinion on the state of British diplomacy today particularly, but not only, as it relates to Russia. The secrets, of course, I'll keep to the end.

ACKNOWLEDGEMENTS

My dad, Cliff Proud, served his Queen and country in an exemplary manner with the British Army for twenty-two years. It was his straight-backed example that imbued in me a strong sense of duty and public service. I have my darling late mum Sheila to thank for my memory and my curiosity. Together, my parents gave me a solid family upbringing the shining example of which I aspire to; if you've not much money but amazing parents, then you have a richer endowment than any millionaire.

My beloved wife Katharine is a far better and more decent person than me. Her unflinching love and support brought much-needed calm into my life - not to mention two beautiful children - and I'm never happier than when I'm with my family. You've got to be special to give up your career and follow your husband on an adventure to Russia for four-and-a-half years, rolling up your sleeves and making the most of the experience.

I thank my dear friend Yulia Vymyatnina, who I first met in St Petersburg in 2016. She has been a great source of advice and insight on the economic and Russia-specific aspects of my narrative, as I pulled together this book.

Thanks to Olivia Beattie and Richard Roper for their help with the copy editing and proof-reading of my manuscript. I have Vanessa Mendozzi to thank for my wonderful book cover and interior design.

Colleagues at the FCDO and the Cabinet Office undertook a process of sensitivity review of my manuscript to ensure its compliance with the Official Secrets Act and the Radcliffe Rules. I should like to thank them for making this process as pain-free as possible, in the circumstances.

Finally, I pay tribute to all my former colleagues at the Foreign Office who, underpaid, poorly led and often ill-equipped, work across the world trying to make a difference in support of UK interests, often in the most difficult of circumstances.

Printed in Great Britain
by Amazon